V.V. Pustogarov

OUR MARTENS

F.F. Martens
International Lawyer and Architect of Peace

Edited and Translated from the Russian, with an Introduction by

W. E. Butler

SIMMONDS & HILL PUBLISHING LTD

KLUWER LAW INTERNATIONAL

The Hague • London • Boston

Published by Kluwer Law International,
P.O. Box 85889, 2508 CN The Hague, The Netherlands
and
Simmonds & Hill Publishing Ltd.
58 Carey Street, London WC2A 2JB
tel: 44 171 405 5145; fax: 44 171 405 7459

Sold and distributed in the U.S.A. and Canada
by Kluwer Law International,
675 Massachusetts Avenue, Cambridge, MA 02139, U.S.A.
tel: (617) 354-0140; fax: (617) 354-8595

In all other countries, sold and distributed
by Kluwer Law International,
P.O. Box 85889, 2508 CN The Hague, The Netherlands
tel: 31 70 308 1562; fax: 31 70 308 1555

ISBN 9041196021 (Kluwer Law International)
ISBN 1-898029 50 4 (Simmonds and Hill)

Our Martens: The Life and Times of F.F. Martens, Russian Jurist, Diplomat and Publicist

CONTENTS

MEETING MARTENS

W. E. Butler

In early September 1990, the height of perestroika, I had taken a day to be in attendance at the Moscow International Book Fair. Inter Documentation Company BV, a Dutch firm specialising in microfiche projects for the academic market, had at my instigation taken a booth in the Fair to demonstrate commercial microfiche projects for the first time to the Soviet market. This was indeed a genuine novelty and attracted large crowds, although by now, notwithstanding previous reports on the Fairs which I had read in the *Times Literary Supplement*, Muscovites had become more sophisticated and discriminating in their choice of foreign publications and the crowds were no longer uncontrollable.

Late in the afternoon, during a general lull in crowd flow, two young men approached me and presented business cards which identified them as staff from the Archive of the Foreign Policy of Russia, attached to the Ministry of Foreign Affairs. I caught my breath, for access by foreign scholars to this Archive had been exceptionally limited throughout the Soviet era and rarely heard of after the Second World War. Just as every other major international institution in the world, they were interested both in preservation and conservation of the Archive itself and means by which programmes for the filming of materials might become at least self-financing. The Archive had a small internal microfiching operation, but found it inefficient, producing microfiche of less than archival standard, and a drain on the budget. Various projects were being explored in the abstract which might enjoy demand in sister institutions abroad.

"Our holdings are truly exceptional," one remarked, "including the Diaries of the Russian international lawyer, F. F. Martens". Now I did visibly express astonishment, for I had searched for years in the hope of finding materials about Martens. He had died in 1909, long before the Soviet era, and I found it difficult to imagine that no effort had been made to preserve somewhere the private records of so distinguished a Russian scholar and diplomat. However, the published two-volume guide with supplement to personal archives in the USSR, the vademecum of all those who sought the existence of personal archives and the data necessary to submit a formal request for permission to use them, did not contain the name of F. F. Martens and no Russian international lawyer to whom I spoke was able to suggest the possible whereabouts of such material.

I pressed for detail. The Martens diaries had come to the Archive of the Ministry of Foreign Affairs from the Martens family before the First World War. They were indeed not listed in any of the research guides and were unknown to Russian and foreign scholars. What followed next was pure perestroika. Would I like to see the diaries? The Archive would be open the following morning from 09:00 hours and I was welcome to present myself for that purpose. I accepted instantly and at 08:55 the following morning appeared in an unpretentious building near an underground station. Admitted immediately without formalities, I was taken up to a comfortable reading room, where seven volumes of diaries awaited me.

Martens' hand is not an easy one, rather a hurried scrawl which I found difficult, as did the Russians. The diaries covered a considerable range of years, entries were intermittent, and usually cursory notes – the sign of a busy and doubtless often exhausted man.[1]

On the small sheets which each user signs to indicate that he has received and returned the volumes I noticed another signature bearing a name well-known to me. I was not the first to use the diaries, for a few weeks previously another international lawyer, Vladimir Vasil'evich Pustogarov, also had read them. This was when I learned that a biography of F. F. Martens was in progress, and I eagerly awaited the results, which appeared in 1993.

[1] Extracts from the Martens' diary have been published, inter alia, as: «Политика России 1905-1907 годов. Из дневника Ф. Ф. Мартенса» [The Policy of Russia in 1905-1907], *Международная жизнь* [International Life], nos. 1-2 (1996).

On 15 October 1998 a Collection of Books and Maps on Russia and Central Asia, the "Property of a Gentleman", came up for sale at Sotheby's in London. Included was a lot containing "rejected and wasted literary matter", unpublished articles and notes by one of Martens' most persistent publicist-protagonists, Charles Marvin (1854-90). It was irresistible, and I didn't. Two of the items contained in the volume were essays written directly against Martens and submitted to newspapers in London and Newcastle. These particular items were not published by the newspapers, although many others by the same writer did appear on the subject. They are offered here for the first time as an Annex to give the flavour of the times and the type of article which Martens inveighed against in his own publicist writings. They also confirm Pustogarov's view that Martens was unique amongst international lawyers of the period in enjoying renown far outside his own international legal community. Articles of this type and similar polemical sallies in books on Central Asia of 1880s featured Martens in a way that ensured any alert student of international affairs was aware of his person and his reputation.

The present edition of Pustogarov's biography of F. F. Martens is the most complete in any language. The original Russian publisher was unable to publish the entire manuscript, omitting two chapters and printing only 1000 copies (which sold out immediately) during the financially-difficult days of early post-independence Russian publishing. The author also took the opportunity to substantially revise Chapter I and make other emendations and additions throughout the text, some of which incorporate additional materials which had come to his attention. Chapters VIII and XII have not appeared previously. None of these additions or adjustments are contained in the excellent French-language translation prepared by M. Mabillard, G. Piron, L. El-Tawil, and A. Volchkov at the University of Geneva, with an introduction by Academician Jiri Toman and assistance from the Institut Henri-Dunant.[2]

[2] See V. V. Pustogarov, *Au service de la paix. Frederic de Martens et les Conferences internationales de la Paix de 1899 et 1907. Biographie d'un juriste et diplomate russe.* Geneva, [University of Geneva], 1999. [iv], 315 p.

Excluding those alterations made by the author himself, no other changes have been introduced in the text except to correct obvious misprints where they were detected and substituting in the footnotes references to English-language editions or translations of Russian secondary materials so that they may be more readily consulted by the reader. In several cases where the author translated material from English into Russian, I have consulted the original source to verify the accuracy of my own version.

The photographs of F. F. Martens have been supplied by the author; they were acquired in 1976 from Professor L. Lesment, who in turn had received them from a descendant of F. F. Martens, M. K. Afrosimova. The photograph of the Bodleian Tercentenary Procession to the Sheldonian Theatre on 9 October 1902, when Martens received an honorary DCL degree, has been provided through the courtesy of The Bodleian Library, University of Oxford and is here reproduced with their permission and my gratitude. I am obliged to Dr. J. S. G. Simmons for drawing my attention to the photograph. Martens received his degree together with Sir Paul Vinogradoff, Lord Strathcona, and A. D. White, of Yale University.

In his Introduction to the present volume, the author notes that in Russia the reputation of Martens has during the past decade begun to receive its due, however belatedly. The centennial of the First Hague Peace Conference provided another occasion to assess Martens' remarkable contribution to the codification of international law. With the support of the Russian Government, a bust of F. F. Martens has been presented for permanent display at the Peace Palace in The Hague.[3] A so-called "Third Peace Conference" to commemorate the 100th anniversary of the Russian initiative to convene the First Hague Peace Conference was held at St. Petersburg in the Smolnyi Institute from 22-25 June 1999, a splendid location where the early slogans of the Bolshevik Government and its Dekret on

[3] Busts of F.F. Martens and Anna Pavlova by Alexander Tarantynov are illustrated in A. Eyffinger, *The 1899 Hague Peace Conference* (1999), pp. 379, 40.

Peace (1917) shared the background with modern posters designed specially for the occasion. The Conference, organised by Judge A. L. Kolodkin, was addressed by the Secretary-General of the United Nations, Kofi Annan. Of lasting value is the collection of documents and commentaries prepared for the occasion, together with the Russian-language texts of the conventions and declarations signed at The Hague on 29 July 1899.[4]

The great merit of Pustogarov's Biography is that it illuminates for the first time in international legal scholarship the "Russian side" of Martens' existence as shown, above all, by the materials of the Archive of the Ministry of Foreign affairs of Russia. While Pustogarov is right to deplore the Cold War perceptions of Martens shared by a tiny minority during the late 1940s and early 1950s in the West and the absolute neglect of his contribution to international law on the part of the Soviet legal community, the Western view of Martens has been far more positive than Pustogarov may appreciate. In his account of Martens' role at the 1899 Hague Peace Conference, Arthur Eyffinger wrote:

> Probably no one in Europe had been so instrumental in slowly but steadily bringing about the rise of the rule of law ... he was the *auctor intellectualis* of the peace and disarmament proposals presented by the Czar at the 1874 Brussels Conference ... Martens, in short, embodies the link between the laws of Geneva and The Hague, as much as indeed he is the visionary precursor to the New York laws on human rights.[5]

In writing these words, Eyffinger is not revising history, but rather eloquently stating the great esteem in which the

---

[4] See V. S. Ivanenko (comp.), *100-летие инициативы России: От Первой конференции мира 1899 г. к Третьей конференции мира 1999 г. Сборник материалов* [100th Anniversary of the Initiative of Russia: From the First Peace Conference of 1899 to the Third Peace Conference of 1999. Collection of Materials]. St. Petersburg, 1999. 168 p. (St. Petersburg Regional Division of the Russian Association for the Promotion of the United Nations/ Law Faculty of St. Petersburg State University). 1000 ptd.

[5] Eyffinger, note 3 above, pp. 178-179.

international legal community generally has held Martens then and now.

ABBREVIATIONS

AVPR	Archive of the Foreign Policy of Russia
ed. khr.	storage unit
l.	sheet
op.	inventory

From the Author

We offer to the English-speaking reader a book devoted to the distinguished Russian international lawyer, Fedor Fedorovich Martens (1845-1909). During his lifetime he enjoyed world renown and accomplished much for the international system. His authority was immense both in Russia and in many other countries.

The *Receuil des traités et conventions, conclus par Russie avec les états étrangers* (1874-1909), in fifteen volumes, would alone have been sufficient to commemorate his name. That work has become a classic which retains its full importance today. The treatise *Современное международное право цивилизованных народов* [Contemporary International Law of Civilised Peoples] (1882-83), in two volumes, was widely read. In Russia the treatise went through five editions and was studied by several generations of Russian jurists and diplomats. The treatise was translated into the German, French, Spanish, Chinese, Persian, and Japanese languages and in 1996 was reissued in modern Russian orthography by Moscow University in a paperback edition.

Martens' popularity was enhanced by his frequent comments in the press on international events. As one of his students wrote later, "his pamphlets, notes, and journal articles with regard to questions of this nature printed in various languages as well as separately, and in general and specialist journals and newspapers in both the Old and the New Worlds were enormous in quantity". Some were a sensational success. The pamphlet *Россия и Англия в Средний Азии* [Russia and England in Central Asia] (1879) was published in the Russian, French, German, and English languages, and the text was transmitted from London by telegraph to the United States. The freshness and originality of Martens' journalistic efforts combined the stirring questions of current politics with scholarly concepts in the domain of international law.

Fedor Fedorovich also was an outstanding diplomat. To be sure, at the time his diplomatic work was to a considerable extent hidden from the general public, and only now, when access to the archives of the Russian Ministry of Foreign Affairs has become possible, has it been feasible to investigate this dimension of his career fully.

Martens was the true author of the programme of the First Hague Peace Conference (1899) which was convoked at the initiative of Russia and set in motion the historical beginning of the disarmament process and the establishment of the rules for conducting warfare and the peaceful settlement of inter-State disputes. Martens proved himself too when preparing and conducting the Second Hague Peace Conference (1907), taking part in the Russo-Japanese peace negotiations (1905) in Portsmouth, New Hampshire, in defining Russian policies with respect to China after the Boxer Rebellion, and others.

As an acknowledged authority, Martens was often invited by various States to settle disputes. His arbitral consideration of the territorial conflict between Great Britain and Venezuela (1899) attracted considerable attention. This arbitration provoked a remarkable polemic fifty years later in legal circles.

Martens' diary entries concerning international conferences, conversations with Tsar Nicholas II, Kaiser Wilhelm II, King Edward VII, King Leopold II, the head of the Russian Government S. Iu. Vitte, the Foreign Minister Sir Edward Grey, and many other State and political figures require us to examine anew certain pages of the history of international relations and Russian diplomacy.

After his death, Martens was rather rapidly consigned to oblivion. He was forgotten in Russia and abroad. The rare voices of recollection merely emphasised this sharp about-face. Of course the phenomenon of unexpected oblivion can be attributed to the capriciousness of history, which wilfully circumvents its heroes. But all the same it is useful to analyse the reasons for this phenomenon in greater detail.

It should be said above all that the legacy of Martens was not obsolete, had not become merely the weal of history. To this day it retains much of value.

The Hague Conventions on the law of war have undergone the severe tests of two world wars and become the foundation for further international legal regulation. They are a monument to a distinguished jurist and diplomat.

The international commissions of enquiry proposed by Martens in 1899 found surprisingly rapid acceptance. They were first used to settle the so-called Hull Incident (1904), which had led to a sharp deterioration in Anglo-Russian relations. There soon followed other examples of the successful use of international commissions of enquiry, and in 1948 the Organization of American States by a special treaty signed at Bogota included them in the arsenal of means for the peaceful settlement of inter-State disputes.

The system of international justice, of which Martens was such a stalwart proponent, has been substantially developed.

The theory of international community and international administration developed by Martens has found confirmation as a whole. The world community has passed from regularly convened international conferences, to the League of Nations, to the United Nations. Having advanced the concept of sovereign States administered by an association, Martens looked far ahead, and his ideas continue to generate real and useful impulses to this day.

All this makes the oblivion of the works of this outstanding jurist and diplomat the more strange. His legacy lives, but his name is virtually forgotten.

One reason doubtless was the enamoration which Fedor Fedorovich had for the science of international law and his faith in international legality and international order. He judged events and actions from the standpoint of international law, and this was not always congenial to Russian and foreign statesmen. In Russia he was repeatedly reproached for "insufficient patriotism", and abroad, for acting as a "Russian politician". It is remarkable that in 1952 one of the articles published in the West held that Martens was at fault for being a "Tsarist writer" and not a "man of law".

In reality those in Petersburg of exalted rank who directed the Ministry of Foreign Affairs – this patrimony of the propertied noble families -- were annoyed by the international authority of an intellectual who was not of gentle birth. Even his professorial rank gave rise amongst the noble aristocracy to scornful attitudes, and in his diary Martens more than once lamented that he was appreciated more abroad than in his native land.

Of the greatest significance was the circumstance that the last decade of Martens' life and activity coincided with the formation of military-political blocs which were preparing for a sanguinary redivision of the world. The cannonade of weaponry increasingly drowned out the voice of law, and Martens, together with other international lawyers, began to experience the impact of the impending catastrophe.

When the guns fell silent and foreign colleagues of Martens set about a peaceful settlement, Russia stood aside from this process. A cordon sanitaire was established around Soviet Russia as a seat of revolutionary plague, and it was subjected to diplomatic and other blockades. Martens and Russia alike were excluded from the international community.

The paradox was that Soviet Russia itself also had a negative view of Martens, indeed a hostile view. In his day Martens had opposed the "anarchists" and the "dynamiters", and with the authority of a lawyer had supported the demand of the Tsarist Government to extradite those participants of revolutionary speeches to Russia, who were criminals according to Russian laws and concealed themselves abroad. It is hardly surprising that in the eyes of Soviet Power, Martens was a "reactionary" and a "Tsarist old hand". When the *Энциклопедия государства и права* [Encyclopedia of State and Law] was published in the USSR (1925-26), the entry on international law contained no reference to Martens. The bias of the article was underscored by the fact that it did mention the German jurist, Georg Friedrich Martens (1756-1821). The name of Fedor Fedorovich Martens also was absent from the first edition of the *Большая Советская Энциклопедия* [Great Soviet Encyclopedia] (1938). Only gradually did fragmentary information about Martens begin to be mentioned in Soviet scholarly writings. Entire domains of his activity continued to remain forgotten. For example, the three-volume *История дипломатии* [History of Diplomacy] published in the 1960s contained not a single word about him.

From the heights of our days we sometimes look back with disdain and arrogantly judge our predecessors. But we have climbed so high and can see so far because we stand on the shoulders of these giants. Their knowledge and experience, their achievements and insight, all nourish the tree of our civilisation, and recourse to the glorious names of the past helps us better to understand our own present and future. This also applies to the life and activities of F. F. Martens.

Collecting materials about Martens was not easy, and the path towards creating an integral picture of this complex and multifaceted individual was a prickly one. Ideological prejudices and the epithets "reactionary" and "Tsarist old hand" were an invisible barrier. The widespread aspiration to fit every public figure into a pattern, to place him in the cage of some sort of scheme, and instead of thinking out the place of Martens in the history of international relations and international law, suddenly commence a discussion (for example, as to which orientation he should be relegated: positivist or natural law?) also was a brake. If Martens did not fit into the scheme, so much the worse for Martens.

A material breach in the wall of silence was made in 1993 by the present writer's monograph in the Russian language.[1] Although the print run was small (1000 copies) and the publisher for financial reasons abridged the work, it aroused interest not only among specialists. The Ministry of Foreign Affairs of Russia where Martens worked for 37 years marked the 150th

---

[1] *«... с пальмовой ветвью мира». Ф.Ф. Мартенс -- юрист, дипломат, публицист* [... With the Palm Branch of Peace. F. F. Martens – Jurist, Diplomat, Publicist]. Moscow, Mezhdunarodnye otnosheniia, 1993. 288 p. The work was reprinted without change in 1999 with a blue binding in 2500 copies by the same Moscow publisher.

anniversary of his birth with a solemn occasion. His treatise on international law was reprinted in 1996 by the Chair of International Law at Moscow University. The Russian Post Office issued a commemorative envelope bearing Martens' portrait. The Russian Academy of Sciences awarded the Russian-language biography of Martens the "F. F. Martens Prize" in the same year. This was the first occasion of awarding the Prize, which had been instituted several years earlier.

I hope that the publication of the unabridged and revised text of my biography of Martens in the English language will help draw attention to this remarkable jurist, diplomat, and publicist, for an English-language version – the most widely used language in the world – will undoubtedly enlarge the circle of readers considerably.

CHAPTER I
THE BEGINNING

The future celebrity was born in extremely modest circumstances, and we have very little reliable information about the early years of his life. The ambiguities and gaps in the early period of his biography have not been eliminated to this day. Notwithstanding the world renown of Martens, reference works still do not indicate his date of birth and say nothing of his parents. The spelling of his name conferred at birth is given variously: Fridrikh-Fromkhol'd, Fromkhol'd; and also the name which he bore subsequently: Fridrikh, Fridrikh-Fromgol'd, Frederik, Frederik-Fromgol'd. Therefore even the most elementary information, such as parentage, place and date of birth, require from those who research the life of Martens the most extensive searches and minute investigations.

Childhood

Common sense says that on this matter one must listen above all to the Hero himself, although for Martens the first ten years of his life were evidently shrouded in the mists. In the collected biographies of the professorial and teaching staff of Petersburg University (1898), the data for which were compiled with his participation, it is said: "Martens, Fedor Fedorovich. Born 15 August 1845 in the City of Pernov, Livonian Province. In 1854 he arrived in St. Petersburg, where in January 1855 he was assigned, as an orphan without father or mother, to the Orphan Home attached to St. Peter's Evangelical Lutheran Church. For distinguished achievements he was transferred from the school of the Orphan Home to St. Peter's Main German School, where he completed the full gymnasium course in 1863."[1]

---

[1] *Биографический словарь профессоров и преподавателей императорского С.-Петербургского университета за истекшие четверть века его существования. 1869-1894* [Biographical Dictionary of Professors and Teachers of the Imperial St. Petersburg University During the Quarter Centrury of Its Existence] (1898), II, p. 6.

As we see, Martens confined himself to the date of birth and city where he was born. He always noted 15th August as his birthday (Old Style, which was used in Russia before 1917 and was twelve days behind the European calendar). This is confirmed by his personal diaries which repose in the Archive of the Foreign Policy of Russia (AVPR) of the Ministry of Foreign Affairs of the Russian Federation.[2] But he wrote nothing of his parents or the names conferred upon him when he was born. It is likely that he became Fedor Fedorovich later, when a grown man. The noted authority V. E. Grabar in his capital work on the history of international law in Russia called him Friedrich-Fromhold.[3] Contemporary Estonian biographers call him by the same name.[4] The most detailed biography of Martens is set out in the novel by the Estonian writer, Jan Kross, *Professor Martens' Departure*.[5]

Although the novel is not a scholarly work but rather falls into the category of belles-lettres, it should be borne in mind that the novelist is a lawyer by education and taught at the Faculty of Law of Tartu University. In 1945-46 he was acting docent at the Chair of Public International Law.[6] According to the novel, Friedrich-Fromholz Martens was the ninth and last child in the family of Friedrich Wilhelm Martens, born in 1795. The latter was for many years the sexton of the Lutheran Church in Audre. A year before the birth of his ninth child, F. W. Martens was dismissed as sexton and moved to Pernov, where he purchased a house on Gartenstrasse 10 and engaged in tailoring. His father died when F. F. Martens was five years old, and his mother, four years later. According to the novel, Friedrich-Fromholz had brothers: Heinrich, who became a cobbler in Riga; August, who graduated from university and became a medical

---

[2] AVPR, opis 787, delo 9, ed. khr. 1-7.

[3] See V. E. Grabar, *The History of International Law in Russia 1647-1917*, transl. W. E. Butler (1990), p. 381.

[4] E. Rahumaa and P. Jarvelaid, «Фридрих Фромгольд (Федор Федорович) Маретнс и юристы Тартусского университета» [Friedrich Fromhold (Fedor Fedorovich) Martens and Jurists of Tartu University], *Tartu ulikeeli teaduslikud sidemed*, XVI (1985).

[5] J. Kross, *Уход профессора Мартенса* (Moscow, 1989); published in English as *Professor Martens' Departure* (1994).

[6] Rahumaa and Jarvelaid, note 4 above, p. 75.

doctor on the Island of Madeira; Johannes, who found employment at a local sawmill; Julius, who began to study pharmacy in Petersburg and later founded a factory for the production of hygiene products. Supposedly the youngest of the Martens family was sent to Julius in Petersburg.[7]

Later, having graduated from University, the young man called himself and allowed himself to be called abroad: Friedrich Fromholz. When, for example, his doctoral dissertation on consuls and consular jurisdiction in the East was translated into the German language and published at Berlin,[8] "with additions of the author," the author was designated as Friedrich Fromholz von Martens. Leaving aside the legitimacy of attaching the noble designation "von", of which we shall speak below, Martens called himself, at least in this German publication, Friedrich Fromholz. Later, when he had become Fedor Fedorovich, Martens used the version "Friedrich von Martens" (in the German language) or Frederic de Martens (in French) on his visiting cards, publications in foreign newspapers, and on documents in foreign languages. The foreign press wrote of him as "Friedrich von Martens" or "Frederic de Martens". When in 1910 the German jurist, H. Wehberg, wrote an obituary about his late colleague, he called him "Friedrich von Martens".[9] This usage has continued to the present, with a slight modification in the English language to Frederic de Martens.

Wehberg wrote that F. F. Martens was the youngest child in a large family and orphaned at the age of nine. Since such information (the youngest child in a large family) was absent in contemporary publications, one must suppose that Wehberg had gleaned information from Nikolai Martens, who had told him about his father.[10]

---

[7] Kross (1989), pp. 317-321, 346-390.

[8] F. F. Martens, *Das Consularwesen und die Consularjurisdiction im Orient*, transl. H. Skerst (Berlin, 1874).

[9] H. Wehberg, "Dr. Friedrich v. Martens und die Haager Friedenskonferenzen," *Zeitschrift für internationales Recht*, XX (1910), no 4.

[10] AVPR, opis 749/1, delo 50, l. 85.

These variant readings give rise to a natural perplexity which is only intensified when in the Archive one finds an exceedingly important document – a petition in the Tsar's name of 1868 in which the young man called himself "Fromholz, son of Fedor, Martens."[11] Not Friedrich-Fromholz, but simply Fromholz, his father being called Fedor ... It is difficult to imagine that in such an important document the supplicant would set out false information about himself. A metric certificate was appended to the petition, and the name designated therein could not diverge from that specified in the petition: "Fromholz, son of Fedor ..." The archival find, however, does not entirely resolve the ambiguities.

The contemporaries of Martens had little interest in the details of his childhood, and they left no information which would elucidate the truth. Recent inquiries have only increased the number of bewildering questions not only with regard to the names given him at birth, but also with regard to the date of his birth. In 1975 an Estonian lawyer published an article which declared that despite the most painstaking searches he could not locate the birth registration of the Martens couple in any of the church registries of Pernov (now Parnu).[12] Such an entry was mandatory when christening a child and then served as the grounds for a metric certificate and other certifications. If there was no entry, does this mean there was no christening and no birth on 15th August?

The reliability of the birth date might be confirmed by the metric certificate which Martens attached to his petition in the name of the Tsar. But, as is evident from the entry in his personal file, the metric certificate was returned to Martens "for a time" on 25 September 1879. It is not to be found in the archival materials of the Ministry of Foreign Affairs of Russia.[13] It should be recalled in this connection that on 18 December 1879 Martens was married. He converted to the Orthodox faith at this time

---

[11] Ibid.

[12] See L. Lesment, «Новые сведения из жизни Ф. Ф. Мартенса» [New Information From the Life of F. F. Martens], *Советское право* '[Soviet Law], no. 5 (1975), pp. 358-360.

[13] AVPR, fond DLC and KhD, opis 749/1, delo 50, l. 86.

and changed names. He became Fedor Fedorovich Martens, and the birth certificate was truly essential to him on that occasion.

The transfer to the bosom of the Russian Orthodox Church combined with the acceptance of a Russian forename and patronymic was a common phenomenon in the Russia of that time. Notable examples were the names given to foreign princesses who married Russian Grand Princes. In marrying the future Emperor Alexander II and accepting the Russian Orthodox religion, Princess Maria Hessen-Darmstadt became Maria Alexandrovna. The Danish Princess Sofia Frederica Dagmar was named Maria Fedorovna when she married Emperor Alexander III, and Princess Alicia Hessen-Darmstadt became Alexandra Fedorovna when marrying Emperor Nicholas II.

Whereas marrying a member of the House of Romanov necessarily entailed accepting Russian Orthodoxy and a change of name, Martens in all probability had other motives. His bride was a Lutheran and remained such until her death. It is unlikely that she and her family preferred a conversion to Russian Orthodoxy.

Why, having become Fedor Fedorovich, did Martens not only not object when he was called "Friedrich von Martens" in German, but he himself placed this name on his visiting cards? In our view this was not a matter of continuing to use the name "Friedrich" but of translating the Russian name "Fedor". Such translations of Russian forenames were common at the time: Ivan-Johann, Mikhail-Michel, Egor-Georg, and others. Martens therefore called himself "Friedrich" in German, and "Frederic" in French. He never did this in the Russian language.

It should be stressed in this connection that having become Fedor Fedorovich in 1879 (or abbreviated "F. F.", as he often wrote to friends and relatives), Martens subsequently was known as Fedor Fedorovich in his family, among colleagues at the University and Ministry of Foreign Affairs, in the Russian press, and generally in public. Thus does he deserve to remain in the memory of his descendants.

Martens' personal diaries might dispel many of the ambiguities of his early years. He kept them regularly from 5

January 1883 until 1 April 1909. However, there is not a single word in them about his parents, brothers, childhood, or adolescence. The diaries do contain thoughts about his wife and children, recollections in passing about relatives of his wife (for example, N. K. Ture, with whom he left his diaries for safekeeping in Germany), but nothing about his own relations. In the diary left by his son Nikolai references are to be found to his mother, but there is complete silence with respect to the relatives of his father.

Doctrinal writings confirm the birth date of Martens as 15 August 1845, and there is no reason to change it. Martens himself observed this date. When he became materially well-off, according to Lesment he purchased his father's house in Pernov and travelled there in the summer for holidays. Lesment found this house in Parnu during the early 1970s. The house had been partially rebuilt, but was preserved. The purchase of his father's house would seem to lend support to Martens' biographical data.

Fate would have it that in 1909, the year of Martens' death, the family of attorney Lesment visited Gartenstrasse. The son of this attorney, Leo Lesment, then seven years old, later devoted considerable time to researching the life of Martens.[14]

In this context it is instructive to dwell upon the nationality of Martens' parents. In foreign doctrinal writings, principally German, it is asserted that this outstanding Russian international lawyer was German in origin. Wehberg explicitly said this in 1910.[15] A Russian reviewer of Wehberg's article did not react to his assertion, and now it is difficult to guess: was this tacit acceptance of the view then widely shared or leniency towards a petty distortion of Martens' biography. The Brockhaus encyclopedia published in Germany in 1971 called Friedrich von Martens a "Russian international lawyer of Baltic-German origin".[16] This data has been repeated in other foreign publications.

Estonian studies reject assertions concerning the German origins of Martens. They cite many arguments in support of the

[14] See note 11 above.

[15] Wehberg, note 9 above, p. 23.

[16] *Brockhaus Enzyklopedie* (1971), XII, p. 190.

fact that Martens was born into an Estonian family. One argument is the social origin of Martens' parents: in Livonia of those years Germans constituted the more privileged strata of the populace. As for the fact that the surname Martens sounds German and that he mastered the German language in his youth, this was not an uncommon phenomenon among Estonians, who had experienced German influence for a considerable period. Suffice it to recall that at Dorpat University, founded in Livonia by Emperor Paul I (which later became Iur'ev, and then Tartu, University when the city was renamed), until 1893 teaching was in the German language. Only after that year did teaching commence in the Russian language. It is therefore not surprising that the German language was mastered by Martens. Jan Kross described the ancestry of Martens in great detail, indicating that the father, mother, grandfather, great-grandfather, grandmother, and great-grandmother of Martens were native Estonians.[17]

As regards the city of Pernov, where Martens was born (now Parnu, in Estonia), at the time it was part of the Livonian Province. Livonia was one of three Baltic provinces of the Russian Empire, with nine uezds, among which there was Pernov Uzed.

Pernov itself was a small (about 15,000 inhabitants in 1896) picturesque community on the shore of the River Pernov, which flowed into the Gulf of Riga. In the year Martens was born it undoubtedly was smaller. The city wallowed in green foliage. There were two parks, two public gardens, and more than one thousand private fruit gardens. On the shores of the Gulf were swimming facilities, which we today would call sanatoriums, rest homes, and boarding homes. Residents could take therapeutic baths and bathe in the sea. Life in Pernov was inexpensive and comfortable, and the climate healthy, as one encyclopedic dictionary observed.[18] Martens later loved to holiday in his native region.

However, this did not mean a free and easy life for Martens himself. He did not like to talk about his childhood, but it was

[17] See Kross, note 5 above, pp. 346-390.

[18] Brockhaus and Efron, *Энциклопедический словарь* [Encyclopedic Dictionary] (1896), XVII-a, p. 844; XXIII, p. 24.

wretched in both Pernov and Petersburg. One may judge this from an exclamation in the pages of his diary: how miserable it was for me even in childhood! Those lines were written fifty years later. His childhood was so wretched that Martens remembered it until the end of his life.

The link of the Martens family with Lutheran circles may explain why after the death of his parents the nine-year old came to be in the Orphan Home attached to the St. Peter's Lutheran Church in Petersburg. He himself publicly recalled that a teacher of the local primary school sent him to the Orphan Home in Petersburg. From there the gifted pupil was placed in the nearby St. Peter's School (German Gymnasium), where he successfully completed the full course. His abilities enabled him to enroll at the Law Faculty of Petersburg University. We do not know why the eighteen-year old youth chose the Law Faculty, whether this was an inclination or an enthusiasm. In the Gymnasium he was disposed towards being an historian and poet.[19] Was this his sole opportunity? Or did the possibility of becoming an advocate or even an official in the justice agencies inspire him? In Tsarist Russia of that day there were not so many opportunities for people of his social origin to make one's way in life. A successful career either in the Army or in the civil service required noble origin, which Martens did not have.

The choice made by the young man from Livonia proved to be remarkably successful. He laid the beginnings of a path which gave to the world a remarkable jurist and brought Martens himself world renown.

Student Years

Martens was admitted to the Law Faculty of Petersburg University in 1863. This was a crucial moment in Russia. Fearing revolution from below, the Autocracy decided to avert it by reform from above. A Manifesto signed by Emperor Alexander II on 18 February 1861 proclaimed the emancipation from serfdom of 22 million serfs. The emancipation of the serfs made transformations essential in State administration. There followed judicial reform, military

---

[19] V. Gribovskii, «Юбилей профессора Ф. Ф. Мартенса» [Jubilee of Professor F.F. Martens], *Вестник права* [Herald of Law], kn. 2 (1896), pp. 42-43.

reform, and changes in public education. The public atmosphere in the country changed noticeably. All of this made the prospects for a gifted but poor student without wealthy parents or the necessary connections more promising. He was not among the "belopodkladochniki", or students of aristocratic appearance and reactionary views (persons so called because of foppish uniforms with a white silk lining), who merely by reason of the renown of their family were secured not only a carefree student life but a future successful career. Martens was a typical Russian intellectual not of gentle birth and could rely only on his own efforts. We know little of his student years. How and where he lived? Who were his friends? What attracted him?

Kross's novel says that while a student Martens lived in an attic loft of the German Gymnasium where he graduated. But in the novel it is unclear on what the young man lived and how he paid for his studies at University.

Judging from the numerous literary sketches of the time, Martens as a student probably did what many others did: he gave private lessons. Tutoring in families of means was a typical feature of student life. V. O. Kliuchevskii, later to become a distinguished historian, gave private lessons, for example, while a student.[20]

Just as Russian society generally, Russian students were sharply divided by material well-being. The perspicacious eyes and literary talent of the Russian writer A. I. Kuprin left us a superb sketch of students of that period in Kiev, which would be equally typical for students at Moscow and Petersburg universities. To appreciate it one must understand that students usually wore a uniform. Kuprin called his sketch "The Student-Dragoon" (1895).

"A service cap of Prussian design without a brim, but with microscopic peak and a black – instead of a blue – cap-band; close-fitting uniform with a turned left flap enabling one to see the white silk lining; pince-nez with a black ribbon; boots without

---

[20] A vivid description of Kliuchevskii's student life in 1861-65 was given by Academician M. V. Nechkina in *Василий Осипович Ключевский* [Vasilii Osipovich Kliuchevskii] (1974).

heels and white gloves – this was the usual dress of the student-dragoon ..." With a secret sadness he thinks that in Kiev one does not wear a sword, as do the Petersburg "student-guardsmen" (only the nobility had the right to wear a sword).

The place of the student-dragoon was in a restaurant, at races, in a public house, or at the theatre, or a fashionable performance. "The university he, of course, sometimes visits ... glancing with a contemptuous smile at those in shabby double-breasted jackets who listen to something there and even write down some trifle."[21]

The young Martens was among those who had "shabby double-breasted jackets", and he diligently outlined the lectures of the professors since there were virtually no printed textbooks in those days and the students wrote down what the teachers said. Sometimes the most complete synopses were reproduced by lithography. This was Marten's lot, and he laboured assiduously. Work, work, and work – this was his destiny.

Student years are an important time in personality formation, in the formation of a scholar. It is during this period that a favourite subject is gradually determined, the first subjects of research, and most important, a world outlook is formed, both scholarly and socio-political. Study in university is not a tense and monotonous process of mastering portions of information given by professors. The future professional, future scholar, is born in the student years.

In Russia one enrolled at university in those days at 17-18 years of age, taking the entrance examination usually in May. Students paid tuition. There were scholarships, but very few and usually were not awarded before the second year of study if the first year had been successfully completed. The course of study was four years. In the fourth year the most able students wrote a candidate thesis (today called a diploma thesis). This was submitted to the Faculty and the degree of candidate of sciences was awarded for it, for example, candidate of law. Certain candidates remained at the University, after completing their

---

[21] A. I. Kuprin, *Собрание сочинений* [Collection of Works] (1964), IX, pp. 5-6.

studies, for two years in order to prepare for the professoriate. During this period the candidate was expected to take the magister examinations and to write a magister thesis (today, the kandidat dissertation). If the dissertation was successfully defended, the Ministry of Public Enlightenment sent the new magister of sciences on a foreign trip for two years "for further study of the subject". Upon returning, he commenced to teach at his University.

It should be noted that the years during which Martens was at University were characterised by the penetration of revolutionary ideas amongst the student body. Petersburg University was even closed in Autumn 1861 by reason of student disturbances, and arrests were made among the ringleaders of the disturbances. However, we have no information about Martens' involvement, even indirect, in revolutionary fermentation. If one judges from his later views (for example, during the Russian Revolution of 1905), he would probably have reacted negatively to student disorders. His attention was devoted to study, to his future speciality.

As regards the future profession of Martens, it should be said that for a long time the Law Faculty of Petersburg University had no special Chair of International Law. It was taught as part of the course of Comparative State law of European States by Professor A. D. Gradovskii, who headed the Chair of State Law until 1889. Contemporaries saw in Gradovskii the "father of the Russian science of State law". Politically, Gradovskii was not a retrograde; many of his views were liberal. At the same time, his legal doctrine was distinctive for the "excessive idealisation of the Russian State system", including idealisation of the "unlimited Autocracy".[22] Gradovskii wrote several works on international law, including on the conditions of a people's war (1878) and on political murder and the right of asylum (1881). His lectures evidently shaped the views of Martens to a considerable extent. That influence might be found especially in the lectures of Gradovskii treating the idea of the rights of

---

[22] *Энциклопедический словарь Гранат* [Granat Encyclopedic Dictionary] (7th ed., 1913), XVI, pp. 367-371.

the individual and Western European constitutionalism. And the idealisation by Martens' teacher of the State system of Tsarist Russia also left its mark.

In accordance with the course of study Martens graduated from the University in 1867. As one of the best students, he submitted to the Faculty a candidate dissertation on relations between Russia and the Ottoman Empire in the Reign of Empress Catherine II.

Here one must dwell on Martens' command of foreign languages. The German language he knew to a certain extent from childhood, and the German Gymnasium from which he graduated in Petersburg consolidated his initial skills. The candidate dissertation testified to his command of the French language, then the traditional language of diplomacy. Later in his mature years Martens spoke English fluently.

Upon graduating Martens faced, just as all other graduates, the question of his future. The industrious Martens had attracted the attention of his teachers. The Dean of the Faculty, Professor I. I. Ivanovskii, liked the candidate dissertation by Martens. Ivanovskii himself (1807-86) headed the Chair of International Law established at the University in 1863. He was educated at the Minsk Gymnasium and the Vilnius University. Then he was sent to perfect his Russian language at Moscow University, and later to a special institute for the training of the professoriate in Dorpat. A foreign trip of three years in duration was spent principally in Berlin. He then became a professor of Petersburg University in the Chair of All-People's Law. His lectures undoubtedly left an imprint on Martens. According to his students, Ivanovskii was the "most brilliant of all the jurists" in the Faculty. His writings and lectures were distinctive for the breadth of views and enthusiasm for the science of international law. The attention of the noted scholar was invaluable support for a rising jurist.

The subsequent events are described in Martens' biography as follows: "Graduated in 1867 with the degree of candidate of sciences, F. F. applied to the then Dean of the Law Faculty, I. I. Ivanovskii, who occupied the Chair of International Law, with a request to remain attached to the University in order to prepare for the professoriate. To the Dean's question: "Which Chair?", the young candidate replied "I would wish to remain at the Chair of Criminal Law." Then the Dean, having sympathetically reviewed the candidate dissertation of F. F. categorically said: "No, remain at the Chair of International Law. Then we will have our Martens", alluding to the two noted European writers on international law and diplomacy in the early nineteenth century who bore this surname."[23]. Ivanovskii had in view the noted German jurist and diplomat, Georg Friedrich Martens (1756-1821) and his descendant and successor in the domain of international law, Charles de Martens (1790-1863), known to this day as the progenitors of collections of international treaties. The "Russian Martens" was made by decision of the Dean.

Having remained at the Chair of International Law, Martens did not disappoint the hopes of Ivanovskii. At the end of 1868 he submitted a magister dissertation on the right of private ownership during wartime. Martens read the dissertation in manuscript aloud during evenings to the Dean and the reviewer. In April it was approved and then printed. After submission of the dissertation Martens took the magister examination. The public defence proceeded successfully in Autumn 1869.[24] Thus Martens did not follow the usual procedure: first he wrote the dissertation, and then took the examinations. This testified to his maturity. Ultimately within two years Martens became a magister.

Foreign Travel Upon the recommendation of the Law Faculty, Martens was sent abroad. He attended lectures in Vienna, Heidelberg, and Leipzig. Judging from his later actions, the lectures of Professor Lorenz von Stein, at the University of Vienna, and of Professor J. Bluntschli, at Heidelberg University, made the greatest impression.

---

[23] Note 1 above.

[24] AVPR, opis 749/1, delo 50, l. 92 contains his Diploma of Magister of International Law for defence of the discourse on the right of private ownership in wartime on 6 October 1869.

Lorenz von Stein (1815-90) had the reputation of a noted jurist, constitutional lawyer, and economist. His path of learning he commenced in Paris with a study of the communist movement. There in 1842 he published a book on socialism and communism in modern France. Thereafter he wrote several works devoted to the communist and socialist movement in Europe. From the time of receiving the professorship in the University of Kiel (Germany), Stein devoted greater attention to the problems of the economy, the State, and law. In his scholarly research he was a follower of Hegel and his dialectical method. In 1855 Stein was invited to take the chair in the University of Vienna and worked there for thirty years, until his retirement.

Stein published works on economics, State administration, the theory of State and law, and administrative and financial law. His seven-volume on the Doctrine of administration (1865-68) was widely admired. Significant attention was devoted to the rights of the individual in his works. Stein developed the notion that the life of mankind is not confined to the State community, which in the modern world is developing as the "social community" and not enclosed by State frontiers. In Stein's view, the measure of the perfection of State power is the freedom of the activity of social organisations, the freedom of the individual. Although Stein's works were devoted primarily to municipal questions, they gave creative impulse to the science of international law, including the international legal doctrines of Martens.

Johann Caspar Bluntschli (1808-81) was born in Zurich and received his legal education and initially worked in Switzerland. He was a member of the Great Council of Zurich, and also a member of the Government of Switzerland. Next he taught at the universities in Munich (from 1848) and Heidelberg (from 1861). He began with a study of Roman and civil law, and then turned to State law. In 1852 his principal work in this field appeared – on General State Law. Finally, he passed on to international law and acquired a world reputation as a specialist. At the height of the Franco-Prussian War of 1870-71 his work appeared on the modern law of warfare of civilised States, in which he undertook to codify the law of war. The codification of the norms of international law along the example of municipal law (civil code, criminal code) was a favourite idea of Bluntschli. The *cours* on international law which he wrote was translated into several European languages. It was published at Moscow (1878) in the Russian language by Professor L. A. Kamarovskii (1846-1912), of Moscow University, under the name "Contemporary International Law of Civilised States Set Out in the Form of a Code". Bluntschli reduced international law to 862 paragraphs.

Bluntschli was one of the founders of the Institute of International Law at Ghent (1873).

Martens interrupted his foreign trip prematurely. In 1870 the Council of St. Petersburg University did not elect Ivanovskii to a new five-year term and the chair of international law was vacant. The Law Faculty proposed that Martens take it (with the rank of docent), and he returned to Petersburg.

Martens treated his university instructors with great warmth. Gradovskii he subsequently quoted in his *cours* of international law frequently, although there were greater specialists on the issues being analysed; Ivanovskii at the proposal of Martens was elected in 1873 an Honorary Member of the Petersburg University.

The foreign trip had a large impact on the scholarly work of Martens. As the immediate future showed, he lost no time in the universities of Vienna, Heidelberg, and Leipzig, but studied assiduously the latest achievements of legal thought and of the social sciences in general. The foreign visit strengthened one of his principal characteristics as a scholar – *the inextricable link with the world science of international law.* The trip was the first, but not the only one. It laid the foundation for Martens' constant communion with foreign colleagues, above all in Europe.

F. F. Martens
1880

CHAPTER II
PROFESSOR OF PETERSBURG UNIVERSITY

Martens' return to Petersburg marked a new era in his life - Professor of International Law of the University in the capital. Before him lay a long road, with many achievements in various domains. But to the outside world until his death he remained above all "Professor Martens".

Young Docent On 28 January 1871 the young docent delivered the first lecture to his students. By tradition a new teacher should deliver his first lecture to the predecessor in the chair. The same tradition required that one lecture on a subject which the predecessor had dwelt upon. Martens acted otherwise. He entitled his first lecture "On the Tasks of Contemporary International Law". It was printed in the journal of the Ministry of Public Enlightenment and then as a separate pamphlet.[1]

The lecture offered a critical evaluation of the state of the science of international law and set out the principal orientations of its future development. Martens was severe as to the state of affairs in Russian doctrine. He concluded that whose who delivered the course on international law before him had no solid scholarly foundations since they did not rely upon an investigation of material factors which conditioned the development of international law nor study the objective laws of societal development contributing to the formation of international law. As Martens said, the science of international law "up to the present has not accepted for research the elements and phenomena of real life, has not even attempted to investigate the internal laws of the community of States and international relations". He pointed out that such work was being carried on in the other social sciences, for example, economics, and that the time had come to "turn to an investigation of the laws of historical development of peoples in their international life".

[1] See F. F. Martens, *О задачах современного международного права* [On the Tasks of Contemporary International Law] (Spb., 1871).

He stressed that "international law only will become a firm foundation when the natural and historical laws of the development of peoples are elicited". Under this approach Martens accorded principled significance to the link between the development of international law and the history of international relations and the study of concrete legal material. In his view only history could provide a firm basis for international legal structures.

If one were to summarise the ideas expressed by Martens in his first University lecture, they might be characterised as a programme for the creation of his own theory of international law. This meant not so much the summary and generalisation of the information that had been accumulated and the factual materials which remained uninvestigated as it did a new methodological approach. This was a bold and innovative statement by a 25-year old docent; not surprisingly, he was critical of everything that had been done previously in the domain of international law. He doubtless went too far in his conclusion that the lectures delivered before his time were unsuitable, proposing to redraw all that had been done before him in the Russian science of international law.

The break with tradition, the massive criticism of the existing situation could not fail to engender a serious reaction. To be sure, many of his most severe statements and especially the tasks he set out reflected to a considerable extent the real state of affairs and were consistent with what was needed. One must agree, for example, that the science of international law in Russia seemed to have lagged behind against the background of the general progress in social thought in Russia.

Russian history was represented by great names. The twenty-eight volume "History of Russia from Ancient Times" had been published by S. M. Solov'ev (1851-79); his writings played an important role in the formation of social thought in Russia. They especially influenced greatly another outstanding Russian historian, V. O. Kliuchevskii.[2] The works of T. N.

---

[2] See the Introduction by S. S. Dmitriev and N. D. Koval'chenko, in S. M. Solov'ev, *Сочинения* [Works] (1988) I, pp. 6-48.

Granovskii (1813-55) were widely read. The Hegelian dialectic underlay his view of the historical process.

The Russian science of State and law enjoyed an upsurge of interest. From the 1860s the volume of politico-legal writings increased noticeably, as did their scholarly quality. Scholars of European reputation emerged in Russia, including in the theory of State and law: M. M. Kovalevskii, N. M. Korkunov, S. A. Muromtsev, P. I. Novgorodtsev, L. I. Petrazhitskii, B. N. Chicherin, G. F. Shershenevich, and others. Most were individuals whose research spanned a vast range of concerns, including the link between Law and the State, morality, and political views. Examples include Petrazhitskii's survey of the philosophy of law (1860), Kapustin's theory of law (1868), and Chicherin's history of political theory in four volumes (1869-1902).

The science of international law was formed in Russia more slowly than in Western Europe; the total number of publicists and works was comparatively small. However, for its time the quality was surprisingly high. It should be added that Martens was not alone in sharply criticising the state of the science of international law. The noted jurist N. M. Korkunov (general theory of law) had appealed for shaking off "the archaic dust" from the science of international law.[3] The desire to raise the standard was shared by a number of Russian scholars of the day. Amongst those who made the most noteworthy contributions were D. I. Kachenovskii, M. N. Kapustin, V. A. Nezabitovskii, A. N. Stoianov, and N. M. Korkunov.[4]

Kapustin was the author of a survey of the subjects of international law (1856-59). Kachenovskii's doctoral dissertation on the law of prize (1855) was translated into English and published in London, which gave the author a European reputation. In a work notable for the sophistication of its historical analysis, Kachenovskii foresaw a number of provisions

[3] Cited in V. E. Grabar, *The History of International Law in Russia 1647-1917*, transl. W. E. Butler (1990), p. 440.

[4] See F. I. Kozhevnikov, *Русское государство и международное право* [The Russian State and International Law] (1947), pp. 135, 141-148.

of the future Paris Declaration on privateering. He delivered a report to the Law Society in London which proposed that international law be codified by a special international collective of scholars. His treatise on international law was published at Kharkov in 1863.

In 1860 Nezabitovskii published his book on the teachings of publicists concerning inter-State possession. Rejecting the views of many scholars, he juxtaposed the view of territory as a thing to his notion of territory as a space within whose limits State power operates.

Korkunov was one of the first in international law to link the ideas of international dispositive legal capacity and sovereignty, international community, and the international protection of rights. He proposed his own system for the structure of international law. He also put forward the idea of international criminal repression. He insisted on the territorial principle in resolving problems of international criminal law. Korkunov left a rich legacy of ideas, including in his book on international law (1886).[5]

If Martens wished to realise his claim to renew the Russian science of international law, he would have to offer works which on the level of theory and a breadth of generalisation of factual material and fundamental research would be noticeably superior to those of his predecessors and be at least at the level of the general progress in the social sciences in Russia and the achievements of the European science of international law. This was an exceedingly complex task for a young docent. But he firmly resolved to combine teaching with scholarly research and did not depart from this resolve. Martens the teacher was organically linked with Martens the research scholar.

Having received the degree of doctor of sciences in 1873, Martens became first professor extraordinarius, and in 1876, professor ordinarius of Petersburg University.

---

[5] See V. N. Durdenevskii, «Вклад русской науки в международное право» [Contribution of Russian Science to International Law], *Вестник Московского университета, Секция общественных наук* [Herald of Moscow University. Section of Social Sciences], no. 4 (1949), pp. 76-78.

"Recueil de traités" In accordance with the tasks set out in his first lecture, Martens worked actively on the problems of international law. He developed his ideas with his students and in individual articles. It happened, however, that Martens realised his scholarly plans mostly in the publication of his capital *Собрание трактатов и конвенций, заключеннчх Россиею с иностранными державами*, but best known under its abbreviated French title, *Recueil des traités*.

For the first time documents of Russian diplomatic history began to be published at the end of the eighteenth century by the noted educator, N. I. Novikov, in his *Древняя Российской вивлиофике* [Ancient Russian Library]. In 1779 Empress Catherine II had signed an Edict concerning the publication of such a collection, the preparation of which was placed on Academician G. F. Müller, who from 1766 had served as the head of the Archive of the College of Foreign Affairs. Müller zealously accepted this mission and quickly submitted to the Empress the "beginning of the *Recueil des traités*", documents of the relations of Russia with the Holy Roman Empire for 1486-1519. He intended to complete the preparation of the *Recueil* within the next five years, but did not succeed in realising his plans. Müller's death suspended the work for an extended period. The project was continued by the administrator of the Archive of the College of Foreign Affairs, N. N. Bantysh-Kamenskii (1737-1814) and A. F. Malinovskii (1762-1840). In 1813 the first volume of the *Собрание государственных грамот и договоров, хранящихся в Государственной коллегии иностранных дел* [Collection of State Instruments and Treaties Kept in the State College of Foreign Affairs] was issued. Work again was suspended. The remaining three volumes were published later, and part of the fifth volume, only in 1894. Almost exclusively internal State acts were placed in these documents, and not international treaties.

In the 1850s publication was commenced of the reports ("*статейные списки*") of Russian diplomats of the fifteenth-seventeenth centuries in the *Памятники дипломатических сношений древней России с державами иностранными*

[Monuments of Diplomatic Relations of Ancient Russia with Foreign Powers]. Other collections of diplomatic documents were also printed. However, they could not replace a systematised complete collection. Given these circumstances, Chancellor A. M. Gorchakov, who headed the foreign policy department, reported in 1873 to Emperor Alexander II the proposed publication of a collection of treaties and conventions concluded by Russia with other States. The Emperor approved the Report of Gorchakov and work on the treaty collection was entrusted to Martens. At the Emperor's instruction, Martens received access to all diplomatic correspondence kept in Russian archives.

Martens set about this task with enormous energy, and by 1874 the first volume of the *Recueil des traités* had appeared. Martens commenced the *Recueil* from 1648, when the Peace of Westphalia was concluded to end the Thirty Years War. In compiling the *Recueil* he decided not to adhere to the purely chronological principle, but rather to order the materials by country. Volume one contained the treaties concluded by Russia with Austria (up to 1762).

Martens rested not only upon the experience of similar publications, but also contributed something significantly new. The international legal acts published were supplied with an historical introduction composed on the basis of archival materials in the Russian Ministry of Foreign Affairs. Sometimes such introductions were substantial (more than twenty pages in small print). In the preface Martens explained that this was due to the "exceptional interest" which the documents represented.[6] Often the historical introductions became independent studies, Martens devoting great attention to the foreign policy initiatives of Russia and the role of Russian diplomacy. The texts of treaties reproduced in the *Recueil* and the introductions to them were printed in parallel texts in the French and Russian languages, which facilitated the use of the *Recueil* in other countries.

---

[6] See *Собрание трактатов и конвенций, заключенных Россиею с иностранными державами* [Collection of Treaties and Conventions Concluded by Russia with Foreign Powers], VII (1885), p. 11.

In the words of Martens' student, Professor M. A. Taube, "intead of the usually dry collection of treaty texts, F. F. offered to give to our and to the foreign reading world, practitioners and theoreticians of international law, diplomats and historians, professors and publicists, and above to the Russian Ministry of Foreign Affairs itself, the living history of Russian treaty relations with foreign powers from the mid-seventeenth century". Taube stressed the enormous importance of the "colossal work", "invaluable – and having no analogue in any State – historico-diplomatic *Recueil*". Noting that the *Recueil* prepared by Martens went far beyond the framework of a collection of the texts of international legal acts, Taube called it an "historical-diplomatic encyclopedia of Russian foreign relations".[7] Another of Martens' students, Professor B. E. Nolde, linked the services of his teacher with the "*Recueil* of enormous historical value, having no equal in foreign scholarly literature either in its wealth of material or breadth of structure".[8]

Having begun work on the *Recueil* in 1873, Martens continued publishing it until his death. Between 1874-1909 fifteen large volumes appeared. The first four volumes were devoted to the relations of Russia with Austria (1648-1877), the fifth to the eighth, with Germany (1656-1888), the ninth through the twelfth, with England (1710-1895), and the thirteenth through the fifteenth, with France (1717-1906).

The *Recueil* rapidly achieved recognition in Russia and abroad. For Russian diplomacy the collection became a useful support in diplomatic activity and occupied a permanent place in the reference materials of the central apparatus of the Ministry of Foreign Affairs and in Russian foreign representations. The Archive of the Ministry of Foreign Affairs has preserved a vast correspondence connected with sending the regular volumes of the *Recueil* to embassies and other representations of Russia in Berlin, London, Paris, Rome, and elsewhere. The editors of the

---

[7] M. A. Taube, *Ф. Ф. Мартенс(1845-1909). Некролог* [F.F. Martens (1845-1909. Obituary] (Spb., 1909), pp. 8-9.

[8] B. E. Nolde, »Ф. Ф. Мартенс« [F.F. Martens], *Русская мысль* [Russian Thought], no. 12 (December 1909), p. 30.

largest Russian newspapers and university libraries received the *Recueil*. In April 1898 the Russian Ministry of Foreign Affairs sent Volume XIII as a gift (the List is given in accordance with the original Chancellery enumeration) to Prince Bismarck, Chancellor Prince Hohenlohe, the Minister of Foreign Affairs von Bülow, the King of Spain, the Emperor of Germany, the King of Denmark, the Prince-Regent of Bavaria, the King of Belgium, The Duke of Saxon-Coburg, the Sultan of Turkey, and others – 41 personages in all.[9] Other volumes newly issued were treated similarly.

The Archive also contains other evidence of the interest in Martens' work. In March 1899 the Director of the Library of Uppsala University (Sweden) reminded the Russian Ministry of Foreign Affairs in writing that upon his petition in 1895 the *Recueil* published by Professor Martens was sent. He requested the sending of regular volumes be continued. The Kharkov Public Library sent an order for the *Recueil*,[10] and so forth. Publication of the *Recueil* truly brought Martens world renown.

It should be noted that in Russia Martens' work was subjected to certain criticial observations, especially from his fellow jurists. Noting the enormous significance of the *Recueil*, they also pointed to certain shortcomings. Taube suggested that the commencement point chosen by Martens, the 1648 Peace of Westphalia, offers a "purely artificial framework for the exposition" since that date was not a noteworthy benchmark in the history of the foreign relations of Russia with foreign States.[11] Nolde wrote of the "many material shortcomings of this publication," to which he, in particular, relegated a "certain hurriedness in processing the material" and also an "exaggerated assessment of the political abilities of many Russian public figures of the nineteenth century". As a whole he reproached Martens for an "excessive deference to our diplomatic tradition".[12]

---

[9] AVPR, op. 336/2, delo 68, l. 33-41.

[10] Ibid., l. 1, 20.

[11] See Taube, note 7 above, p. 8.

[12] Nolde, note 8 above, p. 30.

The critics of Martens' work never denied its high professionalism, but their comments were not always well-founded.

More than a hundred years have elapsed since the appearance of the first volume of the *Recueil*, but the passage of time has not reduced the fundamental significance of Martens' work. Even during his lifetime it had become a classic. So it remains in our day, and no capital work on the history of Russian foreign relations or international relations can fail to refer to that collection. The *Recueil* has passed into the golden fund of international legal literature.

The *Recueil* was sufficient to bring Martens into the group of outstanding international lawyers, as had occured with the "German Martens", also the author of collections of international treaties.

Treatise on International Law

No less, if not greater, fame was achieved by Martens through his two-volume treatise, or *cours*, "Contemporary International Law of Civilised Peoples" (1882-83).[13]

In Martens' day virtually every professor lectured from his own *cours* of international law and, as a rule, in time published it. It is entirely understandable that Martens traversed along the beaten track and intended to embody his idea of renewing the science of international law in his own *cours*.

The methodological approach of the author gave scholarly novelty to the cours. Martens achieved the intention signified in his first lecture in 1871: to supply the study of international law with a solid foundation for the social and political development of States and the history of international relations. As he emphasised, "at the base of international law lie actual, real, vital relations". Therefore it is not chronological positioning of the material nor the form of presentation which is important, but eliciting the societal laws of the development of international relations and the international law regulating them. Martens

[13] See F. F. Martens, *Современное международное право цивилизованных народов* [Contemporary International Law of Civilised Peoples] (Spb., 1882-83). 2 vols.

devoted special attention, in his words, to the evolution of "Russian international policy according to the sources of our archives". In this respect Martens' two-volume *cours* became the first "Russian" (although on a limited scale) cours of international law. Other authors, as a rule, had no such opportunity.

Martens' treatise is distinctive for its fundamentality and the richness of historical and normative material. The endeavour to elicit the internal laws of the societal development of international law inspired him to use a large number of works from the domain of not only international law, but also the history of international relations, the histories of human civilisation and individual States, constitutional law, and law and philosophy.

In the preface to the first edition Martens wrote that Russia had long since acted as a mighty power in international relations. At the same time, in his view, "the science of international law is launching its roots into Russian earth with difficulty" and to date in Russian literature "there is not a single systematic manual relating to this science composed by a Russian scholar". Martens' treatise was called upon to fill this gap. Martens supposed that the value of his work lay in the "system of international law" that he offered, which "best corresponds to the essence and degree of development of contemporary international relations".

The following elements are singled out in Martens' approach to structuring the system of international law. First, the system itself must arise from the essence of international relations. In other words, it must be orientated not towards the logical correlation of principles and norms, but towards the relations which really exist. Second, the system must follow the laws of societal development inherent in the development of international law. Martens singled out the *international community* as a central tenet. He pointed out that "the entire significance of international relations and the entire force of international law is based namely on the community of social, cultural, and legal interests which join together civilised peoples". Third, the system was called upon to take into account the process of the development of international relations and international law. In so doing it may not confine itself to the consistency of the exposition of international events and international legal acts, but must proceed from the peculiarities of a particular historical era. It is in the system proposed by Martens "that the history of international relations occupies a prominent place". Fourth, his system is structured by taking into account the organic link of international relations and international law with municipal life and internal law. A central notion in Martens is that the "degree of the development of social interests and the internal system of a State determines the extent of its participation in international life".[14]

Martens' treatise became a noted phenomenon in the science of international law in Russia and abroad. It was a major contribution to the development of international legal scholarship, for it addressed the changes that had occurred in the world. In Russian doctrine of a later period it was justly pointed out that against the background of the theories of international law which had preceded, Martens' work was of an undoubtedly progressive character.[15]

In Russia many specialists evaluated Martens' treatise as the first fundamental work encompassing the entire system of international law. Taube later wrote of Martens: "The significance of his life and activity consists in the fact that, practically speaking, it was he who transplanted and cultivated ... the science of international law in us ...".[16] Nolde, however, reacted critically to the theory of the international community advanced by Martens,[17] and Grabar, on the contrary, considered a shortcoming of the treatise to be the inconsistent application therein of the "supreme principle of international law", which he considered to be the international community.[18]

---

[14] Martens, note 13 above, 3d ed. (1895), I, pp. iii-v.

[15] D. B. Levin, *Наука международного права в России в конце XIX и начале XX в.* [The Science of International Law in Russia at the End of the Nineteenth and Beginning of the Twentieth Centuries] (M., 1982), p. 19.

[16] Taube, note 7 above, p. 16.

[17] Nolde, note 8 above, pp. 24-25.

[18] V. E. Grabar, *The History of International Law in Russia 1647-1917*, transl. W. E. Butler (Oxford, 1990) p. 464.

The objections of certain scholars led to the proposition that contemporary international law could be applied only in relations between "civilised peoples", that is, the States of Europe and America, whereas in relations with "uncivilised peoples" (Africa, Asia) the principles of natural law must apply. The division of peoples into "civilised" and "uncivilised" was common in the doctrinal writings of the day (treatises by Bluntschli, Heffter, and others). In following this division, Martens proceeded from the real relations in the world. He set out the existing distinctions of principle and took them into account. Martens was far from idealising the colonial orders and favoured respect for the interests of the population of the colonies, protectorates, dependent and semi-dependent States, but on the basis of natural law. His position, however, was assessed by some Russian colleagues as a justification of the policy of colonial oppression.[19]

L. A. Kamarovskii (Moscow University) displayed a suspended approach to Martens' treatise, to which he devoted a special article. Among the merits of the treatise Kamarovskii noted: (1) the originality of the system, the basis of which was the principle of the international community; (2) the abundance of historical and normative material; (3) the numerous citations to the history of Russian foreign relations, which were underscored by the large portion of primary sources, some unpublished. Kamarovskii also praised the independence of Martens' judgments and his polemic with venerable scholars. On the whole, while expressing certain critical remarks, he valued the treatise as a "rich contribution to our fatherland science".[20]

---

[19] See V. P. Danevskii, *Пособие к изучению истории и системы международного права* [Manual for the Study of the History and System of International Law] (Kharkov, 1892), I, p. 105; P. E. Kazanskii, *Введение в курс международного права* [Introduction to the Cours of International Law] (Odessa, 1901), p. 233; L. A. Kamarovskii, *Основные вопросы науки международного права* [Basic Questions of the Science of International Law] (M., 1892), p. 75.

[20] L. A. Kamarovskii, reviewing the first edition of Martens' *cours* in *Юридический вестник* [Legal Herald], no. 3 (1886), pp. 460-486.

Viewed from the vantage point of our day, it is wholly evident that Martens' treatise conferred on the Russian science of international law qualitatively new features. It noticeably advanced the wisdom of the science of international law to the level of the other social sciences, above all the rapidly developing historical and legal sciences.

The vast range of interests of many Russian jurists often led to specialists in international law being deeply engaged with the general theory of law, municipal law, or comparative law, whereas specialists in municipal law made a material contribution to the science of international law. Kapustin, an international lawyer, studied problems of the general theory of law. Tagantsev was concerned with international criminal justice. He left a noteworthy legacy in criminal law, having substantiated in detail the proposition that a criminal act, wherever committed, infringes upon the general good of all States and must be chastised by all States.[21] Kovalevskii developed a lecture course on the State law of European powers.[22] Korkunov taught State law at Petersburg University, but as Grabar justly wrote, "rendered greater service to international law than many of the internationalists *pur sang*".[23]

Against this background the vast range of materials cited by Martens in his treatise on international law – history, political doctrines, philosophy, State law, and others – and his approach as a whole to scientific research, which is a characteristic feature of Russian legal science, becomes the more comprehensible. As regards Martens' method, it should be designated above all as comparative-historical.

The materialistic views of history and social development, to a certain extent inherent in the ideologues of the *narodnichestvo* (N. K. Mikhailovskii, P. L. Lavrov, P. N. Tkachev, and others), in the 1860-70s exerted a noticeable impact on the

---

[21] N. P. Tagantsev, *Курс русского уголовного права* [Cours of Russian Criminal Law] (Spb., 1874), I; id, *Лекции по русскому уголовному праву* [Lectures on Russian Criminal Law] (Spb., 1887), and others.

[22] M. M. Kovalevskii, *Государственное право европейских держав* [Cours of Russian Criminal Law] (Spb., 1883-84).

[23] Grabar, note 18 above, p. 440.

various strata of Russian intellectuals not of gentle birth in the Russian intelligentsia and on the student body. In those years the dissemination of Marxism commences in Russia.

The attitude towards revolutionary transformations in Russia of that period increasingly became a key issue for social thought, especially in view of that fact that the structure of autocracy stubbornly resisted any significant reforms, including evolution towards a constitutional monarchy. Martens too could not avoid an answer to the key question. The treatise on international law provided modest opportunities for evaluations of municipal development, and Martens' views on the position in Russia are to be found only indirectly in it. The general position of Martens, however, can be discerned rather precisely. In speaking of the rights of the individual, legality, the rule of law, he actually opposed the system of autocracy and favoured a transformation of the Russian State. On the other hand, he was an opponent of the revolutionary path and considered it necessary to express this concisely, using the section on emigration and the extradition of criminals. Martens named all revolutionaries "anarchists" and "dynamiters" who threatened the peaceful life and legal order in the Russian State, and indeed the entire world.[24] In Martens' view the revolutionary movement in Russia and other countries was an attempt against the international legal order, and therefore required a rebuff from all civilised States. Marxist ideas, including in their Russian manifestation, did not affect the oeuvre of Martens.

The treatise on international law achieved widespread recognition surprisingly quickly. In Russia it went through five editions between 1882-1905 and became the most widely used textbook. As such it lasted up to the First World War, that is, for thirty years. Emperor Nicholas II studied it as the future heir to the throne. V. I. Ul'ianov (Lenin) read it in 1891 when he took his external examinations for the university course of study in Petersburg (Martens' treatise was on the list of compulsory reading, and Martens himself was a member of the examination commission). A. F. Kerchenskii (1881-1970), head of the

---

[24] See Martens, note 13 above, II, pp. 162-180, 381-417.

Provisional Government in 1917, G. V. Chicherin (1872-1936), People's Commissar of Foreign Affairs of Soviet Russia, and also a large number of other State figures of prerevolutionary and postrevolutionary Russia, studied Martens' treatise.

One manifestation of the international recognition of Martens' treatise was its translation into many languages of the world. A German translation of the treatise appeared in Berlin (1883-86), a French translation followed (1883-87), and then a Spanish (Madrid, 1895). The treatise also was translated into Chinese, Persian, Serbian, and Japanese – in all seven languages. The *Encyclopedia Britannica* (1946) called Martens' treatise the "best-known in the world".[25]

It is remarkable that abroad Martens' treatise is accepted not only as a textbook, but also as the exposition of the position of an authoritative jurist.

In completing an evaluation of the role and place of Martens' treatise in Russian and foreign literature one may quote the words of Taube, who wrote in the year of Martens' death that his manual "has primacy of place – and is predominant to this day – without any serious competitors in the sense of depicting a general system of contemporary international law in the course of exactly 27 years".[26]

To be just, it should be noted that in the view of a number of writers Martens, after the publication of his treatise, not only created no new scholarly works but did not even rework the treatise itself. This, however, does not mean that there was no further development of the scholarly concepts which he proposed. Suffice it to draw attention to the works, categorised as publicist, to discover rich lodes of ideas which deepen and enlarge upon the scholarly propositions in the treatise: "The Egyptian Question and International Law" (1882); "The Nationality Policy of Prince Bismarck" (1883); "The African Conference in Berlin and the Colonial Policy of Contemporary States" (1885); "The Hague Peace Conference" (1900), and certain others.

---

[25] See *Encyclopedia Britannica* (Chicago, Ill., 1946), XIV, p. 982.

[26] Taube, note 7 above, p. 6.

Martens' intensive practical work on the codification and future development of international law can not be regarded as lacking scholarly importance. In the course of such work Martens not only realised his scholarly conceptions, but developed them under the influence of the specific formation of international relations. This relates, in particular, to his reports submitted to the Institute of International Law in Ghent.

The fifth edition of Martens' treatise was published in 1904-05 without revision. The fact that Martens did not consider it necessary to update the treatise can, in this writer's view, be explained by the fact that he did not see qualitatively new changes in international relations. In this Martens was right. Qualitative changes in international relations matured latently, but they led to radical movements only in connection with the First World War, the Revolution of 1917 in Russia, the Revolution of 1918 in Germany, and other revolutionary shocks. Martens did not live to see these changes, and his scholarly oeuvre is linked with the prerevolutionary epoch.

Historical Essays

While working on the *Recueil* and the treatise on international law Martens, given his scholarly views, could not fail to be steeped in the history of international relations and Russian foreign policy. The history of international relations was extensively set out in his treatise, and the history of Russian foreign policy illuminated in the *Recueil*, which was justly called an "historico-diplomatic encyclopedia of Russian foreign relations". Less known are Martens' excursions into history, which abound in his publicist works such as "The Eastern War and the Brussels Conference" (1879); "Russia and England in Central Asia" (1880), and "The Nationality Policy of Prince Bismarck" (1883).

Virtually forgotten are the historical essays which he regularly published between 1882 and 1905 in the journals *Вестник Европы* [Herald of Europe] and *Русская мысль* [Russian Thought]. The essays were a sort of by-product of the *Recueil*. However, this does reduce their significance. An undoubted merit of the essays is the abundance of the archival materials used, including those introduced into scholarly circulation for the first time. They contain many original assessments and conclusions of the author. One feature inherent in the essays is extremely rare in historical research: the view of world events and foreign policy from the standpoint of international law.

The list of historical essays by Martens is rather extensive: "Russia and Prussia under Catherine II" (1882); "Russia and Prussia in the Era of the Restoration" (1883); "Russia and England in the XVI-XVII Centuries" (1891); "Russia and England at the Outset of the Nineteenth Century" (1894); "Emperor Nicholas I and Queen Victoria" (1896); "Russia and England in the Reign of Emperor Nicholas I" (1898); "Russia and England on the Eve of Rupture" (1898); "Alexander I and Napoleon. Last Years of Their Friendship and Alliance" (1905).

Unremembered is the fact that Martens was a member of the Russian Imperial Historical Society, indeed a member of the Council of the Society, which annually held its sessions with the participation of the Tsar (under Alexander III, in the Anichkov Palace).

In Martens' diaries there are curious sketches of these sessions. In February 1892 at the yearly meeting there were nineteen persons present: Alexander III; N. K. Giers, the Minister of Foreign Affairs; A. A. Polovtsev, a public figure, senator, and one of the founders of the Society and then its President; P. I. Bartenev, an historian interested in the reign of Tsar Aleksei Mikhailovich and founder in 1863 of the journal *Русский архив* [Russian Archive]; K. P. Pobedonostsev, formerly a professor of civil law and tutor of Alexander III, ober-procurator of the Holy Synod; N. F. Dubrovin, academician and military historian. Those assembled heard several brief abstracts, including K. N. Bestuzhev-Riumin on the character of Tsar Aleksei Mikhailovich. In April 1895 Martens again was present at the yearly meeting of the Society, now under the chairmanship of the new Tsar, Nicholas II. At the yearly meeting in February 1896, this time in the Winter Palace, Martens himself reported on relations between Russia and England in the period 1832-1840 on the basis of the reports in the archives of the Russian Ambassador in London, Count K. O. Pozzo di Borgo and the Envoy Baron (later Count) F. I. Brunov. Martens wrote that his address "was exceedingly pleasing to them". The Tsar especially was interested by the early years of rule of Queen Victoria and the circumstances of her taking the throne and the coronation.[27] For the new Tsar, whose coronation had been held in May of the preceding year (the well-known catastrophe on Khodyn Field, involving numerous human casualties), the information communicated by Martens was evidently of great interest.

Martens the historian also became well-known abroad. In December 1896 he was elected associate member of the Institut de France, a high honour for a foreign scholar. The election took place in the Académie des sciences, morales, and politiques, the section for universal history and philosophy, headed by the pre-eminent French historian, Albert Sorel. Martens had close personal contacts with Sorel.

Martens' reknown as a jurist undeservedly has overshadowed his significance as an historian. His historical legacy awaits a researcher.

Social Activity Active participation in social life was traditional for a university professor of those years, especially for noted specialists in the social sciences. International lawyers were no exception.

The Professor of International Law at Moscow University, L. A. Kamarovskii, had won great popularity as a pacifist. He founded the Society of Peace in Moscow and unflaggingly gave lectures which propagandised the ideas of international peace, disarmament, and an international court. In 1909-12 he was a deputy of the Moscow City Duma. Kamarovskii was very lively in reacting in the press to current international events: the Eastern question, colonial policy, military rivalry of the powers, the Hague Peace Conference, and others. He was an active member of the Law Society attached to Moscow University, where he gave dozens of reports.

[27] See AVPR, op. 787, delo 9, ed. khr. 2, l. 29, 122; ed. khr. 5, l. 22.

A student and later successor of Martens in the chair of international law, A. A. Pilenko, became a noted publicist. For *Новое время* [New Times], one of the leading Russian newspapers of that time, he wrote an enormous number of articles, feuilletons, and notes on questions of international law, current world politics, and the history of diplomacy.

Against this background Martens was somewhat aloof. It can not be said that he stood aside from social life. But his official position, the nature of his activity, and personal inclinations meant that he did not follow the crowd in social matters.

A position as an official of the Ministry of Foreign Affairs obliged Martens to refrain from participation in domestic politics and from public criticism of the Russian foreign policy. Martens was too independent in his opinions and too responsive to events to strictly follow the traditional rule. But all the same a certain pattern emerged. His speeches with regard to domestic policy were rather rare, although it happened that they led to conflicts with the leadership of the Ministry of Foreign Affairs (for example, his publication in 1905 in *The Times*, where he actually favoured dissolution of the State Duma). Martens' publicist works on questions of foreign policy were devoted not so much to an analysis of the actions of Russian diplomacy as to international events with a direct link to international law.

In his scholarly works Martens proceeded from the fact that the peaceful life of peoples corresponds to the ideals of international law. In his practical activity he did much to bring order to the joint life of peoples and, thereby, a stable international peace. At the same time, Martens, unlike, for example, Kamarovskii, stood aside from pacifist movements.

Duties with regard to the Ministry, frequent and rather extended trips abroad, together with teaching at the university left Martens little time for social activity. Nonetheless, he took part in the work of the Russian Imperial Historical Society, as recounted above. He actively promoted the founding in 1880 of the Russian Society of International Law and became its secretary. He was a member of the Société de histoire diplomatique in Paris, the Royal Academy of Belgium, and an honorary member of the Berlin and Dublin law societies.

Colleagues and Students In speaking of Martens as a professor of Petersburg University, one must not fail to mention the fact that he also taught simultaneously in some other educational institutions. The combining of jobs to lecture was at the time a rather widespread phenomenon, and not only for material reasons. Principally the most highly qualified, well-known specialists were, naturally, able to combine positions.

By 1871 Martens had been invited to take the post of Professor of Public Law in the Imperial Alexander Lycee. The invitation evidently came upon the recommendation of I. I. Ivanovskii, who had held the position there for many years.

The Alexander Lycee was then the most privileged and prestigious educational institution of the boarding-type. Founded in 1810 as the Tsarskoe Selo Lycee (located in Tsarskoe Selo), in 1844 it was moved to Petersburg and renamed the Alexander Lycee (after its founder, Emperor Alexander I). The Lycee always had a strictly limited number of pupils (in 1877, that is, when Martens worked there, 186 persons) exclusively from the nobility. The children of other estates were not admitted to the Lycee. From within its walls came A. S. Pushkin, the noted scholar N. Ia. Danilevskii, the State Chancellor and one of the greatest diplomats of the nineteenth century, A. M. Gorchakov, and an entire pleiad of other State and social public figures of Russia. Future ministers in particular were educated at the Lycee: M. N. Reitern (Finances), Count D. A. Tolstoi (Enlightenment, Internal Affairs), and others. A significant number of graduates of the Lycee were in the Ministry of Foreign Affairs. The ministers of foreign affairs with whom Martens came to work – A. M. Gorchakov, N. K. Giers, A. B. Lobanov-Rostovskii, V. N. Lamzdorf – all were trained at the Alexander Lycee. Not without reason did the great satirist, M. E. Saltykov-Shchedrin, himself a former pupil at the Lycee, call it the "breeding-ground of ministers". Emperor Nicholas II paid a traditional visit to the Alexander Lycee in March 1899. He entered the class where

Martens taught. When he saw the Martens' treatise on international law lying on the table, he said that in his day he had studied it.[28]

Teaching in the Lycee was entrusted to the greatest and most politically reliable or, as they said then, well-intentioned, specialists. A professorial post in the Alexander Lycee, besides additional earnings, served as a valuable recommendation not only to the University leadership, but to even higher circles. Graduates of the Lycee held, as a rule, high posts.

In addition to the University and the Lycee, Martens also accepted service at the Petersburg Imperial School of Jurisprudence. Many future officials studied at this educational institution. Among the graduates was, for example, K. P. Pobedonostsev. Attendees of Martens' lectures at the School were K. A. Naryshkin, subsequently Major-General, and Head of the Military-Field Chancellery of His Majesty, and certain other future generals and highly-placed bureaucrats.

In recalling all this, one can only be astonished at the young professor's capacity for work. It was in those years that Martens published, volume by volume, the *Recueil*, worked out the treatise on international law, wrote a series of books and scholarly articles, drew up memoranda for the leadership of the Ministry of Foreign Affairs, participated in international conferences, and others.

Martens' capacity to work undoubtedly was facilitated by the fact that teaching and scholarly work had become his calling. He gave himself to them with enthusiasm. There where diplomats and bureaucrats, Russian and foreign State figures with whom he communed, saw only boring, routine labour, Martens found satisfaction and spiritual joy. He entered in the diary in 1895 at the top of his professorial news: "Lectures often give me spiritual delight when my attendees follow the course of my thoughts with attention and feeling. Archival work always interests me and gives great satisfaction".[29]

---

[28] See AVPR, op. 787, delo 9, ed. kh. 2, l. 113.

[29] Ibid., l. 32.

No detailed information about Martens' attitude towards the University has been preserved in the literature and archival materials. In any event he can not be classified among those University professors who were idols of the student youth of Petersburg and Moscow. For that he was comparatively far-removed from an active social and political life and too overloaded in this speciality and in the affairs of the Ministry of Foreign Affairs. Martens' character and manner also did not encourage this: reserve, efficiency, and a certain pedantry. At the same time there is reason to believe that Professor Martens enjoyed the respect of colleagues and those who attended his lectures. An episode which occurred in 1887 testifies to this. The Petersburg newspaper *Новости* [News] reported that on 26 March 1887 Professor F. F. Martens of Petersburg University had taken his leave of the graduates and students of the fourth year and according to his custom offered parting words at the end of his lecture. As set out by the newspaper, these words were sufficiently brief to quote them in full: "Exactly 20 years ago I left, as do you at the present time, the University school days. Many questions worried me; many hopes and ideal aspirations inspired me and my comrades. But life for each who acts prepares a multiplicity of disappointments, endeavours to extinguish cherished cultural ideals, and from each requires many deprivations and struggle. All this lies before you. Many disappointments await you, much firmness and force of conviction is required of you to persevere in the forthcoming struggle for existence. How does one emerge the victor from such a struggle? How does one save oneself from the oppressive and grievous force of circumstances? Only a steadfast faith in the ultimate triumph of our moral ideals as developed by the cultural life of our Motherland and all other peoples may serve you as an anchor of rescue; only loyalty to them and steadfastness in the defence of the ideas of truth and justness everywhere may serve you as the guiding thread in your labourious path of life. Recall the mythological tale of the struggle of Heracles – the representative of physical strength – with the Giant Antaeus, son of Gaia, of Earth. The strength of the last did not weaken, but was constantly renewed since only he could touch mother

Earth. For you science, the University, the Motherland are the same mother, the same life-creating power to which you must adhere, to touch always when the boldness of spirit leaves you for further struggle and when life is ready to grind you into powder. Then recall the University, return to the cultural ideals imbued in you - you will serve the faith and truth of our dear Motherland".[30]

According to the newspaper report, the remarks of the professor made a profound impression on the attendees and were followed by continuous applause and cries of "Thank you!" along the entire University corridor. Moreover, at the entrance to the building on the Neva Embankment the students formed two rows, escorting the professor. As Martens wrote in his diary on the occasion of this manifestation of student devotion, "I myself was touched almost to tears".

In January 1896 Martens marked the twenty-fifth anniversary of teaching at the University. On the afternoon of 18 January his colleagues honoured him, and in the evening there was a banquet at the noted Petersburg restaurant, the Donon (Pushkin had lunched at the Donon). The honoree was unpretentious and happy. In his speech at the banquet he related with humour certain episodes from his life, his successes having been achieved thanks to an exceptionally happy confluence of circumstances. The speech was a success, and information from it was published in the press report about the jubilee.[31] The instances from life which Martens jokingly related actually occurred, but the honoree did not speak of the main matter - the diligent daily labour which was the sole source and basis of his success. Closer to the truth was the address which he gave on the following day to his students who honoured him. He said that those who attend University usually have nothing except their knowledge and their labour. Therefore they must labour unceasingly and in labour find their reward for all the adversities

---

[30] Новости [News], 27 March 1887.

[31] See V. Gribovskii, «Юбилей профессора Ф. Ф. Мартенса» [Jubilee of Professor F.F. Martens], *Вестник права* [Herald of Law], kn. 2 (1896), pp. 42-43.

and vicissitudes of fate. He called upon the students always to love the University and science. As we see, Professor Martens, who had earned at that time high rank and material sufficiency, had not forgotten his non-noble origins as an intellectual and displayed a spiritual link with those students who not by birth or capital but by labour and talent would traverse the road of life.

A. A. Pilenko greeted the honoree in the name of the students; Martens knew him thanks to his work on international law, for which had received a gold medal. He later became a professor himself. An attendee from Chernogoria (Serbia) also spoke. At the end the students raised their professor on their shoulders and carried him to the exit.[32]

Professor Martens was well-known in many foreign universities. Edinburgh, Cambridge, Oxford, and Yale universities bestowed degrees *honoris causa* on him. The universities of Bern and Dublin invited him as a guest of honour to their jubilee celebrations.

Martens could leave the Chair of International Law of Petersburg University with a feeling of satisfaction. There he had trained a worthy replacement in the person of a number noted scholars. His successor in the Chair became M. A. Taube (1869-1960), who not only successfully taught, wrote several scholarly works relating to the theory, history, and individual branches of international law, but also took an active part as a representative of Russia in international affairs: in 1904-05 as a member of the Commission of Inquiry in Paris relating to the Hull Incident, in 1908-09 as a participant in the Conference on Maritime Law in London, and from 1909 as a member of the Permanent Court of International Arbitration at the Hague, and others.

After Taube's departure from the University in 1911, another student of Martens replaced him in the Chair of International Law – A. A. Pilenko (1873-?). His works on private international law (protection of authors' and inventors' rights)

---

[32] See AVPR, op. 787, delo 9, ed. khr. 3, l. 119.

received recognition in the world of scholarship. His calling he found in publicist writings.

B. E. Nolde (1876-1948) was one of the most talented students of Martens. His life and creativity were similar to the biography of his teacher, above all in the fact that he combined extensive scholarly work with practical activity: he participated in the 1907 Hague Conference, the 1908-09 London Conference on Maritime Law, the 1910-12 conferences on Spitzbergen, and others. He continuously held the Chair of International Law at the Petersburg Polytechnic Institute.

A. N Mandelshtam (1869-1949), a pupil of Martens, also graduated from the Oriental Faculty. Remaining at Petersburg University to prepare for the professoriate, he took up service in the Ministry of Foreign Affairs and devoted his principal attention to diplomatic work, in particular the Ottoman Empire. In 1905 he was one of the representatives of Russia on the International Commission of Enquiry into the Hull Incident, in 1907 secretary of the Second Hague Peace Conference, in 1913 a delegate at the International Commission on Reforms in Turkish Armenia. He wrote a number of works on the theory and history of private international law. The degree of doctor of law (bypassing the degree of magister) was conferred on him at once upon the recommendation of Martens for a two-volume work on "The Hague Conferences and the Codification of Private International Law".

Yet another student of Martens, L. A. Shalland (1870-1919), took the Chair of State Law in Iur'ev University. His scholarly works were in significant measure devoted to private international law.

In addition to the jurists named above one may mention certain other followers of Martens who acquired fame. As Grabar justly observed, "Martens left after himself a rich legacy in the form of an entire pleiad of young international lawyers".[33]

Martens retired from the Chair of the University in 1903, having worked there more than thirty years. In the same year

[33] Grabar, note 18 above, p. 310.

he ceased to teach at the Alexander Lycee. He taught in the School of Jurisprudence until his death.

CHAPTER III
INTERNATIONAL LEGAL DOCTRINE OF MARTENS

In devoting himself to international law, Martens immersed himself in it entirely. Even international relations and the history thereof he studied to the extent to which international law and the history so required. State and law as a subject of research did not attract his attention specially, and they remained outside his purview unless they led him to international law. In seeking the societal laws of the development of international law, Martens came to the "unshakeable conviction that the internal life and order of a State reveal fatefully their effect on international relations and politics. International relations always represent a mirror which exactly reflects the internal condition of State societies at a certain epoch of their existence, and likewise the principles which underlie the social and political structure thereof".[1]

The state of international law turns out to be dependent upon the social and political system of States that make up the world community, the development of State and Law being primary, and international law, secondary. Therefore the exposition of international law Martens considered it necessary to link closely with the theory and history of State and Law, and in his treatise on international law set out the principles and norms thereof against the general background of municipal life and municipal law. "Only by knowing the internal life of a country and its State institutions can one comprehend the principles and rules by which it is guided in relations with other peoples," he stressed.[2]

On the other hand, Martens declared the influence of international relations on the development of a State and of municipal law to be inevitable. Whereas the mutual relations of

---

[1] F. F. Martens, *Современное международное право цивилизованных народов* [Contemporary International Law of Civilised Peoples] (Spb., 1883), I, p. iv.
[2] Ibid., I, p. 23.

peoples are built on the basis of peace and law, they exert influence in the same spirit on the internal life of individual countries. "Only on such a structure of international relations can respect for law and order be affirmed in a State," Martens concluded.[3] On the whole the development of States and the world community consisting of them, just as the development of municipal and international law, was to him a single process in which both constituent elements were inextricably linked and constantly interacted with one another. This view determined the approach of Martens to the nature of the State and to municipal and international law.

On the Nature of the State

In Martens' understanding, the State is an objectively existing social organism which is formed in the course of the development of civilisation. The State arises when mankind goes beyond the stage of primitiveness, the origin of the State being conditioned by material causes, above all, the formation of social production. Economic development creates the foundation for the development of culture, art, and orderly relations between the members of society. All this requires defence, and then the State arises and assumes the protection of relations in society, social production, and the defence of spiritual values.

Martens saw the source of social progress in the growth of the material and spiritual requirements of man. Here he sketched a dialectical process: requirements stimulate the growth of the economy and culture, and the higher standard of social life creates new requirements demanding satisfaction. "Historical experience in everyday life persuades us that only with the full development of all intellectual and moral forces is the satisfaction possible of all material requirements. The more such requirements, the more essential are the means to satisfy them. The development of requirements makes necessary the improvement of the means to satisfy them. The more the people

[3] F. F. Martens, «Россия и литературное общество западноевропейских народов» [Russia and the Literary Society of Western European Peoples], *Вестник Европы* [Herald of Europe], no. 3 (March 1881), p. 237.

have requirements, then the members thereof stand on a higher rung of cultural development," Martens noted.[4]

This dialectical process which underlay the uninterrupted development of the State and human history is simultaneously the history of State development: from simpler forms to more complex. Therefore Martens stressed the importance of an historical approach to the State. In the era of absolutist monarchies the State was one thing, and under conditions of parliamentarianism, another.

Mutual relations between various strata and groups of society have determinative significance for the development of the State. Martens wrote that "the life of the State is concentrated primarily in the activity of social circles into which each people is divided, and therefore the changes to which the State life of a people and the structure and administration of a country are subjected always depend upon relations which the social classes have towards State power".[5] The division of society into social groups reflects not only the differences but also the contradictory nature of their interests. Therefore the vital activity of a nation, society, and the State as an integral organism is based on compromises between diverse interests, compromises which are consolidated by law and realised by the State. "The life of civilised society is a constant chain of such compromises between opposed interests which find sanction in law and in the social power protecting it", Martens wrote.[6] State power stands above all groups of society, ensuring the achievement of agreement among them and thereby the preservation of the integrity of society.

Martens attached special significance to the level of development of society and the State. He divided in principle all peoples contemporary to him into "civilised" and "uncivilised". To the first he relegated the peoples of the European countries; to the second, many peoples of Asia. The African continent and a significant part of the American continent were territories colonisied by European peoples. Understanding by "civilisation"

[4] Martens, note 1 above, II, p. 97.
[5] Martens, note 1 above, I, p. 21.
[6] Martens, note 3 above, p. 236.

a "certain aggregate of acquired knowledge and conditions of culture",[7] Martens allocated "civilised" peoples into one "educated" or "civilised society", with which he personally was engaged. He was among those few jurists of his time who had worked out the relations between "civilised" and "uncivilised" peoples.

The measure of civilisation of a society and the State in Martens' understanding was the status of the individual. In his view a single principle is a law of the development of human society and passes through the entire historical life of peoples: "the principle of respect for the human individual".[8] If respect is great, if the human individual is recognised to be a source of civil and political rights, then the role of law and the stability of the State system are considerable. "The more the Governments are aware of their duties with respect to all of their subjects, the more they treat with respect their rights and legal interests, and the more stable is the internal State order", Martens stressed.[9] But there is no order, no compliance with legality, if the State denies that inalienable rights are inherent in man. As Martens suggested, "the task of the State consists of granting to its subjects all means for the fullest possible development of spiritual and physical abilities and powers".[10] It is the fulfilment of this task that made the State responsive to the requirements of the new era.

Martens evaluated European States of the seventeenth and eighteenth centuries from these positions. He pointed out that the social order which existed at the time, in particular absolute monarchies, did not secure human rights. "In the eyes of the European monarchs of that epoch subjects had no rights with respect to State power as represented by the person of the sovereign", Martens wrote. The municipal life of absolute monarchies is distinguished by the fact that "social needs and aspirations were not satisfiable at the time in any European continental State" and "disrespect for the rights of the individual person" predominated there. As Martens declared, "unlimited

[7] Martens, note 1 above, II, p. 131.
[8] Martens, note 1 above, I, pp. 23-24.
[9] Martens, note 1 above, I, pp. iv-v.
[10] Martens, note 1 above, I, p. 17.

royal power arbitrarily disposed of the ownership and life of its subordinates".[11] Martens juxtaposed the orders which predominated in absolute monarchies with the States of the parliamentary type contemporary to him.

The significance which Martens attached to the State in regulating the rights of the individual should not create the impression that he was a proponent of the statisation of social life. He, for example, in the spirit of the liberal economic doctrines of his era, favoured the limitation of State interference in economic life. He pointed to the duty of governments to create favourable conditions for industry and trade, including by using the advantages of international communion, but simultaneously wrote: "Governments must repudiate the idea inherent in the police State to make the national economy productive through direct participation of State power therein, which only holds back natural economic growth and the development of the people".[12]

Martens regarded the notions of his time concerning the "national State" from the standpoint of the individual. In his era the national liberation movement in Europe was on the upsurge, and this left a visible imprint on the development of social thought. Alexander Herzen wrote that for the leaders of the Italian national liberation movement, for example the noted politician and jurist Manzini (1817-88), the ideas of nationality had the character of religious conviction. Everything was subordinated to the national idea.[13] Martens adhered to another approach to this issue. He regarded nationality relations within the State through the prism of respect for the rights of the individual and opposed any impingement of these rights because of the nationality affiliation of a citizen (or subject). The more the State respected the rights of the peoples and nations populating it, the less reason they had for dissatisfaction, to endeavour to isolate themselves from this State, and the more stable the structure of the State itself. At the same time, Martens

[11] Martens, note 1 above, I, p. 93.

[12] Martens, note 1 above, II, pp. 201-202.

[13] See A. I. Herzen, *Собрание сочинений* [Collected Works] (1956), V, p. 324.

treated with considerable reservations and, one may say, prejudice, the very principle of a national State.

In his *cours* on international law Martens acknowledged that in the nineteenth century the "principle of nationality" had become a salient one in international relations. In his view, the proponents of this principle demanded "to set in the place of a State which is a creature of power or arbitrary transactions a State based on the natural element of nationality". The uprising of the Greeks against Turkish domination, the separation of Belgium from Holland, the unification of Italy into a single kingdom, and other analogous examples served as confirmation of the aspiration of peoples to create independent national States. "The idea of nationality," Martens wrote, "was a protest against the arbitrary disposition by fate of a particular people, against the sale of State territory together with its populace, against being given as dowry and other similar transactions previously common".[14] In this respect he completely recognised the justness of national self-determination.

The national idea, according to Martens, comes down to the fact that the State must relate "with complete respect to national elements". Respect for the rights and interests of citizens "of whatever national origin they are or whatever language they speak", Martens believed to be the duty of each contemporary civilised State. At the same time, Martens wrote: "To see a panacea in the principle of nationality for the settlement of all international difficulties seems to us to be unfounded and the conviction that it has exclusive supremacy over all the leading ideas of our time is dangerous". In his view the stable foundation of a State is not the national idea, not "historical legends", but "identical cultural interests", "identical State ideals", an "identical understanding of political freedom", and "identical respect for the highest values of human civilisation". In his opinion the "principle of nationality, having no historical foundation, will create nothing stable, but it is in a condition to destroy much".

---

[14] See Martens, note 1 above, I, p. 150.

The danger of the realisation of the principle of the national State Martens saw, in particular, in the fact that it would lead to a "radical change of the political map of Europe and, consequently, unavoidably would cause international wars".[15]

Another of Martens' objections against the realisation of the "national idea" came down to the fact that he did not see guarantees of compliance by national States with the provisions of international law. He suspected them of pursuing their own ultra-egoistic interests.

If these propositions of Martens are carried over to the political life of Russia of that time, they signify the preservation thereof as a unified State with all of its multinational composition and ensuring in all of its provinces equal rights to all subjects irrespective of their nationality affiliation. For him there was no doubt that the nationality question was to be decided by ensuring the rights of the individual, including the right to the development of national culture. If a citizen or subject was secured the right to use the national language, to propagate his religion (which frequently is closely linked with national life), and also to adhere to his national customs, if a citizen or subject had equal rights irrespective of national and religious affiliation, for Martens the nationality question no longer had any foundations.

An analysis of Martens' views on the nationality question confirms that he viewed municipal life primarily from the standpoint of international law. The concept of the State itself originated for Martens in his international legal views. For him it was a "society of people living on a determined territory under one supreme power".[16] He approached from an analogous position the internal structure of States, which he divided into simple and complex. To the last he relegated unions of States, confederations, and federations. In so doing the principle of national self-determination played no dominant role for him, the territorial structure being used as the basis. Russia fell for

---

[15] Martens, note 1 above, I, pp. 151-152.

[16] Martens, *Восточная война и Брюссельская конференция* [The Eastern War and the Brussels Conference] (1879), p. 47.

him into the category of simple States since it was a unified monarchy, whereas the United States was in the category of complex because it was a federal State. He saw that specific States were the "products of a determined historical process" but considered as deserving research only those factors of this process which told directly on the development of international relations and international law, for example, the creation of new States, change of their territories, their "death", and the like. The specialist in international law always gave priority to them.

Although the term "rule of law State" was not used in Martens' works, one may conclude that he saw the rule of law State in the civilised State. The legal character of the State had in Martens' eyes such a determinative significance that he pushed into the background such factors as the form of State structure or national self-determination. One does not encounter in Martens' works, for example, a comparison of the virtues of the republic and the monarchy. We quoted above a condemnation by him of the arbitrariness of absolute monarchies in Europe, but he did not draw from this conclusion the need to replace monarchies with republics. For him most important was the establishment of legal order, and monarchical England was for him as civilised a State as was the French Republic.

On the Nature of Law [jus] As in the approach to the nature of the State, when determining the essence of law Martens endeavoured to rely on its material basis and elicit the societal laws of its development.

Law for Martens reflected the relations actually existing in society. When these relations are changed, legal norms which regulate them also are altered. Therefore law is never regarded separately from real municipal life, and for an understanding of the nature of law it is essential to investigate carefully the social relations actually existing. Referring to the noted work of the French philosopher and writer of the Enlightenment, Montesquieu (1689-1755), *De l'esprit des lois*, Martens wrote: "The venerable definition of Montesquieu is still the best of many new ones. Laws, he said, are those necessary relations which arise from the nature of things, and in this sense all their essence is subordinate to laws. If in place of the word 'relations' one places the word 'rule' or 'norm', then we have the complete concept of Montesquieu's definition. He truly throughout his classic work constantly endeavours to elicit the existing living relations, to investigate them in their historical meaning and reasonable purpose with a view to comprehending those laws to which they are subordinated. From this point of view it is not difficult to understand the task of legislative power in the State. If all living relations have their own laws arising from their very nature, if all people are bound in relations with one another by determined rights and duties, the task of the legislator must consist of the comprehensive study of these real relations and a precise determination of the rules arising from them and laws corresponding to them".[17]

At the same time Martens did not consider the function of law merely as a simple consolidation of real relations in society. The basis of law he saw in the moral values of society, in its moral norms. "Despite the diversity of political institutions and the civil and criminal laws of contemporary civilised States, one and the same source underlies their rights and legislation – the idea of justice and justness inherent in human nature", wrote Martens.[18] In his view moral values are the source of law [lex], and not legislative power, and the task of the legislator is not to invent rights but to conscientiously study living relations, the mutual interests of people, which are reflected in norms of morality. Therefore laws denying these norms (in particular, the right of man to life, honour, and freedom) and laws contrary to good reason and justness, have no right to existence.

Thus, on one hand, legal norms reflect real relations in society; on the other hand, they arise from the moral values of mankind and develop in accordance with its ideals. History offers a multitude of examples. "Napoleon conquered Europe by force of arms and by the propaganda of new free ideas proclaimed by the Declaration of the Rights of Citizen and Man. French forces extended these ideas to those States which they occupied and

[17] Martens, note 1 above, I, p. 14.

[18] Martens, note 1 above, I, p. 10.

everywhere met with the sympathy of peoples for the free political orders which they established in the conquered lands. Napoleon understood superbly the significance of such propaganda; in instructions and manifestoes he constantly announced that war was being waged against feudal orders despised by all peoples and wished to base his power not on the enslavement of peoples, but on their sympathy", Martens wrote.[19]

Martens accorded an important role to economic, political, and cultural development. The degree of the civilisation of a people served him as the measure of maturity of municipal relations and, respectively, municipal law. "The life of savages knows neither trade, nor cultivation, nor artisanship. In their milieu each individual person is his own guardian" Martens stated.[20] Undeveloped productive forces and social relations condition the embryonic state of State institutions and legal relations. For example, war was a law of feudal society. There one observes, Martens noted, the "complete, unlimited, and day-to-day supremacy of arrogation and the law of the fist. One may say that the entire Middle Ages was nothing other than a constant series of wars which were waged not only beween States, but also within them, between various parts of territories and between individual subjects".[21] Social progress carries with it the development of law and an enhancement of legal culture, Martens concluded.

Martens pointed out that the application of the norms of domestic law was secured by State coercion which stood behind them. At the same time, he sharply polemicised with those scholars who saw in power a source of law. "The view that power is a basis of law we deem to be unworthy of man, dangerous to social and state life and pernicious for international life" he stressed.

In his view the proponents of the theory of power as a foundation of law confused the means of the realisation of norms

---

[19] Martens, note 1 above, I, p. 126.

[20] Martens, *Россия и Англия в Средней Азии* [Russia and England in Central Asia] (1880), p. 15.

[21] Martens, note 1 above, I, p. 26.

of law with the nature and sources thereof. "The procedure for protecting law here is confused with law itself and is made an organic, constituent part thereof. If law may be protected by power, authority, or coercion, it does not follow that this power, authority, and coercion directly enters into the concept of law, that law is inconceivable without it", Martens wrote.

In his concept a civilised State is characterised by the supremacy of law [lex] and respect for legal provisions and institutions. And the most important indicator of such an attitude towards law is respect for the rights of the individual. The rights of the individual are not a gift of the State, but a manifestation of the realities existing in nature and society. The "inviolability of life and honour is recognised as the right of each not because it is protected by a criminal law, but because each has, on the basis of his nature, an inalienable right to his life and honour. A law must protect a right, but it is not the source of the entire aggregate of rights which belong to a person", Martens noted.

By the reference to inalienable rights Martens again stressed that law rests on an objective foundation in the form of social relations actually existing. Therefore the power of coercion can not arbitrarily change legal norms; they remain so long as the social relations which gave rise to them are preserved. The subordination of the development of law to the objective laws of societal development implanted in Martens the assurance that social progress would constrict force in the life of society. "We hope that in the near future the defenders of unlimited physical force in the domain of social life will be pilloried and the concept of law be deprived of its contemporary materialist interpretation and content. We believe in the ultimate triumph of law even where it is being violated most outrageously because we believe in the ideal power of law", Martens emphasised.[22]

Here one should stipulate that while opposing a "materialistic interpretation" of the nature of law Martens never criticised a materialistic understanding of social processes. His objections were directed against the efforts of vulgar materialism to find grounds for social phenomena in the world of beasts, in

[22] Martens, note 16 above, pp. 38-39, 41.

the physiology of man, and the like. He in particular vigorously opposed the then fashionable carry over of the theory of natural selection of the English natural scientist, Charles Darwin (1809-88) to human society. He pointed to the reactionary character of such attempts: "Thus, the theory of the 'struggle for existence' transforms mankind back into the times of [Thomas] Hobbes [(1588-1679)] and [B.] Spinoza [(1623-77)], who in the seventeenth century had proclaimed the very same principle being advanced at the end of the nineteenth century as a great discovery made for the good of suffering humanity. Spinoza had placed at the base of his entire world outlook and entire political philosophy the principle that the struggle between people is as inevitable and lawful as it is lawful in the organic world. Large fish, he said, devour small ones because they are stronger".[23]

In Martens' conception social progress steadily changes the correlation of law and power: the history of antiquity, feudalism, and the renaissance testify to the diminished role of physical coercion and the growth of the role of law. The growth of the role of law, in turn, confirmed the rule of law in the State and society. The rule of law was the Martens' ideal. "In fact, our 'practical' century which sees the purpose of human life in easy gain and the accumulation of all possible material benefits and finds the means to achieve this aim in the wrongly comprehended theory of the 'struggle for existence' can not set on the low degree of understanding of law which falsely is presented as the sole true and reasonable one. This unconditional admiration of physical power corresponds to times past but is at odds with the future. To be sure, we are inclined to study and devote exclusive attention to the past, forgetting that the future has its own rights. But such an orientation can not continue; it is contrary to the basic law of development of all culture and modern civilisation. This law is the law of progress, of the advancing and unrestrainable development of man, society, the State, and international life. Development can not consist of turning back; it is inconceivable when there is domination of physical power and an admiration thereof; it is impossible in the absence of

[23] Martens, note 16 above, p. 14.

rights and order. Progress is conceivable only in an onward movement forward; its purpose and its ideals are in the future", Martens wrote.[24]

In Martens' eyes the general level of economic and cultural development of the State had decisive significance for the state of the law. The civilised nature of a society incorporated a high standard of legislation, law enforcement practice, and legal culture. Savagery, lack of civilisation doomed society to legal chaos and the arbitrariness of brute force. The measure for Martens here too was securing the rights of the individual. Legal defence of the individual was, in his opinion, the best indicator of the civilisedness of society and the development of its legal norms and institutions.

On the Nature of International Law In Martens' conception international law, just as municipal law, was not merely the fruit of the creative activity of jurists. Its origin and development were conditioned by factors actually existing which were not subordinate to the will of people. Therefore he directed his efforts first to eliciting the objective base of international law by means of investigating the "laws of historical development of peoples in their international life".

He stressed: "Since the subject of the science of international law is the aggregate of living relations existing between contemporary educated States, then the system thereof must obviously be the system of these relations and not those laws and principles which in the course of time have been worked out in international life".[25]

The central idea of all Martens' theoretical structures was the conviction that international law reflects in its norms and principles the international relations actually existing. He drew the conclusion that: "at the base of international law lie the actual, real, living relations which exist at present between peoples".[26] The actual relations between States are primary, and

[24] Martens, note 16 above, p. 41.
[25] Martens, note 1 above, I, p. 179.
[26] Martens, note 1 above, I, p. 17.

the norms of international law reflecting them are secondary. "Change the mutual relations of peoples, change the conditions of their mutual relations, and you change at the same time the basis of the principles of law whose obligatory force was recognised by them", Martens emphasised.[27]

When in connection with the Russian proposal for an international conference in 1874 discussion unfolded as to whether a law of warfare existed and was necessary, for Martens the chief argument in favour of adoption of a convention on the laws and customs of warfare was that such rules already actually existed in international life. The task was not, while being guided by humane considerations, to speculatively work out and adopt some norms, but rather to elicit customs in existence and, being guided by them, to formulate, codify, and establish generally-recognised norms of behaviour which met the principles of humanity. Turning to history, Martens showed that war begins to be subordinated to certain rules when a social order is worked out that is based on respect for man and his rights. The rules of warfare developed in the Middle Ages to the extent that in States "law and properly organised State power gradually built barriers against the unbridled will of the person".[28] Thus the rules for waging warfare are born objectively as a consequence of the development of State and international life, and international law consolidates such development.

The second fundamental idea of Martens was that international relations and the international law corresponding to it developed not chaotically but were subordinate to their own internal laws, and the task of the science of international law was to elicit these societal laws of development and not create artificial systems which had no support in actual life.[29]

Martens considered the basic law to be the "law of progress, the advancing and unrestrainable development of man, society, the State, and international life".[30] The law of the progressive

---

[27] Martens, note 20 above, p. 14.
[28] Martens, note 1 above, II, p. 463.
[29] Martens, note 1 above, I, p. 178.
[30] Martens, note 16 above, p. 45.

development of international law derived from this, which Martens strengthened with the history of international law. Antiquity, feudalism, the new era which began with the 1789 French Revolution – these in Martens' understanding were an era of the advancing development of human society and the international law corresponding to it.

The standard of economic, political, and cultural development of peoples was a decisive prerequisite for the birth and formation of international relations and international law. Martens pointed out that international relations arise from the need of peoples to satisfy their physical and spiritual requirements by means of communion with other peoples and that such requirements originate not at once but after the achievement of a determined level of civilisation. On this basis he denied the existence of international law in primitive society, in antiquity, in the early period of feudalism, and among the tribes and peoples contemporary to him which had not reached the necessary level of development. As Martens suggested, in his day the "space of the operation of international law was limited only to those peoples who recognise the basic principles of European culture and are worthy of the name educated peoples".[31] We recall that he titled his own *cours* the "contemporary international law of civilised peoples".

It should be noted that Martens was not alone in dividing peoples into "civilised" and "uncivilised". This was at the time the dominant position in international law. Martens' conception corresponded to the level of the development of international law, although he did not adhere to the extreme, expansionist views of a number of jurists who were his contemporaries.

The steady and irresistibly growing requirements of peoples in communion with one another was another law singled out by Martens. He stated that the development of society increasingly required the communion of peoples, the unification of their efforts, and agreement of rules of behaviour. In his view, the "real grounds of international activity of States lie in the sufficiency of the power and means of an individual people to

[31] Martens, note 1 above, I, p. 181.

achieve their vital aims". To the "elementary powers uniting peoples" he relegated religious beliefs and ideas, intellectual and moral interests, economic interests and trade relations, political interests. He pointed to the unprecedented "correct and continuous exchange of their industrial, economic, and business activity", the establishment of stable communications (for example, the creation in 1874 of the Universal Postal Union), the free movement of people from one State to another, the intensive exchange of cultural valuables, as a result of which "virtually all Western European peoples now constitute a single international society" where, in particular, any literary figure, scholar, artist, performing artist, or composer enjoys an identical right to the defence of his literary and artistic property. Martens came to the conclusion that "the entire significance of international relations and the entire power of international law is based on the community of social, cultural, and legal interests which link civilised peoples".[32]

Since international relations and the law regulating them are developing without interruption, international law should be analysed directly from the standpoint of historical change and in connection with the evolution of international relations. In his *cours* Martens repeatedly pointed to the role of the history of international relations. One may say that his entire *cours* is permeated with historicism.

Resting on such fundamental ideas, Martens saw in international law the "aggregate of legal norms which determine the conditions of the achievement by peoples of their vital aims in the sphere of their mutual relations". Since international law reflected the real relations between States, Martens suggested that the "science of international law has as its task to constantly watch over the changes of these relations". In his view it should not lag behind the progress of international life and since "life remains the criterion for prevailing international rules and laws" and "the provisions advanced in the science of international law should constantly illuminate and set normative standards for the actual procedure of things predominant in the domain of

[32] Martens, note 1 above, I, pp. 2, 5-6, 18.

international relations, this order will give content to international law". The rules of international communion agreed by States and the community of jurists play their own role. As Martens emphasised, the science of international law should be guided "not only by those rules and laws which have been worked out and adopted by States and jurists, but also by the living relations which have actually been established between peoples".[33]

Martens devoted considerable attention to the moral foundations of law as a whole and of international law in particular. As already noted, he passionately polemicised with those who saw the basis of law in power. For Martens the foundation of any law is – justness, conformity to moral norms worked out by civilised peoples. For him "power is more than an element of unjustness than of justness", and as a whole the foreign policy of a State based on power is the antipode of international law. In stressing the moral basis of law, he wrote that he believed in the "ideal power of law", having in view the power of the idea of justness and humanity. He asserted: "Neither the idea of disconnection, nor the idea of admiration for physical power, nor the idea of political equilibrium, nor, finally, the principle of nationality can be deemed to be guiding principles of a properly structured international life. Its guiding principle is the idea of law [jus]".[34] Martens pointed out that international law arose and survived the formation of moral ideas as confirmed in the life of peoples and believed that the development of human society in the future would intensify an awareness of the solidarity of peoples. "The time is coming too in the domain of international life when the great law of social life will be executed, when each people will exist for the world and the world for them", he wrote.[35]

Theory of the International Community A distinctive feature of Martens' doctrine of international law which noticeably

[33] Martens, note 1 above, I, pp. 16-18.
[34] Martens, note 1 above, I, pp. 9, 29.
[35] Martens, note 16 above, pp. 23, 45.

distinguished him in the Russian and world science of international law was the proposition concerning the international community as the basis of international law. "At the base of a scientific system of contemporary international law", he wrote, "must be placed the *idea of the international community*, according to which each autonomous State is an organic part of a single whole, connected with other States by a community of interests and rights".[36] This idea received such important significance in the works of Martens that his entire doctrine passed into history as the theory of the international community. Thus has he been characterised too in Russian scholarly doctrinal writings.[37]

Substantiating his theory of the international community, Martens wrote: "The majority of representatives of international law to this day hold another view, that the rights and duties belonging to States in the domain of foreign relations have as their sole basis sovereignty, mutual autonomy, and the independence of States. We reject this point of view ...". In his opinion the idea of State sovereignty indicates merely that a State is "an original juridical personality" in international intercourse. But it does not show in what relations various States are found and which rights and duties unite them. The idea of sovereignty, Martens believed, presupposes enmity and hatred of individual peoples, their isolation. But no civilised State contemporary to Martens was in such a position. The "permanent relations in which educated peoples find themselves compel the last to mutually limit the absolute application of their autocracy ...", he wrote.[38]

According to Martens, the international community arose as a consequence of the awareness by States of the need for mutual assistance and collaboration in order to achieve by common efforts the satisfaction of their reasonable requirements.

---

[36] Martens, note 1 above, I, p 178.

[37] D. B. Levin, "Русские юристы-международники о сущности международного права" [Russian International Lawyers on the Essence of International Law], *Советский ежегодник международного права 1975* [Soviet Yearbook of International Law 1975] (1976), p. 218.

[38] Martens, note 1 above, I, pp. 201-202.

The purpose of the State - comprehensive development of the powers and abilities of their subjects - forced them to seek in the domain of international relations the means to satisfy the spiritual and material interests of their peoples which could not be found within the State itself.

Summing up his theoretical structures, Martens declared: "The international community is the free alliance of States in order to achieve by common actions the complete development of their powers and the satisfaction of their reasonable requirements. The aggregate of legal norms determining the effectuation of the idea of the international community comprises the law of the international community; this is international law".

Self-limitation of sovereignty does not mean a reduction of the rights of States, to which Martens relegated: the right of self-preservation ("a people not wishing to defend their life do not have the right to autonomy"), the right of territoriality (exclusive dominion of the State throughout the entire space of its territory, the right to the inviolability of this territory), the right of independence, the right to respect and honour, the right to international communication and the right of coercion (the right to protect by all lawful means their rights and interests with respect to both other States and their subjects).[39]

When setting out the right of independence Martens devoted great attention to questions of unrequested interference both in the internal affairs of another people and into its foreign relations. According to him, such interference is "always illegal". In great detail he refuted the proposition that a change of State system was an occasion for interference. He wrote: "If all States of whatever form of rule are within the international community, of course every State may freely change at its discretion and need its own internal orders and its structure and administration. All State transformations, however material and in whatever spirit they were undertaken, are questions of domestic policy and not of international law. It is essential only that the particular people have existed as an independent political organism having

[39] Martens, note 1 above, I, pp. 202, 296-310.

all the attributes of a State. Such people under the new internal orders retain their qualities of international personality and will be a subject of international law. As a consequence of changes made within a State it does not lose its previous international rights nor acquire new ones".[40]

Martens' belief in the progressive development of international relations and international law should not be understood as utopianism. On the contrary, Martens, so closely linked with the practice of inter-State relations, always displayed sober realism. He proceeded from the fact that international conflicts born in the contradictory interests of States will continue in the future. He wrote that the "struggle of interests and mutual conflicts are the operation of an immutable law". The task of international law is to establish by common consent the limits of the freedom of action of each State to find common ground for the development of various interests of States.[41] In Martens' conception the norms of international law embody the balance of interests of various peoples. He pointed out: "All of European civilisation is founded upon this power of the combination and mediation of opposed interests. The pledge of the development of civilised European peoples lies in this idea of mutual spiritual dependence and in this cognition of its unattainability by their individual powers".[42]

Proceeding from the inevitability of conflicts in inter-State relations, Martens should have given a scientific answer to the eternal question of international law: how by legal means does one secure a universal and indestructible peace between peoples? Here he could have relied on centuries of tradition and an extensive literature. In his *cours* on international law Martens singled out this question specially, pointing to the proposals for perpetual peace of the King of France, Henry IV, the Abbé Saint-Pierre (submitted to the Congress of Utrecht in 1713), the French philosopher J. J. Rousseau, the English philosopher and jurist, Jeremy Bentham, and certain other writers.

[40] Martens, note 1 above, I, p. 276.
[41] Martens, note 16 above, p. 33.
[42] Martens, note 3 above, p. 236.

Is perpetual peace possible and is war between States inevitable? Martens pointed to the indisputable realities: "The history of mankind is nothing other than an uninterrupted series of sanguinary wars, victories, defeats, and peace treaties". This development testifies to the fact that war breaks out for profound reasons imbedded in human society. Without eliminating these reasons, perpetual peace is utopian. However, Martens opposed the view of war as the operation of an immutable law which no one can influence. In Martens' perception social progress carries with it a number of "victories of the soul over matter, law over physical power, order over anarchy, justness over lawlessness. On the basis of this law and in the domain of international relations little-by-little law and justness must be introduced where arbitrariness and coercion exist.

International war must be converted into a struggle in which an awareness of one's physical power never drowns out the voices of conscience and reason".

Martens allotted a large role in this process to the growth of the civilised nature of society, an awareness by peoples of the perniciousness of wars, and also the positive influence of international law. He noted the profound changes in public opinion: whereas for savage peoples war was a lawful means, a manifestation of valour and honour, civilised peoples contest the legality of wars and see in them a terrible evil and calamity.

Martens considered that neglect of international law was one of the reasons for wars and other international conflicts. His words were imbued with genuine passion: "Even now, at the end of the nineteenth century, proud of their high culture and civilisation, the view has currency that the domain of international relations is intended by its very nature to be an arena of unlimited arbitrariness and exploits of physical power. There is no domain in which one comes into contact with more vital interests of mankind, but there also is no field in which arbitrariness and brute force have greater latitude and freedom. All on this planet are subordinate to certain laws – only relations between peoples are unaware of them. Here lawlessness dominates in place of law, and arbitrariness instead of rights!"[43]

[43] Martens, note 16 above, pp. 1, 20, 22, 35.

In the well-known controversy between two great German philosophers, Hegel and Kant, Martens inclined towards the latter. Immanuel Kant suggested that at a determined level of social development war is the sole means for effectuating rights in relations between States. However, as humanity progresses wars become less frequent and with time they should completely disappear. Kant wrote a special work "On Perpetual Peace".[44] Criticising Kant's theory, Hegel actually proceeded from the inevitability of wars. He wrote: "A dispute between States, insofar as special wills do not lead to an agreement, may be decided only by war". Moreover, he saw a positive role for wars: "People come out from war not only fortified, and nations too within which there is an implacable antagonism acquire an internal tranquillity thanks to external wars".[45] The assessments of Hegel manifest, naturally, his philosophical views, and in Russian writings it is justly pointed out that the Hegelian theory of State and law and of war and peace are rather contradictory and give broad scope for use by various legal schools and political currents. At the same time it is beyond doubt that the Hegelian conceptions do not attract proponents of the peaceful development of international relations.[46]

It should be noted that one of Martens' teachers, Professor A. D. Gradovskii, whom he cited frequently, was critical of the Hegelian approach to war and peace.[47] However, in the *cours* of the German jurist, A. W. Heffter, which Martens considered one of the very best, the views of Hegel on war and on international law permeate the entire work. Heffter wrote: "In

---

[44] I. Kant, *Сочинения* [Works] (1965), VI.

[45] G. Hegel, *Сочинения* [Works] (1934), VII, pp. 344, 351.

[46] See I. S. Andreeva, *Проблема мира в западноевропейской философии* [The Problem of Peace in West European Philosophy] (1975), pp. 145-146; V. S. Nersesiants, *Гегелевская философия права* [The Hegelian Philosophy of Law] (1974), p. 119; D. I. Fel'dman and Iu. Ia. Baskin, *Учение Канта и Гегеля о международном праве и современность* [The Doctrine of Kant and Hegel on International Law and Modern Times] (1977), pp. 98-101, among others.

[47] A. D. Gradovskii, *Собрание сочинений* [Collected Works] (1906), III, pp. 304-306.

generating spiritual emotion, war undoubtedly strengthens the forces which during peacetime atrophy or are expended uselessly. It gives protection against injustice and thereby leads to the restoration of peace".[48] Martens did not share this conclusion. He remained true to his approach and inclined towards Kant, and not Hegel.

In assessing war as an inevitable evil for the international relations contemporary to him, Martens saw the task of States and international law as, first, the development of the law of warfare so as to reduce its perniciousness and, second, to reduce the likelihood of war by means of creating and improving mechanisms for the peaceful settlement of international conflicts. He wrote: "In acknowledging war under existing relations between States to be completely inevitable, we, however, at the same time affirm that the law of warfare is not an idea of idle fantasy but the result of historical experience and the modern state of international life. Being deeply convinced that the time is coming when war truly will be an exception and when States will find a more advisable means for resolving quarrels which arise between them, we are convinced that until that time as there is greater familiarisation and mutual understanding of peoples the law of warfare is the sole means of removing from war its barbaric character and limiting the calamities connected with it".[49]

Theory of International Administration Since international law was for Martens the law of the international community, he devoted great attention to working out questions of the administration of international relations. He pointed out that the practice of international relations already had created the forms, methods, and organs of international administration. The task of the science of international law was, in his view, to elicit the developmental law in this domain and to facilitate by means of law the further development of the administration of the

[48] A. W. Heffter, *Европейское международное право* [European International Law] (1880), p. 6.
[49] Martens, note 16 above, p. 44.

world community. The second volume of Martens' *cours* was devoted to international administration. He wrote: "In this volume has been set out for the first time the entire law of international administration in all the various spheres of international life of contemporary civilised peoples. The attempt to envelop in a single system the entire immense wealth of international relations and to turn more or less well-known facts into the content of organic international activity of States is difficult to such a degree that I do not doubt a multitude of more or less substantiated objections will be encountered. But my attempt to create a new system for the science of international law having little in common with all existing systems of this science is merely a first step on the path along which the science of international law, in my view, must develop in the near future".[50]

Martens supposed that the progressing development of mankind inevitably would lead to a more intensive community of States and thereby to the strengthening and improvement of international administration. In his eyes international administration was the real path towards the elimination of military conflicts. If one follows Martens' ideas, then the constant work of international law with regard to the creation of legal order in the world community which corresponds to the achievements of human civilisation and the gradual development of international administration which strengthens the peaceful cooperation of peoples is the path towards the establishment of perpetual peace on earth, a path complex, not quick, but the sole true and real path.

Martens attached great significance to the theoretical comprehension of the organisation of the international community. He in principle separated the foundations of municipal and international administration and the foundations of municipal and international law. Whereas in a State supreme power exists and behind domestic law there stands the coercive force of this power, in international relations independent sovereign States are the subjects which are not subordinate to

[50] Martens, note 1 above, II, p. 1.

any supreme power. There are no organs of supranational power in international relations – no legislative, no executive, no judicial power. Behind the norms of international law there is no coercive force of executive power; its force is based on the common interest of States, on their solidarity. By its nature the international community of States "does not need permanent organised international power" Martens suggested. In his view, the world community is and may by its essence only be an "alliance of peoples", a "free association of independent States". The legal order in such a community is based "on full respect for the individuality of each people" and compliance with the norms of international law.[51]

"International administration by its essence has a treaty character", Martens wrote. But he did not exclude the significance of other sources of international law, to which he relegated national legislation, administrative acts, judicial decisions, and even the instructions of governments to their plenipotentiaries at international negotiations. Martens relegated only States to the subjects of international administration. Social groups and individual persons play their role in international relations, but their activity, in his view, was "under the control, patronage, and responsibility of the State". The "aggregate of all vital relations between States, social groups, and private persons, who require assistance, protection, and the defence of State power, are the object of the law of international administration", Martens wrote.

To organs of international administration he relegated international conferences and congresses, and also State agencies which participate in international relations (foreign representations, ministries of foreign affairs, armed forces). In his view, "every person appointed by a State to perform a particular international administrative task should be considered to be an organ of international administration".[52] Martens was sympathetic to the idea of creating an international court with decisions binding upon all States but doubted the reality of such

[51] Martens, note 1 above, II, p. 219.
[52] Martens, note 1 above, II, pp. 9, 11.

a scheme since he did not see the material power which would ensure the compulsory execution of decisions of the court (the creation of an "international army of execution" he at the time regarded as unlikely).[53]

Endeavouring to encompass the entire aggregate of international relations, Martens included in his *cours* on international law the following sections:

1. International administration in the sphere of spiritual, physical, and economic interests of peoples. To this he relegated questions connected with religion, science and art, emigration, public health, customs, and other economic unions, means and routes of communication, industry, and trade.

2. International administration in the domain of legal interests of subjects and peoples. In this section Martens included private international law and international criminal law.

3. International administration in the domain of the compulsory protection of the interests and rights of subjects and peoples. Martens relegated to this the means for the settlement of international conflicts, the law of warfare, and the law of neutrality.

Martens did not confine himself merely to an exposition or systematisation of the norms of the international community being formed. He endeavoured to elicit the trends of its development so as in accordance with them to determine the most promising forms and methods of international administration. For example, the tasks of international administration in the spiritual domain he did not reduce to agreements concerning literary property or other analogous concrete measures, but regarded them on a broad plane, both temporal and spatial. He saw in the development of spiritual powers and abilities the "common aim and reasonable purpose" of the individual, people, and the entire world community. "Under normal conditions not a single educated State was in a position to perform its duties or to settle its tasks without the assistance of other States", Martens wrote.[54] In his concept the

[53] Martens, note 1 above, I, p. 225.

[54] Martens, note 1 above, II, p. 7.

objective requirements of human civilisation dictate the freedom of international exchange of spiritual values. Limitations on such exchange also harms those States which establish the limitations and the world community as a whole. The achievements of culture and science of individual peoples are becoming the weal of all peoples and benefit all of civilisation. "Science recognises no territorial boundaries for itself", he wrote, "and has no nationality. It may be constrained in its development only by police barriers erected by a government. It is 'national' only in the sense that each people taking an active part in universal scientific work is obliged to contribute its own mite, being endowed with the individual abilities inherent to it".

In Martens' view, with the development of spiritual life peoples increasingly become an organic part of world civilisation. Mankind acquires the features of a unified, integral community which increasingly needs a developed international administration and international law as the basis for the regulation of relations in such a community. "At present," Martens pointed out, "a society of civilised peoples truly exists; its limits are the limits of the binding force of international law; its purpose is to give to each member the possibility of comprehensive spiritual development; its means are the contributions of intellectual and artistic labour to be made by each people, and the greater such contribution, the greater benefit, material and moral advantage, received by all peoples". The task of international administration is to promote in every possible way the achievement of such a position and its further development. Analogous tasks confront international administration in other spheres of communion and the cooperation of peoples and activity of the world community as a whole.

In working out questions of international administration, Martens opposed the various schemes for the creation of a world State, whether in the form of a confederation or a federation. In his *cours* on international law he analysed in detail such projects (Abbé Saint-Pierre, Rousseau, Bentham, Kant, Bluntschli, Kamarovskii, and others). As Martens noted, "underlying this type of scheme are proposals whose effectuation is inconceivable and in general undesirable. They all presuppose either the complete refashioning of the political map of Europe or the subordination of autonomous States to a common supreme power".[55] But it was not only political considerations which persuaded him to reject such schemes. Here it is important to note the methodological approach of Martens. He proceeded from the fact that the foundations of municipal life and international relations have different roots. Therefore he in principle rejected the attempts to squeeze the international community into State forms. Referring to historical experience, he pointed out that "attempts to organise an international community in the sense of a State community, in the form of a world monarchy or world republic, must be rejected as futile. It is unlikely that any sort of international community would be organised according to the schemes and plans drawn up at various times by analogy with the forms of the State".[56] He saw the prospects for a world community in an association of sovereign, equal States.

The Individual in International Relations In recognising the State to be the sole subject of international law, Martens in accordance with his theory of the international community devoted significant attention to other "subjects of rights in the domain of international relations", namely: (1) social groups, partnerships, companies, and other organisations, if they have been deemed to be operating legally in their States; (2) private persons. As Martens wrote: "the international community grants to each person the right to seek satisfaction of his vital and legal requirements everywhere in the domain of international turnover".

The central idea of Martens lay in the fact that the human individual has rights in the domain of international relations and is under the protection of international law. He stated: "All contemporary civilised States are agreed that man is a person, that is, a subject of certain inalienable rights which must be respected in the domain of their mutual relations. Therefore

[55] Martens, note 1 above, II, pp. 131, 199-202.
[56] Martens, note 1 above, I, p. 220.

every person, irrespective of citizenship or nationality, presently finds protection of his person and ownership throughout the entire space of the operation of international law. The ultimate purpose of the State and the purpose of international relations is the protection of the person." In his *cours* he proposed the systematisation of the basic rights of man which have found recognition in international law irrespective of citizenship and national affiliation. In the digest of the basic rights of man Martens included: (1) the right to existence and development of the physical person (freedom to acquire means necessary for the maintenance of life within the limits set by a law); (2) the right to the development of spiritual and intellectual abilities (including the right to use all means for the satisfaction of such aspirations: schools, libraries, museums, and others); (3) the right to communication and free movement "within the limits of the international union of States" (including the right to emigration; the "attachment of man to land", in his view, was contrary to contemporary international law).[57]

Martens' digest of the rights of man is not so extensive as it would be now. Yet the very idea of the protection of the rights of man by international law and attempts to codify these rights undoubtedly had pioneering significance.

For Martens the protection of the rights of the individual in the international community had key significance. As noted, the development of the individual and respect for his rights he considered to be the measure of the civilisation of a State and of the entire international community. "We are persuaded", he wrote, "that if in a State the human individual as such is deemed to be a source of civil and political rights, then international life represents a high degree of development, order, and law. On the contrary, in a State in which the human individual enjoys no such rights, where he is without rights and oppressed, international relations can neither develop nor be established on stable grounds".[58] The further progressive development of international law Martens made dependent on strengthening the

[57] Martens, note 1 above, I, pp. 327, 335-336.
[58] Martens, note 1 above, I, p. v.

legal protection of the individual in individual States and in international life.

Law-Creation An important feature of Martens' activity was that he closely linked the theoretical working out of international law with the practice of its formation and application in international relations. The fact that he had the opportunity to experience this in real life affected Martens' doctrine. For him norms of international law were not an abstraction arising out of logical principles. They were born in the requirements of a specific stage of international relations, and Martens took part in working out some of them.

In his works he repeatedly pointed out that the task of international law is to single out and consolidate the legal norms of relations which actually exist in the life of peoples. Martens thereby stressed that the functioning of a legal norm depends not only upon being postulated in an international legal act as being in existence in real life; in other words, on whether the norm exists objectively. He was aware that merely declaring does not create an actual right. Martens wrote that "each international law [lex] has a reasonable grounds and right to existence insofar as it corresponds to the actual, reasonable vital relations between peoples".[59] If a norm was adopted, and the respective relations did not arise in practice, this means there was an attempt to create a right, but the attempt was unsuccessful. Therefore Martens constantly sought support and orientations for law-creation in actual international relations.

Martens' approach did not mean, however, that he reduced the role of international law merely to determining which relations have arisen or are arising, and the role of the State to one of passively watching over the development of international life. He allotted to States an active role in law-creation, having in view that such law-creation would facilitate the formation of bringing order to international relations and their progressive development.

Martens saw, naturally, a theoretical problem in the process of law-creation. This problem he in practice resolved not only

[59] Martens, note 1 above, I, p. 17.

on the basis of theory, but also pragmatically. His pupil Nolde described Martens' method thus: "existing" law he saw through the prism of "proper" law. Being guided by the "proper", he discovered in international relations much that other scholars had ignored. As a result, norms were born which moved international law forward.[60] In my view Martens approached law-creation not only as a science, but also as an art in which talent and experience play a large role and intuition and skill soberly assess the situation. Success in law-creation (to be discussed below) undoubtedly testifies to the fact that Martens had a command of this art.

Understanding international law as the consolidation of actual relations between States, Martens attached significance of principle to such factors as the adequate embodiment of vital realities in legal consciousness. If a State does not understand or does not respect the needs of its people, then the obligations assumed by them quickly discover they are unconstituted. "Only those treaties withstand the onslaught of circumstances and serve the development of international relations which are concluded by States in the awareness and for the satisfaction of a right and for the benefit of their peoples", he wrote. International relations progressively develop when peoples are aware of their requirements which they may satisfy only by means of international communion. In Martens' view, the "task of the science of international law is to elucidate the legal consciousness of contemporary educated peoples expressed in their aspiration to secure their legal spiritual and material interests by an exchange of services and consent".[61]

Great influence was exerted on Martens' position with regard to questions of law-creation by his view of the correlation between international and municipal law. Unlike many Russian and foreign international lawyers, Martens did not fence off international law from municipal, but proceeded from their close interlinkage and interaction, which actually existed in reality.

---

[60] B. E. Nolde, "Ф. Ф. Мартенс" [F. F. Martens], *Русская мысль* [Russian Thought], no. 12 (1909), p. 26.

[61] Martens, note 1 above, I, pp. 177, 187.

Although limiting the "autocracy of States" in international communion, Martens acknowledged such autocracy in the municipal domain. But here he proceeded from the interaction of international and national law. On one hand, he relegated to sources of international law not only municipal legislation, but also governmental decisions and judicial practice. On the other, he noted as an undisputed fact the influence of international law on municipal law. "Rather frequently international relations gave the initial stimulus to certain legislative work within a State or to a change of legislation" he pointed out.

Actual relations were for Martens the major orientation point in the theory and practice of law-creation, but not the sole orientation point. He saw in the moral values of civilisation yet another guiding thread.

Martens opposed the mixing of legal and moral norms and stressed the need to strictly delimit them. "International law, being the aggregate of legal norms, has law as its subject, and not moral or religious laws by which peoples are or were guided in their mutual relations in various epochs of their life. Moral principles and religious views beyond doubt even now affect international life, but they do not comprise the subject of study of the science of international law", Martens wrote.[62] He pointed out that international law can not sanctify all facts of international life, for example, the use of force. Reflecting actual relations of the present, law is only vital when it has aspired to the future, towards the achievement of moral ideals. In his view, if contemporary law does not meet full moral ideals, this is not its weakness and shortcoming, but its pledge of future development. Moral ideals which also are embodied in scientific conceptions act as the moving force in the progress of international law.

Of decisive significance for law-creation in international life, in Martens' view, is the circumstance that its participants are sovereign States. And he pointed to the "difficulty comprising the distinctive peculiarity of the process of the formulation of international laws". The fact is that, as Martens noted, "relations between States are based on the idea of complete independence.

[62] Martens, note 1 above, I, p. 16.

They can not acknowledge as above them and supreme either legislative or judicial power. They themselves have power and do not subordinate themselves to an outside authority. If this mutual independence of States does not exist, one can not speak of relations between them. It follows that in the domain of international relations laws which should have binding force for States may be established not other than by means of joint agreement between them".[63] Achievement of the agreement of States is the major rule when working out international legal norms. And in his activities at international conferences Martens insistently and cleverly achieved this. For his successes in law-creation he was in no small degree obliged to his skills in achieving the broad agreement of the participants of the conference and even unanimity or, as we say these days, consensus.

Martens attached great significance to the codification of existing international rules. The Hague conventions on the laws and customs of warfare are a persuasive example. Martens saw one of the tasks of the Institute of International Law, created at Ghent in 1873, as the codification of international laws.[64] It should be noted that codification was for Martens not only the bringing of existing norms together, but also of reworking and renewing them. The very meaning of codification comprises this to a significant extent. Therefore Martens suggested that the "codification of international law to such a degree is a complex and difficult matter which can hardly be fulfilled successfully by a single person". He pointed to the unsuccessful attempts to resolve the task thus and suggested: "... the combining of scientific legal forces is necessary, and in view of the fact that international law is developed by the cultural life of various peoples, it is desirable that learned representatives of all educated nations be involved in this common labour". As an additional measure Martens suggested the creation in European States of a number of "private societies for the purpose of studying international law".[65]

[63] Martens, note 16 above, p. 49.
[64] Martens, note 1 above, I, p. 198.
[65] Martens, note 1 above, I, p. 196.

Systematics of International Law In creating the *cours* on international law, Martens devoted great attention to its system. Such attention was in the tradition of the Russian School of international law. It should be noted that from the mid-nineteenth century questions of systematics acquired significance. The majority of writers encompassing the entire aggregate of international law considered it necessary to touch upon the problems of the system of its structure. We refer above all to German and Russian jurists. Among the early works specially devoted to this problem was the book by Professor A.M. Bulmerincq (1822-90), of the University of Dorpat.[66] The French and other representatives of the Romanic-language literature devoted much less attention to systematics, and to Anglo-American writers it remains alien to this day.

When Martens began to write his *cours* on international law there already were the works of a number of predecessors in the domain of systematics, including Georg Friedrich Martens, which F. F. Martens regarded highly. G. F. Martens had structured his *cours* as follows: introduction, then the part concerning the subjects of international law and the part affecting the objects of international law, by which he understood the rights and duties of States. His system advantageously differed from those which divided international law only into the law of war and the law of peace. It was comparatively symmetrical. But objections arose because he called the aggregate of the rights of States, which actually constitute international law, the objects of international law. The system proposed by G. F. Martens was the best of its day, but its weaknesses inspired further work, and the distinguished German jurists, R. von Mohl (1799-1875) and L. von Stein (1815-90), created their own systems.

F. F. Martens put foward his own system which differed from those already existing. He wrote: "The system by which we set out the science of international law materially differs from others existing in the rich Western European literature ... During

---

[66] See A. Bulmerincq, *Die Systematik des Völkerrechts von Hugo Grotius bis auf die gegenwart* (1858).

eleven years of teaching activity this system was and remains, in our extreme understanding, that sequence which best corresponds to the essence and the degree of development of contemporary international relations". Martens had in view that the consideration of only legal norms, even taken together and in historical sequence, could not elicit the profound causes which gave rise to them. He pointed out that the majority of scholars contemporary to him structured the system of international law as a continuation of ancient Roman Law, which in essence was civil law, and he considered this approach to be unscholarly. An understanding of the societal laws of development of international law required an analysis of those actual relations which bound States as members of the international community. He stressed: "Thus the subject of the science of international law is the aggregate of vital relations existing between contemporary educated States, that is, the system thereof must evidently be the system of those relations and not those laws and principles which in the course of time are worked out in international life".[67]

In accordance with such a methodological approach Martens structured his *cours* on international law as follows: in the preface to Volume One he set out his view on the nature and subject of international law, and also the tasks of the science of international law. The exposition of his own positions was accompanied by a critical analysis of other views. The Introduction to the *cours* he divided into three parts: (1) the basis of international law; (2) the definition of the concept of international law; (3) the history of international relations and law.

In accordance with the said scheme Martens adhered to the following periodisation: first period – from antiquity to the 1648 Peace of Westphalia; period two – from the Peace of Westphalia to the 1815 Congress of Vienna; period three – from the Congress of Vienna to the present time. Next came the development of the science of international law in which he singled out: (a) the period of the dominance of natural law

[67] Martens, note 1 above, I, pp. iv, 179.

(Grotius, Vattel, and others); (b) the period of the predominance of a positivist orientation (Mably, Moser, and others); (c) the periods of the combining of philosophical principles with elements of positive international law (G. F. Martens, R. J. Phillimore (1810-85), L. von Stein, A. W. Heffter, P. Mancini, D. I. Kachenovskii, and others).

The Introduction was completed by the following sections: the spatial operation of international law; the relationship of international law to other legal and political sciences; the sources of international law; the codification of the principles of international law.

The General Part of Volume One consisted of four chapters: the law of the international community (including its organisation and organs); the subjects of international law and subjects of international relations (including the rights of private persons in the domain of international relations); State territory and routes of international transport (including the high seas, straits, rivers), and international treaties.

The Second Volume of the *cours* Martens devoted to international administration. Chapter One of this volume he entitled: "On International Administration and the Organs Thereof". Chapters Two and Three comprised the section "International Administration in the Sphere of Spiritual, Physical, and Economic Interests of Peoples". Chapters Four and Five comprised the Section "International Administration in the Domain of the Legal Interests of Citizens and Peoples" (including private international law and international criminal law). In Section Three ("International Administration in the Domain of Compulsory Protection of the Interests and Rights of Citizens and Peoples") were the three remaining chapters: the law of international enforcement and international conflicts, the law of war, and the law of neutrality.

The system proposed by Martens was a novel one. It is not surprising that among specialists it, together with general recognition, also gave rise to certain comments. As with respect to other parts of Martens' doctrine, his compatriots were his most severe judges.

Grabar regarded as a shortcoming of Martens' *cours* the fact that in his system he, to the detriment of consistency and symmetry of exposition, also included ambassadorial and consular law. Grabar believed the entire Martens system to have been borrowed from Stein, and further believed that Martens had made it worse, introducing the law of international enforcement, including war and neutrality. In Grabar's view, war and neutrality have little in common with international administration.[68]

As a whole, however, Martens' system received extensive recognition and exerted a notable influence on subsequent works. Grabar himself, giving a general assessment, acknowledged: "This was a revolution in the systematics of international law".

The above were the basic features of Martens' legal doctrine. It is impossible in a brief summary to illuminate the great wealth of thoughts and ideas advanced by the outstanding jurist. Willy-nilly there were mixed accentuations in Martens' doctrine: at the forefront he advanced the propositions and ideas which attract attention these days, and not those which were of lively interest to contemporaries of Martens (for example, the special rights of sovereigns and the church in the international community, polemics with the natural-law school, and certain questions of the law of war).

Undoubtedly Martens' international legal doctrine is of interest to the modern reader. There are many propositions which correspond with surprising freshness to the concerns and problems of international relations and international law of our time. Against the background of headlong historical change it is remarkable that a significant part of Martens' doctrine retains scholarly importance. A number of provisions which seemed to contemporaries of Martens to be secondary or utopian have acquired actuality in our era. A considerable number of phenomena of international life to which Martens referred in

---

[68] V. E. Grabar, "Из истории систематики международного права" [From the History of the Systematics of International Law], *Советский ежегодник международного права 1963* [Soviet Yearbook of International Law 1963] (1965), pp. 486-489.

confirmation of his conceptions and which at the time were embryonic or underdeveloped (for example, international organisations, ensuring the rights of man by international legal acts, and others), have survived stormy development and in our era play a larger role than was dreamed of in those days. The entire theory of international administration proposed by Martens has acquired now, when the United Nations has truly taken on a universal character and plays an active role in settling inter-State and regional conflicts, in principle a very different sound.

Martens' international legal doctrine is not merely the legacy of history. It continues to give useful impulses when investigating modern problems. It is from this, in my view, that one should proceed when assessing the place of F. F. Martens in the science of international law.

CHAPTER IV
THE PLACE OF MARTENS IN THE SCIENCE OF INTERNATIONAL LAW

In the science of international law scholars are traditionally divided into representatives of the natural law and of legal positivism. Martens did not escape this approach.

Legal Positivism

Martens himself rather concisely outlined the place of his doctrine in the general development of the science of international law. He singled out three principal stages in this development: prior to the eighteenth century the dominant orientation in the science of international law was natural law, the progenitor of which was Hugo Grotius (1583-1645). In the eighteenth century natural law increasingly absorbed the principles of positive law, which soon became the predominant orientation. Representatives of the positive law orientation placed at the base of their structures the treaties and practice of international relations. Whereas the natural law school suffered from an abstract, natural-philosophical approach which divorced it from the realities of international life, the positivist school frequently fell in to the opposite extreme, becoming the "servant of practice". Objective development advanced the task of synthesising the achievements of both schools. The realisation of this task Martens considered to be the substance of the third period of the development of the science of international law contemporary to him.

Thus Martens relegated himself to the positivist orientation in the science of international law, but to the higher stage thereof, the beginning of which, in his view, was laid by the German jurist, G. F. Martens. F. F. Martens valued highly the contribution of his colleague of the same surname. Of his followers he singled out Professor A. W. Heffter, of the University of Berlin. Martens believed that the school whose beginnings were laid by his German colleague with the same surname had exhausted itself by the 1860s. He noted the merits of this school: the aspiration to elicit on the basis of critical analysis and the generalisation of international customs, treaties, and historical examples those legal norms by which States determine their relations; attempts to create "one organically integral system of positive international law". Martens simultaneously subjected this approach to fundamental criticism. In his assessment G. F. Martens in the approaches of his worldview had adopted basically the positions of natural law.

In addition, in his works a lack of autonomous analysis of the facts of international life is noticeable, indeed "excessive partiality to facts". He "thought and summarised insufficiently", summarised F. F. Martens.[1] He classified as similar the works of Anglo-American, French, German, and Latin American representatives of the positivist school of that time. In Russian literature he noted the general poverty of autonomous works.

In the science of international law positivism takes root in the first half of the nineteenth century, having supplanted the natural law orientation and extended roots so deep that to the present day it occupies the predominant position. The spread of legal positivism could not fail to strengthen the separation out of divergent currents and schools.

Positivism always has been a diverse and multi-faceted phenomenon, and those features are clearly traceable at the end of the nineteenth and beginning of the twentieth centuries. By his doctrine Martens merely added to the diversity in positivism. All this should be taken into account when comprehending the ideas of Martens and classifying his doctrine as positivist.

The Special Characteristics of Martens' Positivism

When considering the international legal doctrines of Martens one is struck by the fact that certain aspects of his theory and the individual international legal propositions advanced by him diverge from the postulates of positivism. Martens not only did not spurn theoretical generalisations, he saw their absence as a weakness of the conceptions of his predecessor, G. F. Martens. He aspired to cognition of the objective laws of the development

[1] F. F. Martens, *Современное международное право цивилизованных народов* [Contemporary International Law of Civilised Peoples] (1882), I, p. v.

of international relations and through them, the societal laws of the evolution of international law. Following the French philosopher Auguste Comte, one may say that Martens attempted to answer not only the question "how" (how do international legal relations develop), but also "why" (why do they develop thus). He did not always succeed in this, but the endeavour was deliberate and purposeful. Martens' departures from positivism were remarked upon by his contemporaries. Nolde wrote: "His viewpoint was far from the vast and poorly substantiated utopian structures and from strict legal positivism". The author of an article about Martens in an encyclopedia, while concurring with the relegation of his doctrines to the positivist orientation predominant in the literature of international law, expressed several reservations.[2] He considered it necessary to stress that Martens did not confine himself to stating what were the prevailing legal norms and institutions; he attempts by means of historical research to discover their laws of development, and he sought by means of analysis of the state of international relations contemporary to him to elicit the significance and vitality of these norms and institutions. Martens studied them not in isolation from but in connection with the legislation and legal institutions of individual States and the diverse spiritual and economic interests of these States.

When assessing the scientific position of Martens, his realism should especially be singled out. His scientific conceptions undoubtedly tell on the approach to individual facts and theoretical questions. But he did not bend real developments to fit them. On the contrary, international life constantly adjusted his theoretical views. The sober realism of Martens at times gave rise to a certain uncoordination and even inconsistency both in his own works and in international legal doctrine as a whole. As an example one may cite his theory of the international community: on one hand, respect for the sovereignty of the State, the inadmissability of interference in internal affairs; on the

---

[2] "Мартенс, Ф. Ф." [Martens, F. F.], *Новый Энциклопедический словарь Брокгауза и Ефрона* [New Encyclopedic Dictionary of Brokhaus andd Efron] (1916), XXV.

other, the steady growth of the world community which gradually led to the knitting of the world community into a single whole and conditioned the establishment of precise rules for the behaviour of States in the community and regulation of their rights and duties. Martens saw that the absolutisation of sovereignty, independence, and autonomy of the State would lead to an "insoluble legal form of conflict". Therefore he also drew a conclusion of principle, that the sovereignty of a State can not be the sole grounds for the rights and duties of States under international law. As participants of the international community, as members of the world community, States depend on one another, and such interdependence, placing the interests of the international community higher than the interests of individual States, is gradually increasing. The "autocracy" of States is turning out to be self-limited in the process of the progressive development of international law. Such conflicts reflected the real contradictions of international life, and they can not be resolved "legally". The realism of Martens inspired him to treat scientific concepts in all of their true contradictions.

Contemporaries understood Martens' aspiration to preserve a close link with the living fabric of international relations, with the practice of the functioning of international law. "He proposed to raise himself above the superficiality of the daily facts of international life, but at the same time recommended a flight close to the surface thereof", Nolde wrote.[3]

Martens opposed confining research solely to normative material. His scientific conclusions he endeavoured to base on the development of international relations. He allotted primary significance to the history of international relations and international law. On the whole he was an adherent of the comparative-historical method. When one recalls the constant references of Martens to the "inalienable right" of the individual and examines his theory of the international community, one can not fail to discover the existing elements of adherence to natural law. This is entirely consistent with his aspiration to synthesise the positive aspects of both orientations.

---

[3] See B. E. Nolde, "Ф. Ф. Мартенс" [F. F. Martens], *Русская мысль* [Russian Thought], no. 12 (1909), pp. 24-25.

Taking into account the foregoing, in my view Martens can conditionally be regarded as being within the positivist camp. Martens' doctrine, at times so complex and multi-faceted just as international life itself, is difficult to fit within the framework of a single concept even so broad a one as legal positivism.

The New International Law

If one compares international law at the beginning and at the end of the nineteenth century, one may speak of different eras, so great are the differences between them. Development proceeded, naturally, rather gradually with the accumulation of quantitative changes, with the preservation of succession, but the last quarter of the nineteenth century and beginning of the twentieth century (up to World War I and the revolutionary shocks connected with it) stand out increasingly as a boundary signifying a qualitatively new stage in the historical evolution of international law. A comparatively brief space of time (30-40 years) accommodated so many innovations that with full justification it can be called a revolutionary stage. It was precisely then that much which comprises the foundation of modern international law was formulated. This relates, in particular, to his theory of international administration.

The theory of international administration proposed by Martens was as follows. At the base of international law lies the requirement of peoples for communion with one another. This constitutes a guarantee of the sovereignty and independence of States. From international communion arises the need for international administration, that is, the activity of States with regard to coordinating the interests of themselves and their social organisations and citizens, and also relating to the organisation of the community. The aggregate of legal norms regulating this activity comprises the law of international administration, situated at the centre of the entire system of international law. It regulates the cooperation of States in the sphere of their economic, scientific-technical, cultural, humanitarian, and legal interests, and also regulates the structure and activity of agencies of the State in this domain (ambassadorial and consular law), and likewise the means of resolving international disputes arising in the course of the cooperation of States, including the law of warfare and neutrality.

The scheme proposed by Martens is not distinguished by impeccable symmetry; complexity and multiplicity are inherent in it. But its undoubted merit is that it singles out and systematises in international law those norms and institutions which regulate peaceful international cooperation. The theory of international administration was an attempt to reply to those questions which were put to international law by the progressing internationalisation of the life of peoples and the process of the formation of an international community into a single whole. This was an innovatory and genuine attempt. The fact that after the appearance of Martens' *cours* all writers except the Anglo-Americans took into account to some extent the formation of international administrative law testifies to the success of the conception.

In my view one can not reduce the significance of Martens' doctrine on the international community and international administration solely to the formation of international administrative law. Martens design, it seems to me, is broader and its realisation in the *cours* of international law, more substantive. In essence we are speaking about an interpretation of the problems of the formation of an organically integral world community and the management of that world community. Here Martens not only generalised the normative material which existed but saw far beyond, so far that in our day his theoretical postulates have not lost their significance.

Within the framework of the present book there is no reason to delve into characterising the changes of international law and an analysis of the reasons for this development. Suffice it to note that the rapid renewal of international law is conditioned by the fact that the developed States of that period (civilised States, in Martens' terminology), and together with them the entire system of inter-State relations, had entered a new stage of development. The scale of the changes is evidenced by the fact that thanks to the works of a number of researchers, above all of a Marxist orientation (R. Hilferding, Karl Kautsky, V. I.

Lenin, and others), the boundary of the nineteenth and twentieth centuries came to be characterised as the beginning of a new era – the epoch of imperialism. The changes in international law of that time were expressed by the insistent requirements of changing international relations.

As always, the objective requirements were not realised directly in specific legal norms. They should have been thought out in advance, and it is not surprising that in the last quarter of the nineteenth and at the beginning of the twentieth centuries the rise of the science of international law represented by outstanding jurists occurred.

The activity of Martens coincided with this revolutionary stage in the development of international law and its science. This development was stimulated by many objective and subjective factors and is linked with many names. It is beyond doubt that Martens both as a scholar and as a practitioner played an outstanding role in this process. He was then one of the most significant creators of international law.

Many of his contemporaries were aware of the pre-eminent place of Martens in the science of international law and in the formation of a new international law. Nolde, for example, drew the conclusion that at the moment of Martens' arrival in the scientific and practical milieu contemporary international law "actually did not exist" and it was Martens who did so much for its formation. Nolde's assessment is the more weighty in that he was not sparing in his criticism of individual ideas and propositions of his teacher. A large number of Russian and foreign specialists shared Nolde's opinion. The German jurist Wehberg called Martens one of the founders of modern international law. He pointed out that Martens' theoretical works had accelerated the transformation of the old international law into the modern.[4]

The Roots of Success

In his day, that is, in the period from approximately the 1874 Brussels Conference to his death in 1909, Martens was the greatest specialist on international law in Russia. Now, almost a century

[4] See H. Wehberg, "Friedrich v. Martens und die Haager Friedenskonferenzen", *Zeitschrift für internationales Recht*, XX (1910), 25.

later, this is especially obvious. His renown accordingly was and remains.

But to this day unabated discussions of Martens obscure his stature as a scholar. An example is the assessment of such a great specialist as Grabar. Giving his due as a whole to the services of Martens, Grabar wrote that his position in science he achieved "not only because of his gifts, but by hard work". As expressed by Grabar, "Without the brilliance of Kachenovskii or the penetration of Nezabitovskii, he gave to the Russian science of international law a breadth which his more talented predecessors had not succeeded in doing. His motto ran: "Labour conquers all".[5] Another writer, while noting Martens' "business-like character, good faith, and sincerity", joined Grabar.[6]

Such assessments alluded to a certain decline of Martens as a scholar. Evidently some of Martens' contemporaries saw him as more an indefatigable toiler than a scholar outstanding in his talents. From the standpoint of our day such judgments seem one-sided, excessively emotional, too linked to current events. Talent and labour are inextricably linked to one another. And the fact remains that the activity of Martens exerted great influence on his contemporaries and later generations, and his works, above all his *cours* on international law and his *Recueil des traités*, retain significance to this day. D. I. Kachenovskii (1827-73) at Moscow University and V. A. Nezabitovskii (1824-83), at Kiev University, for all of their gifts did not leave so profound a trace on the science of international law as did Martens. Time incontestably has made its adjustments here. To the view of Grabar one should add that following Martens in the Russian science of international law of that time were not Kachenovskii and Nezabitovskii, but L. A. Kamarovskii (1846-1912), a professor of Moscow University.

Grabar also drew the conclusion that Martens did not leave a school to succeed him since he, in Grabar's view, was not one

---

[5] V. E. Grabar, *The History of International Law in Russia 1647-1917*, transl. W. E. Butler (Oxford, 1990), p. 387.

[6] A. L. Sakketti, "Федор Федорович Мартенс" [Fedor Fedorovich Martens], *Советский ежегодник международного права 1960* (1961), p. 257-9.

himself. It is impossible to concur with this assessment. Martens left not only a pleiad of pupils who played a leading role in the Russian science of international law, not only conceptions which shaped its future development, but also traditions which left a deep imprint. One of them should, in my view, be especially singled out: the combining of scholarly work with practical activity in the domain of international relations, in particular, with participation in the progressive development of international law. It was law enforcement practice, real international life, so familiar to Martens from personal experience, that deprived his scholarly conceptions of that academic brilliance which was inherent in the works of certain professors who did not venture beyond the university walls. The flight of their theoretical thought and the symmetry of logical structures were not interfered with by the contradictions and inconsistencies of real life, as was the case with Martens. In assessing his place in science, in my view, closer to the truth is the article in the *Encyclopedia Britannica*, which considered that Martens "determined the character of the Russian school of international law".

We also do not accept the assertion that the "ideas of Martens in and of themselves were not distinguished by originality".[7] In this connection it is essential to note the following. Martens was profoundly right when he saw his task as being to elicit and interpret the objective bases and societal laws of the development of international law. But this approach left little room for originality since the actual basis of international law is identical for all researchers. Their originality may be expressed in the degree of cognition of objective phenomena, and not in the invention of speculative constructions. Martens would have changed his fundamental views had he proceeded along that path. His "originality" lies in the fact that he undeviatingly engaged in investigating the real foundations of international law and the societal laws of its development. The very "original" aspect of his theory – the theory of the international community

[7] Sakketti, note 6 above, p. 258.

- emanated from the state of international relations and the prospects for their development.

The extensive use by Martens of the works of Russian and foreign writers, the synthesis of their ideas, are an important contribution to the development of the science of international law. The use of the conceptions of Stein and Mohl, and of other scholars, are a virtue and not a weakness of Martens. His virtue is that he created his *cours* of international law as an integral part of world science, or world legal thought. In so doing he used the wealth of his knowledge, the breadth of legal views, a close familiarisation with European culture, and a command of several languages. There are no grounds to reproach him for insufficient originality. We are increasingly convinced of the correctness of the position of Martens, who saw that the development of science recognises no national boundaries. He himself facilitated the internationalisation of the science of international law.

One should note in this connection that the *cours* of international law by Martens was not in any way orientated towards the works of Stein or Mohl. The first citation in his *cours* is to an Englishman, Robert Joseph Phillimore, and it is Phillimore who, measured by the number of citations, is referred to most frequently. Another author often cited in the *cours* is J. Bluntschli. But why does this give grounds to assert that Martens merely relates the ideas of Phillimore and Bluntschli? One must not forget that Martens was rather critical of the works which he used, not hesitating to direct critical remarks at recognised authorities. He quoted rather often the "noted German jurist" Rudolf von Jhering (1818-92). But he polemicises sharply with him in relation to defining the essence of law, above all the role of coercion and force. Martens pointed out that Jhering "confuses two different things: law itself and the coercive procedure for its effectuation". Martens objected in principle to a theory which saw the basis of law in force.

He treated similarly the conceptions of Professor Georg Jellinek (1851-1911), of Heidelberg University. Martens referred to his works in substantiation of his theory of the international community, his approach to the sovereignty of the State, and when setting out other international legal questions. But he also disagreed with him.[8]

In general Martens was never a docile pupil in science. He displayed a critical intelligence and inclination towards autonomous judgments. His doctrine on international law he developed by relying on his own conclusions. In so doing the orientation point was not so much the conceptions of other scholars as the real processes which occurred in international relations.

In speaking of "civilised peoples" Martens placed real relations at the base of his theoretical conceptions. And the relations of colonial oppression were a reality of that time. At the time, the liquidation of the colonial system was not proceeding, and Martens opposed this, being guided in legal regulation by norms which arose not from real relations, but from conceptions about the future.

Grabar noted the weak places in the Martens system. But one must observe that Grabar in his own work criticised all systems of international law which existed then. It is remarkable that ultimately he praised most the system proposed by the pupil and successor of Martens, M. A. Taube.[9] Martens evidently reflected successfully in his system the real international relations and the real level of the science of international law of those years, which did not leave much expanse for its improvement in the immediate period thereafter.

Opponents frequently reproached Martens, and at times reproached justly, for the inconsistency of individual tenets of his theory and the inconsistency of his argumentation. The reasons here were various: the inconsistency of Martens' philosophical views, individual inadequacies and omissions. But the principal reason for many contradictions peculiar to individual positions of Martens was hidden in the fact that the sober realism so characteristic of him did not enable him to smooth over or evade the objective contradictions of international life, and he reflected them in his conceptions.

---

[8] See Martens, note 1 above, I, pp. 8-9, 202, 246, 288.

[9] Grabar, note 5 above, p. 483-484.

The assessments of the scholarly labours of Martens, in my view, inadequately reflected the fact that this outstanding Russian scholar personified the European community, in particular the legal community of Europe. His conceptions were permeated with a general European approach, and in his works – scholarly and publicist – Russia always is an integral part of European history and European culture. His critical remarks against Slavophiles, against national exclusivity, were conditioned by an adherence to the European community. To be sure, Martens reacted negatively to schemes for a general-European State formation, for example, against the scheme for a United States of Europe. However, he did not object to European integration. Moreover, he proceeded from the steady approximation of European countries and the arising on this basis of some form of association of the European States. He merely cautioned against the unreality of a mechanical extension of State structures and State law to international relations. In his concept international and municipal relations and international and municipal law have a different basis in principle and develop according to their own immanent laws. Martens emphasised their very close interconnection but regarded them as autonomous magnitudes. And he always pointed to the unifying role of international law, including in the European region. In our times when the pan-European process occupies a noteworthy place in the politics and social consciousness of the European peoples, the pan-European orientation of Martens' scholarly conceptions takes on a new actuality.

The international legal doctrine of the outstanding Russian jurist is noteworthy for another quality: the close combination of scientific thought with the rich experience of teaching international law, intensive law-creation activity, diplomatic practice, and publicist publications. In 1896 Martens already was spoken of as a well-known practising lawyer who had made a noteworthy contribution to the development of the norms and principles of international law. In the literature on Martens it was pointed out with full justification that he had "created international law". Moreover, the opinion was expressed that "a leading role belongs to Martens in the cause of the creation of contemporary international law".[10] In so doing they had in view his participation also in the preparation of documents of the Institute of International Law and in arbitrations, and especially in working out legal acts of international conferences. This diversity of interests, especially the combining of legal science with practice, could not fail to produce a remarkable creative fusion. This fusion we find in the works of Martens.

Some of the more perspicacious contemporaries understood the special nature of Martens' position in science. Nolde, close to him, wrote: "Martens was undoubtedly a great figure, but precisely because he was great, less attention was given to assessments from the standpoint of our usual classifications".

Discussions, polemics, criticism, perplexing issues – and the steady growth of the authority, the world recognition, of Martens. Where is the explanation for this phenomenon?

All remark on the enormous capacity for work and the diligence of Martens. Only a few display an understanding of the fact that in his scholarly creativity and in his practical activity Martens foresaw the essential requirements of the international community. The growth of international communion, the progressing intertwining of peaceful links and interests required that inter-State relations be put in order, above all by the so-called civilised States, and Martens worked towards this purposefully. It is so important to note that he proved to be able to perceive in international relations those rules which already had been formed, which had ripened and were latent. The laws and customs of warfare, arbitration, commissions of enquiry, organs of international administration – they all enjoyed success because they had matured and fallen on productive earth. Martens imparted to the science of international law an unprecedented scope, and the rise of the science in turn brought him to new heights. Nolde was right when he wrote: "The secret of Martens' success lay in the fact that from the very beginning he served one idea, that in serving it he invested exceptional

---

[10] Nolde, note 3 above, p. 25.

energies, and that the idea to which he dedicated himself turned out to be fruitful. To the extent that this idea strengthened and grew, and historically it could not fail to grow, so too matured its faithful and active servitor".[11] The diversity of interests, broad horizons, multi-faceted activities – these did not dissipate the powers of the scholar, but merely concentrated his energies and merged them into one mighty flow.

Discussions on the subject of Martens generate a question: what is the reason for this? Why did the uncontestable authority of a scholar yield with difficulty to a general assessment? Why did his international reputation cause misunderstanding on the part of contemporaries?

In my view the controversies surrounding Martens arose above all by virtue of his originality. The multi-facetedness of his activities did not fall within the customary framework: professor and diplomat, jurist and historian, advisor and publicist ... These days such combinations have become more usual, whereas then they were accepted with difficulty. Martens did not fit well into the existing hierarchy of subordination. He objectively claimed a role which according to notions of the day was clearly "above his rank" and hereinafter in this discourse we will encounter similar judgments. As a whole Martens personified the new, and the new is not always readily accepted.

In conclusion it is appropriate to devote several lines to the personal qualities of Professor Martens. From the assessments of Grabar and certain other specialists, and even from the utterances of Martens himself, one may have the image of a dried-up man who day and night pored over books. There comes to mind the characterisation given by the sharp eyes and literary talent of A. I. Kuprin: "Scholarly specialists usually are the most boring, dry, closed, and arrogant people in the world". Fedor Fedorovich Martens hardly was of this type. He loved mixing and constantly moved in society, and he had many friends at home and abroad. As regards his way of life and his style of work, he was well-organised, worked intensively, and had a high capacity for concentration. As his son Nikolai wrote in a diary,

[11] Nolde, note 3 above, pp. 20, 22.

Martens was "wholly harmonious. He had a vast memory and was very systematic". Of the work pace of his father, Nikolai Fedorovich wrote: "He rose early and was moderate in everything, even work, that is, did not prejudice his health".[12] Martens worked intensively, but rested during the summer months. His dacha in Livonia, near Wolemar, became in time his favourite place of leisure. There he was amongst his family and played tennis. He regularly travelled to resorts in Germany (Baden-Baden, Bad-Neuheim), where he sought relief from severe rheumatism.

Martens' life-style does not confirm the conclusion that his scholarly achievements came to him only through exhausting labours. The originality of his scientific conceptions, theoretical propositions, and the abundance of published works are to be explained not only by unceasing labours, but also by his capacity to work, his organisational skills, knowing how to rapidly and precisely set out his thoughts, and an ability for profound analysis and rapid generalisation. And all this makes up the person of a scholar and his talent.

The Works of Martens Today

The international legal doctrine of Martens exerted influence on scholars not only in Russia, but also in other countries. When the noted Cuban jurist, A. Bustamante, published his capital treatise in the 1930s on international law, he borrowed much from Martens and specially noted his role in the development of the contemporary science of international law, in particular, the significance of his theory of the international community.[13] The German jurist W. Kobarg in a work devoted to the deportation of foreigners cites the memorandum of Martens to the Institute of International Law in 1880 as the most authoritative source.[14] In a study of State succession conducted by Gruber, Martens is cited frequently as a "classic writer", in particular his *cours* on international law.[15]

---

[12] AVPR, opis 787, delo 8, l. 4.

[13] See A. S. Bustamante, *Droit international public* (1935), I, p. 7.

[14] See W. Kobarg, *Ausweisung und Abweisung von Auslandern* (Leipzig, 1930).

[15] See A. Gruber, *Le droit international de la succession d'Etats* (Paris, 1986).

Foreign authors point out that Martens became the first Russian international lawyer whose works were so frequently translated into foreign languages.[16] In reality it was Martens who formed the watershed in the interaction between Russian and foreign doctrinal writings: whereas before the appearance of his work a one-sided movement predominated – the publication in Russia of foreign authors (Bluntschli, Heffter, Klüber, Rivier, and others), a revolution occurs with its appearance in the field of scholarship – Martens' works appeared in many countries.

The books by Martens to this day have their place in the scholarly libraries of the world and especially in the libraries of various universities. Fifteen works by Martens are represented in the catalogue of the Harvard Law School (United States) on international law and relations.[17] When visiting the University of Ruhr (Bochum, Germany) in 1989 the author of this book was given a list of Martens publications in the university library containing twelve titles in the German, Russian, and other languages.[18] During a Soviet-Swedish symposium at the University of Stockholm in 1991 the complete set of the *Recueil de traités* compiled by Martens was shown to me in the library, and in the Royal National Library I was informed that they also had the *Recueil des traités* and the Martens' *cours* of international law in French and in Russian, as well as the German translation of his doctoral translation.[19] The works of F. de Martens also are found in the library of the Peace Palace in The Hague, built with his assistance, including the memoranda prepared on behalf of the Institute of International Law.[20] The works of Martens connected with the activities of the Institute are kept in the

---

[16] See Boris Meissner and A. Uschakow (eds.), *Sowjetunion und Völkerrecht 1917 bis 1962* (Cologne, 1963), p. 30.

[17] See M. Moody (comp.), *Harvard Catalog of International Law and Relations* (1966), XIII, p. 115.

[18] The author expresses his gratitude to the then Rector of the University of Ruhr, Professor K. Ipsen.

[19] The author is grateful to the Dean of the Law Faculty of the University of Stockholm, Professor K. Lindenkrone.

[20] See the *Catalogue de la Bibliothéque du Palais de la Paix. Index Alphabetique (1916-1929)* (Leiden 1932), p. 846.

Institute archives in Ghent and continue to serve the science of international law.

From the vantage point of our times when historical development has singled out the most important events and individuals the contribution of F. F. Martens to international law and to the science of international law is especially evident. Martens is among the cohort of outstanding jurists of the world who formulated the science of international law at the end of the nineteenth and beginning of the twentieth centuries, that is, the science with which mankind approached the new millennium. Their labours have proved to be so stable that it is now part of the foundations of contemporary legal science. Among the jurists of prerevolutionary Russia, F. F. Martens left the most notable trace in international law. He became one of the most eminent representatives of the Russian school of international law of the new era. At the turn of the nineteenth and twentieth centuries he was one of the best known specialists on international law in the world. A number of legal norms in whose establishment he took part continue to retain force in our day, and many legal conceptions which he advanced have not lost their actuality.

CHAPTER V
JURIST, DIPLOMAT, PUBLICIST

In modern writings F. F. Martens appears as a jurist, a specialist on international law. The reputation as a jurist has so pushed into the background the other aspects of his activity that now nothing is remembered of them. Especially "forgotten" is his diplomatic activity. Little was written about this during his lifetime, and now it has been forgotten entirely. Martens proved to be an exceptional diplomat, and his success in the development of international law can not be separated from his diplomatic abilities and experience. He was involved in major foreign policy actions of Russia, the greatest international events. Without illuminating Martens' diplomatic activity, his profile inevitably would be one-sided. The international lawyer and diplomat are inextricably combined in his life and activity. To this must be added a strong publicist element.

Collegium Secretary In the Archive of the Foreign Policy of Russia there is preserved the request of "candidate of law Fromgolts, son of Fedorov, Martens" to Tsar Alexander II concerning his enrolment in service at a department of the Ministry of Foreign Affairs, dated 21 December 1868.[1] The request, as was the practice then, was written on a large sheet of stamped paper and not by Martens (his bad handwriting is imprinted all over the diaries), but by a professional scribe. The address of the petitioner is specified on the request: the home of Loginov, Teriaeva Street, near Karpovka, Petersburg side. That district of the City was clearly not aristocratic, being a typical place of residence for junior bureaucrats and others of various ranks. There the young graduate had rented an apartment (or room, corner?).

On 6 January 1869 Martens was enrolled in service at the Ministry of Foreign Affairs, as we would now say, taking a second job, with the rank of a collegium secretary. The head of the

---

[1] See AVPR, opis 749/1, delo 50, l. 85.

foreign policy department, the State Chancellor, Prince A. M. Gorchakov, had conversed personally with the new official.

According to the Table of Ranks established by Peter the Great and in force in Russia until 1917, all persons in the military and civil service were divided into fourteen classes. The highest, first, class was allocated to the State Chancellor. The lowest, the fourteenth, to the collegium registrar. The rank determined for Martens was the tenth class and in the Army corresponded to a lieutenant.

The twenty-four year old Martens had come to the Ministry of Foreign Affairs at a moment when they had begun to work there under new conditions. The scheme for reorganising the Ministry had been submitted by Gorchakov to the State Council on 7 September 1867, was confirmed by Alexander II on 22 May 1868, and entered into force from 1 January 1869, several days before the enrolment of Martens.

Later in his own design for reorganising the Ministry of Foreign Affairs (1895) Martens was rather sceptical about the transformations effectuated under Gorchakov. In Martens' view, the principal purpose was to increase the salaries for the personnel of the Ministry by reducing the numbers in the personnel establishment. In fact the reduction was significant: instead of 306 officials according to the personnel establishments of 1838-40, only 179 remained in 1869. The maintenance for the director of a department had increased significantly (this corresponds approximately to an administration within the present Ministry of Foreign Affairs of the Russian Federation) from 3362 up to 5000 rubles a year. Martens considered the reduction to be the sole result of the reorganisation and wrote that it "did not breathe new life into the old inherited forms of this department".[2]

Martens' view was exaggeratedly severe and one-sided. Gorchakov's measures amounted to more than the fiscal-organisational side. The reorganisation of the Russian Ministry of Foreign Affairs in 1868 undoubtedly was a consequence of those changes which had given rise to the Great Reform of 1861

[2] AVPR, opis 731, delo 28, l. 4-5.

in Russia. A new spirit had been achieved in the Ministry of Foreign Affairs. Suffice it to say that the new Statute on the Ministry precisely determined its tasks, releasing it from a large number of functions not within its purview. The document confirmed by Alexander II established that in future the Ministry of Foreign Affairs would: (1) effectuate political relations with foreign States; (2) protect Russian trade and Russian interests in general abroad; (3) petition concerning the legal defence of Russian subjects abroad; (4) assist foreigners in their affairs in Russia. Before that time the Ministry of Foreign Affairs had been engaged, in particular, in arranging palace ceremonies and entertainments, and the "Orenburg Kyrgyzy and Small Horde", among others, had been within its jurisdiction.

As a consequence of the 1868 transformations the activity of the Ministry of Foreign Affairs took on a modern image. And the appearance of Martens in the Ministry was a consequence of the new spirit. At a time of a radical reduction of personnel establishments when officials used any opportunity to keep from being cast aside, they had hired a raw magister of law, not of the nobility, a man who, as they said then, "was without kin and tribe". There was no high protector, and the leadership of the Ministry of Foreign Affairs could be attracted by only one thing in Martens – knowledge of international law, foreign languages, and his talent and diligence. They did not require from Martens when hiring him that he concentrate on practical, current tasks of the Ministry. On the contrary, it was suggested that he continue his teaching and scientific-research activity. Martens recalled the words of Prince Gorchakov uttered at the first meeting: "Occupy yourself with your scholarship, and you will be our Ewers and Sacken".[3] (Prince Gorchakov had in mind J. F. G. Ewers (1781-1830), a noted jurist and historian, rector of Dorpat University, corresponding member of the Russian Academy of Sciences, who left works on State law and Russian history, and also F. R. Osten-Sacken (b. 1832), a graduate of the Law Faculty of St. Petersburg University who came immediately to the Ministry of Foreign Affairs upon graduation and held

[3] AVPR, opis 731, delo 28, l. 2.

executive posts there, combining service in the Ministry with extensive scholarly research).

They expected from the young official that he in time would become a highly-qualified expert of the Russian Ministry of Foreign Affairs on international law. Such a personnel decision must be acknowledged to have been wise and farseeing. Thereafter it brought great fruits. Martens had come to the Ministry of Foreign Affairs when noteworthy new approaches were being taken connected with the name of Gorchakov, one of the greatest Russian diplomats.

Martens later changed his initial assessment of the reorganisation undertaken by Gorchakov. In November 1905 he entered in his diaries the results of many years of observations: "The executive personnel of the Ministry of Foreign Affairs are not to be compared with thirty years ago under Gorchakov".[4] Whereas for Gorchakov himself, his deputy Giers, Zhomini, and certain other leading diplomats he had many words of approval, the diary characterisations of officials of the Ministry of Foreign Affairs at the turn of the twentieth century are replete with expressions of "ignoramus", "worthless", and the like. A certain nostalgia is in evidence here and possibly the usual old man's grumbling. But the change in the initial assessment of the reorganisation of the Ministry of Foreign Affairs is quite startling. Undoubtedly it testifies to the excessively categorical and onesided previous view of Martens reflected in his project for transforming the Ministry in 1895.

In January 1869 Martens was admitted to the Ministry of Foreign Affairs, in January 1871 he delivered his first lecture to students, and in 1874 he was to perform his first responsible task for the Government in the international arena – as a member of the Russian delegation to take part in the Brussels Conference for the Codification of the Laws and Customs of Land Warfare.

Brussels Conference (1874) Russia had taken the initiative in convoking the Conference, the point of departure being the Franco-Prussian War of 1870-71 in which the belligerents had not applied uniform rules for

[4] AVPR, opis 787, delo 9, ed. khr. 3, l. 115.

waging warfare and from time to time resorted to harsh reprisals. The underlying idea of the Russian initiative was in peacetime, when there were no hostile emotions, to agree binding rules for waging warfare and thereby to mitigate its grave consequences. This was a routine step for Russian diplomacy in a traditional direction. Martens described the initial course of events (in the Preface to the French edition of his work *The Eastern Question and the Brussels Conference*): "During the War of 1870-71, being close to the theatre of war, I collected from the newspapers of all countries and through personal contacts all the facts which established a violation of the laws and customs of war. Already I had come to the conclusion that the establishment by the governments themselves of these laws and customs was entirely necessary in order to prevent endless accusations and merciless reprisals. In 1873 I had the honour to submit this idea to my noted superior, Chancellor Prince Gorchakov. General Count Miliutin, at the time War Minister and one of the most outstanding Russian public figures, not only reacted sympathetically to this matter but hastened to extend his influential support for it. The initial draft convention on the laws and customs of warfare, prepared by myself, was subjected to detailed and attentive discussion in a commission of eminent Russian military officers under the chairmanship of General Miliutin himself".[5] Taking into account the views of Miliutin (1816-1912), the commission headed by him prepared a second draft convention, Martens taking a very active part. By instruction of Alexander II, other States were familiarised with the draft convention by a Circular Note of the Russian Ministry of Foreign Affairs.[6]

Later a hot discussion raged in legal doctrine and the general press with regard to the authorship of the draft. The discussion has not quieted to this day.

The polemics divided the participants into two groups: one pointed to the key role of Martens, whereas the other reproached

[5] F. F. Martens, *La paix et la guerre* (Paris, 1901), p. i.

[6] See Martens, "Гаагская конференция мира" [The Hague Peace Conference], *Вестник Европы* [Herald of Europe], no. 2 (Feb. 1900), pp. 15-16.

him for nothing less than usurping authorship. It is instructive to recall in this connection that Martens never put himself forward as the author of the idea to legally consolidate the rules for waging warfare. The treatise by Bluntschli mentioned above on the modern law of warfare of civilised peoples, published at the height of the Franco-Prussian War, was itself an attempt to codify the entire law of warfare. There were other publications on the same topic. The idea, as is said, was in the air. It can not be denied that in Russia it was the young jurist Martens who prepared the draft international convention on the laws and customs of warfare and that it was the Russian Government which initiated convocation of the international conference to adopt such a convention. That the untiring efforts of Martens advanced it in time to the centre of the struggle for the adoption of the convention is an undisputed fact. To him belongs the uncontested authorship of many of its provisions. These provisions were created by Martens not in a void, and his service lies not in the fact that he, neglecting the accumulated material, invented something original, but rather that he generalised all of the legal experience which corresponded to the real international relations which had formed. A number of norms were rethought and worked over by Martens himself. Finally, he imparted to the provisions of the future convention the necessary legal form.

To better understand the sense of the discussions which raged around the draft convention submitted by Russia to the Brussels Conference it is necessary to briefly set out their substance.

The Convention determined that the laws of waging warfare apply not only to armies, but to irregulars and voluntary detachments if they met the following criteria: (1) have at the head a person responsible for his subordinates; (2) have a distinctive marking; (3) openly bear arms; (4) comply in their actions with the laws and customs of warfare. This was a serious innovation: detachments of volunteers ("partisans" in the terminology of the day) received legal status which determined their rights and duties.

The rights and duties of prisoners of war relative to their ownership, conditions of recruiting them for work, nourishment, release under word of honour, creation of information offices, subordination of prisoners of war to laws, instructions and regulations operating in the army of the State under whose power they were situated, and the like were regulated in detail. All provisions were directed towards prisoners of war being treated "humanely".

With respect to the means for causing harm to the adversary it was stressed that belligerents do not enjoy an unlimited right of choice. In particular, it was prohibited to use poison and poisonous weapons, and also weapons, projectiles, or substances capable of causing unnecessary suffering; to destroy or seize enemy ownership without military necessity, and illegally use a flag of truce or national flag, military markings, or uniform of an adversary. In the event of sieges and bombardments it was prescribed to spare, insofar as possible, historical monuments, buildings servicing the purposes of science, art, and philanthropy, and military hospitals with wounded. It was prohibited to hand over a city or locality for looting, even if taken by storm.

The draft convention contained provisions concerning scouts, envoys under flag of truce, capitulations, and armistices. Significant place was given to the actions of military authorities on the territory of the enemy State. If territory was occupied by an enemy, the authorities were obliged, insofar as was possible, to restore and secure public order and public life and to respect the laws existing in the country. The belligerents were obliged to respect the honour and life of individuals, family rights, religious convictions, private ownership ("private ownership shall not be subject to confiscation", "stealing is absolutely prohibited"). Rules for recovering taxes on occupied territories, other monetary requisitions, contributions, and requisitions in kind were determined.

The Convention was directed towards establishing agreed rules for mitigating the suffering of the peaceful populace, reducing destruction caused by military actions, and limiting the means and methods of waging warfare. If the Convention were adopted, a legal foundation would emerge to limit the arbitrariness traditionally inherent in military actions and the behaviour of the victor on captured territories.

Notwithstanding the obvious humanitarian aims of the Russian draft, the very idea of convoking a conference encountered guarded and partially negative attitudes. In French political circles the draft was viewed as machinations by Bismarck, who recently had sought France's military defeat. Rumours were spread that the draft itself had been prepared in Berlin. The British Government openly displayed a negative attitude towards the draft and required, in particular, that the planned conference not touch relations between belligerents at sea. When the Russian Government gave such an assurance, England sent her delegate with an instruction not to take part in the discussion and not to sign any act. The Englishman sat in silence at all sessions. The United States avoided participating in the Conference, declaring that exclusively European affairs were being considered in which the United States does not interfere pursuant to the Monroe Doctrine.[7] The view was sometimes expressed in the European press that the codification of the law of warfare not only was inconceivable, but even very undesirable. In particular, the "idealism of international law" was juxtaposed to "military realism". However, the initiative of the Russian Government found too broad a response amongst the general public to reject it from the outset. Ultimately the Conference opened at Brussels on 15 July 1874.

Initially it was established that the participating States would send, in accordance with long tradition, one diplomat each and one military officer each to Brussels. However, having regard to the numerous legal questions which were to be discussed, Belgium, Germany, and Russia included additionally in their delegations one specialist each on public international law. In Petersburg the choice fell on Martens, who had participated so

---

[7] See Martens, *Восточная война и Брюссельская конференция* [The Eastern War and the Brussels Conference] (1878), pp. 51, 110-129. The Monroe Doctrine was proclaimed in 1823 by the President of the United States, James Monroe.

actively in preparing the draft convention. Baron A. G. Zhomini (1814-88), a noted diplomat, headed the Russian delegation. Besides Martens, Major-General G. A. Leer (1829-1904) was included. In giving due to the initiative of Russia, the Conference elected Zhomini as the Chairman. The work of the conference was structured on the basis of the Russian draft.

The draft convention did not give rise to any radical comments. When it was decided to draw up a Declaration based on it, the text virtually reiterated the provisions contained in the draft.[8] Sharp debate unfolded around the very idea of codifying the laws and customs of warfare. As a result, both the Convention and the Declaration were left unsigned. The matter was limited to the adoption of a concluding protocol in which the importance of codifying the law of warfare was acknowledged as was the need to continue work.

In his final evaluation Martens said the Brussels Conference ended as a "complete failure".[9] Modern Russian doctrine adheres to the same assessment. The history of diplomacy[10] published in the Soviet era does not mention the Conference either in the section devoted to the 1870s nor as a precursor of the 1899 Hague Conference. Nor is their information about the Conference in the diplomatic dictionary.[11] The information in foreign doctrine is very sketchy.

Such neglect is unjustified. First, a Russian foreign policy initiative is ignored which commenced the codification of the law of warfare and was continued at the 1899 and 1907 Hague conferences. Second, the objections of the Conference participants testified to the unreadiness of the ruling circles and public opinion in many countries to accept the very idea of codification; an important role of the Brussels Conference consisted of overcoming the atmosphere which existed and laying the basis for further creative work. Third, the draft convention submitted by Russia proved to be so successful that it served as the basis

---

[8] Martens, ibid., Annexes 1 and 2.

[9] Martens, note 6 above, p. 16.

[10] See *История дипломатии* [History of Diplomacy] (Moscow, 1963), II.

[11] *Дипломатический словарь* [Diplomatic Dictionary] (Moscow, 1984), I.

for the respective 1899 and 1907 Hague conferences. Finally, fourth, as future events showed, the Russian digest of the rules for waging warfare were so in keeping with public opinion, at any event in Europe, that deviations from it or violations thereof were already accepted as a violation of international law. The behaviour, for example, of the Russian and Turkish forces in the Eastern War of 1877-78 was assessed by many from the standpoint of those norms which had been formulated in the draft for the 1874 Brussels Conference.

As regards Martens himself, his opinion concerning the "utter failure" does not reflect the results of his labours. Moreover, he personally could experience a certain satisfaction from the general recognition of the international legal document which Russia had submitted to the Conference and in whose preparation he as a jurist and diplomat had taken such an active part. It already has been noted that the Declaration prepared at the Conference retained virtually all the major provisions of the initial draft convention. In addition a resolution of the Institute of International Law (1875) adopted by all of its members (except the Englishman) contained support for the codification of the law of warfare, and the provisions of the Russian draft were characterised as "practical, humane, and progressive principles". Such an assessment by the greatest jurists of the world could not fail to give satisfaction to Martens, especially, that part of the resolution which said that the Brussels draft "stood at the apex of contemporary science".[12]

Propagandist of Laws and Customs of War The lack of a readiness on the part of governmental circles and the general public to accept new international legal norms so clearly manifest at the 1874 Brussels Conference put in relief the question of the extensive and persuasive propagandising of new approaches, of shaping new political thinking. The situation inspired jurists and diplomats to become publicists.

Martens reacted tactfully to the public requirement. He took up his pen in order to bring scientific theories, the

[12] Quoted from Martens, note 7 above, p. 140.

conclusions of science, and the needs of international practice to the Russian and foreign reader. In 1875 Petersburg journals published his articles on the results of the Brussels Conference and a pamphlet on the need to define the international rules of warfare.[13] Demonstrating the need to adopt the convention discussed in Brussels, he expressed the hope that the 1874 Conference would become the "crossing point", a turning point in the history of the numerous attempts to ameliorate the misfortunes of warfare.

The Russo-Turkish War of 1877-78, also known as the Eastern War, imparted a new urgency to the problem. Russia rendered assistance in this War to the Christian population of the Ottoman Empire, opposing the oppression and genocide practised by the Turkish authorities. According to the San Stefano preliminary peace treaty of 3 March 1878, which ended the War, Bulgaria received the status of an autonomous principality and the Turkish forces were withdrawn from the country; the complete independence of Serbia, Czernowitz, and Romania was established; and Ardahan, Kars, Batumi, and Baiazet acceded, which had important significance for the fate of the Armenian and Georgian peoples; Turkey was obliged to introduce an administration in Epirus, Thessalonika, and Albania which better secured the safety of the populace, and also to effectuate reforms in the Armenian regions.

Russia had entered the War without allies. France and Germany were exhausted by their conflict. England and Austro-Hungary took an anti-Russian position. They conducted negotiations about entering the War on the side of Turkey. London intended to send a fleet to the Straits of the Bosphorus and Dardanelles and proposed that Vienna strike the rear of the Russian Army which had liberated Bulgaria. A frenzied anti-

---

[13] See Martens, *О необходимости определения международных правил войны* [On the Necessity to Determine the International Rules of Warfare] (n.p., 1875); id, "Брюссельская декларация о законах и обычаях войны" [Brussels Declaration on the Laws and Customs of Warfare], *Военный сборник* [Military Collection], no. 6 (1875); id, "Брюссельская международная конференция 1874 года" [The 1874 Brussels Internaitonal conference], in *Сборник государственных знаний* [Collection of State Knowledge] (1875), I.

Russian campaign was conducted in the English press, in the atmosphere of which the most incredible conjectures were painted, including fictitious "Russian atrocities".

Martens' publicist work, an historical study of Russian policy on the Eastern question, which he wrote in the French language for a specialist international legal journal published in Belgium was linked with the outbreak of the War. In it he substantiated the right of Christian powers, especially Russia, to come to the defence of the Christian population of the Ottoman Empire. The subject proved to be so current that the work was published in Berlin and Paris as a separate pamphlet, and at Petersburg, in a translation into German.[14]

The course of the Eastern War drew attention again to the conducting thereof. Reports about the evil deeds of the Turks, especially their irregular forces similar to bandit gangs (so-called bashibuzuki) with respect to Russian prisoners of war and the peaceful population, and particularly about the slaughter of the Armenians and Bulgars, stirred up the general public in Russia and many other countries.

Martens actively advocated compliance with the laws of warfare in the Institute of International Law. As noted above, the Institute was created in 1873 at Ghent (Belgium) and called upon to promote the study of international law and its codification. The most eminent jurists from a number of countries were members of the Institute, which imparted to it great authority and enabled it to influence the development of international law and the deciding of specific legal problems. Martens had become the member of the Institute from Russia in 1874. With his active participation the Institute in 1877 adopted an Appeal to the belligerents and the press and a Declaration in connection with the Russo-Turkish War. Drawing attention to the information about the crimes committed in the course of the War, the Institute pointed out that the Russian Government had familiarised its forces with the rules for waging warfare,

[14] See F. de Martens, "Étude historique sur la politique Russe dans la question d'Orient", *Revue de la droit international*, IX (1877); F. von Martens, *Die russische Politik in der orientalischen Frage: Eine historische Studie* (Spb., 1877).

whereas the Turkish Government had done nothing of the sort. The Institute expressed the wish that all States undertake treaty obligations to comply with the laws and customs of warfare which had been discussed at the Brussels Conference. Press organs were called upon to objectively illuminate the events and to refrain from attempts to fan nationalist and hostile feelings.[15]

The current nature of the subject and the attacks on the Russian Army, on one side, and the manifestations of heroism by the Russian soldier, on the other, so strongly gripped Martens that soon after the end of the war and the Congress of Berlin which determined its results (June-July 1878) rapidly, within two months, he wrote a substantial book of six hundred pages entitled in Russian "The Eastern War and Brussels Conference". The book was published in St. Petersburg, the preface dated by the author on 21 January 1879.

In a popular form understandable to the general reader the author endeavoured to set out not so much the terrors of war as to answer in a scholarly way the fundamental questions: where lie the sources of war? Is it possible to eradicate wars? By what means may this be achieved? What are the priority tasks in so doing?

Martens was obliged to state: the history of mankind is nothing other than an uninterrupted chain of sanguinary wars. The destruction and suffering caused by wars, their senselessness, has long since raised the question of whether international wars can cease completely so that peoples live in love and friendship.

Martens delved into the history of international relations and recalled: "Attempts actually were made in this direction, commencing from ancient times up to the present moment. In antiquity an international court was used to settle international disputes. Rather strong agitation is occurring at present in favour of this means of preventing wars. However, this means has been acknowledged by some thinkers to be inadequate. They have engaged in composing vast treatises on structuring a 'perpetual peace'. The Abbé Saint-Pierre had laboured on resolving this issue, as did such a profound thinker as Kant.

---

[15] See Martens, note 7 above, Annex 4.

Together with these utterances on instituting a 'perpetual peace' sharp attacks on international war in general have been made. It is not only the composers of projects for 'perpetual peace' who were sworn enemies of war. No, their numbers are many, and we encounter them in antiquity, in the Middle Ages, and in the modern day. But especially in this century, thanks to exhaustion from constant wars at the beginning of the century and the continuous development of international trade turnover, the war against wars has taken on enormous dimensions. 'Peace societies' have been founded, special publications disseminated for the purpose of propagandising everywhere a feeling of revulsion against international war, and many works issued in which international war is absolutely refused the right to exist".

Martens came to the conclusion that continuous enlightenment propaganda for peace and against war brought certain fruits. A gradual change was occurring in the public consciousness from extolling war to condemning it. Scholarship played its own role in effectuating such a change, and in particular the science of international law. In Martens' view, "whereas war among primitive peoples is a legal means for capturing property of the enemy and the complete eradication thereof, whereas for them it serves as an occupation for the most honourable and worthy person, civilised peoples to the contrary unanimously condemn war as a most terrible evil and calamity which destroys the fruits of many years of peaceful activity and extinguishes the lives of millions of people. Whereas primitive peoples deified war, and according to the great warriors of the ancient world – the Romans – the spear was the symbol of the right of ownership, and in the Middle Ages war was the 'law of feudalism' and the normal state of international and State life, no modern people, to the contrary, consider it possible openly to acknowledge war as the sole purpose of its aspirations and an advisable means for the settlement of conflicts which arise. No, public opinion increasingly is against the legality of war. Parliaments and people's assemblies unanimously proclaim arbitration to be the most worthy means for the settlement of international disputes. Noted thinkers and publicists energetically propound the need to devise an international arbitration tribunal. One may suppose that modern civilisation is incompatible with international hatred and that war is condemned not only by Christian love, but also by science and the conscience of civilised peoples".

However, one change in public consciousness is not enough. Wars continue, and this testifies to the fact that the reasons for this too are profound. One reason is the conflict of opposed interests of States and peoples. It would be utopian to expect that such contradictions will disappear in the near future; the task is to settle the inevitable conflicts not by war, but by peaceful means. The formation of a proper legal consciousness has important significance to this end. Martens pointed out: "The more that peoples are imbued with an awareness that the full developments of all their abilities and powers is possible only with mutual assistance to one another and absolute respect for the rights and conditions of the life of other peoples, the fewer conflicts of interests there will be and the less often will their own rights be violated".

In forming the legal consciousness of peoples the most prominent place belongs to science, and Martens noted that there are still thinkers who substantiate not only the inevitability, but also the usefulness, of wars. Therefore Martens devoted greater attention to polemics with the apologists of wars, above all the French philosopher and sociologist of a socialist orientation, P. J. Proudhon (1809-66), whose work "War and Peace" represented, in his view, "the most edifying example of the delusion of a bright mind and great talent". Proudhon had proceeded from the proposition that "war is divine, that is, primitive, inherent in life, for man himself and for society". Moreover, for him war is the "revelation of justice". "War," Proudhon solemnly exclaimed, "is our history, our life, our soul; it is legislation, politics, the State, fatherland, social system, international law, poetry, theology; once again, it is everything".

Led in his ecstasy to such a conclusion, it remained for Proudhon to take but one step to bring the right to use physical force to the level of an ideal for human society, and he actually declared openly that the "right of force" exists, on the basis of which the strongest has the right to preference over the weakest. "On this side is force, and on that side is truth", Proudhon concluded.

Martens passionately objected to Proudhon: "If one concurs with the basic thesis of Proudhon, then we must acknowledge to be just and legal such pathetic crimes as the Sicilian Evening, the Bartholomew's Night, the killing of the Duke of Angiens by Napoleon I, all the wars of Louis XIV against Napoleon I. Moreover, we must, in this event, also bow down to the divine right of the Turks to systematically murder and eradicate all their Christian subjects. Or, perhaps, the Christian population of Turkey only because there is a right to inviolability of life and honour that such a mighty power as Russia stands up for it? To come to such a conclusion means to laugh bitterly about the fate of the unhappy Christian population in the Ottoman Empire. Meanwhile it logically follows from the sophistry of Proudhon that the Turks still have the right to eliminate the Christians, dishonour their wives and daughters, and plunder their property, because the Christians themselves do not have the forces to resist and drive their tormenters for centuries into Asia".

Martens polemicised with the proponents of the theories of Thomas Malthus (1766-1834), the English philosopher and economist who saw in war "a great boon and saving of mankind from death by starvation"; with the proponents of "social-Darwinism" who declared the "struggle for existence" to be the principal law of social development; and with the German historian, H. Treitschke, who wrote about the "majesty of war".

A similar approach to war was widely shared among jurists. Basing himself on the words of the noted English philosopher, Sir Francis Bacon (1561-1626), a representative of the English school of international lawyers, Phillimore, defined war as a "terrible conflict between States". No less an authority on international law, Bluntschli, in acknowledging war to be the "armed self-help" of a State, averred that "war in general is a dispute concerning a public right between States as belligerent parties". Many other writers of the time expressed themselves in this vein. Actually they equated war between States to a civil proceeding between individuals. Martens sought to show that an international war is not merely a dispute about a right between belligerent States. War more often was the consequence of an irreconcilable opposition of interests and aspirations. Much less often did it arise from a violation by one of the Contracting States of its obligations. Therefore, Martens postulated, to define war as a dispute concerning a right is unjustified: such a definition was at odds with existing experience. The purpose of the definition, in Martens view, is most noble: a dispute concerning a right must occur within the limits of law. It followed that all phenomena of war, the slightest orders of the military command, all movements of forces must be determined by precise legal means. But experience showed that this is impossible. Martens concluded: there is very little in common between a civil proceeding conducted according to a known procedure and a war between independent States.

Especially dangerous in Martens' view were the utterances by certain scholars that the basis of law, including international law, is force. Martens pointed out: "It remains only to consistently develop this deplorable theory of law to be convinced of its utter bankruptcy. In fact this entire theory evidently is based on a misunderstanding. The procedure for the protection of a right here is confused with the right itself and is made an organic constituent part thereof. If a right may be protected by force, power, or coercion, it does not follow from this that force, power, and coercion are directly part of the concept concerning the right, that the right is inconceivable without them. It would be laughable to deny the right of the creditor to payment of the amount due to him if this right is unrealisable because the debtor has no property. The right of the creditor exists all the same, may be recognised by a court, and be defended by the entire power of the State.

That is why we refuse to stand under the banner on which the words are painted: "Law without force is a dream!" We proceed from the basic proposition that, just as the human individual, a people also are a source of certain inalienable rights. Just as vital relations within a State must be studied, elicited, and determined by legal norms, so too relations between peoples are subject to the operation of specific laws. If the opinion is correct that where there is no awareness of duty there also is no awareness of law, then obviously the task of life and science is to come to an awareness of these mutual rights and duties. A method consisting of the establishment of this awareness in the domain of private, social, and State life and a denial of the possibility of such awareness between civilised peoples" is incomprehensible to us.

Martens established neglect of these vital issues, disdain or magnanimous condescension towards the science of international law, and a fatalistic admiration for a confirmed fact. "With great zeal and assiduousness the slightest phenomena of the organic world are studied; any speck of dust of any flora is researched with unbelievable care through natural experiments, but the phenomena of international life are considered still to be unworthy of either comprehensive study or of precise definition", Martens wrote.

With great emotion he wrote: "Even now, at the end of the nineteenth century, proud of its high culture and civilisation, the view has gained currency that the domain of international relations was intended by nature to be the arena of unlimited arbitrariness and feats of physical force. There is no domain with which more important interests of mankind are associated, but there is no walk of life in which arbitrariness and naked force would have such scope and freedom. All on this planet are subordinate to certain laws – only the relations among nations do not know such. Here instead of law, lawlessness dominates, and in place of rights, arbitrariness!".

For Martens it was obvious: only the rule of law in international relations was capable of eradicating wars. Paradoxically perhaps, but this also applied to the law of warfare. "We allow ourselves to think that when a consciousness of the law of warfare is made the weal of every defender of the Fatherland, when a violation of its prescriptions will be an exception, when the armies are themselves convinced that execution of generally-recognised customs of warfare will not paralyse the successful course of military operations, – then a feeling of solidarity among peoples will be reliably strengthened and by the power of events themselves the number of international wars must decrease", he wrote.

Here it is appropriate to depart from the discourse of Martens and recall that at the moment when the book on the "Eastern War and Brussels Conference" was published, war was considered to be a lawful, legal means for the settlement of international disputes. It is strange now, when mankind seeks a world without wars and nuclear weapons, to read the soothing assurances of Martens that the codification of the law of warfare would not impede military operations. But such was the world outlook then. Both in ruling circles and military commands, and among the general public there were many who did not acknowledge the applicability of any legal norms to war. What could be law during a war?! What might be the "law of warfare" if war is the apotheosis of force?! Many regarded the very question to be absurd, for example, the German, General Julius von Hartman (1817-78) or the Swiss, Colonel F.W. Rüstow. The last laughed at the requirements to comply with any rules of warfare and asserted that in principle a belligerent was allowed to do anything. As Rüstow wrote, the victors, if they felt so disposed, might cut off the ears of the vanquished.

It is not surprising that so much attention is devoted in Martens' book to a justification of the very requirement to comply with certain rules during a war. In his context the pathos with which he wrote is understandable: "This is the law of warfare. It has historical experience of several centuries, the consciousness of all civilised peoples, and an incorruptible feeling of truth and justness.

In reality the law of warfare will exist so long as States are aware of their duties to one another. It constantly is developing and changing in conformity with the changes of cultural concepts of peoples. In the name of this law there is required from the victor the inviolability of life and honour of peaceful inhabitants of a non-enemy country; in the name of this law even the vanquished enemy remains a person deserving of respect and sympathy".

Martens sets out the origins of the law of warfare in detail, with citations to Hugo Grotius and his work "On the Law of War and Peace" (1625), the King of Sweden, Gustav Adolf (1594-1632), and other authorities:

"Peoples of the classical world could not be aware of their mutual rights and duties because they did not understand man to be a subject of inalienable rights ...

But as culture and civilisation develop, as respect for the person, for his personal freedom, aspirations, feelings, and rights is confirmed in States, the domain of international relations and war little-by-little are subordinated to determined rules and order. Peoples who have laid down as the basis of their entire social system and culture respect for the person as a person can not fail to acknowledge certain inalienable rights in other peoples. Thanks to this circumstance, during warfare certain limits are placed on brute force not only in the name of religion or humanity, but they exist in the consciousness of certain customs and laws of warfare, the failure to comply with which on the part of the enemy leads to reprisals and gives the victim grounds for satisfaction.

It is by this means that the law of warfare has been worked out over centuries, and why it has binding force".

Martens persistently proved that in the Declaration discussed at the 1874 Brussels Conference nothing new had been thought up; it merely codified those laws and rules of warfare which had been formed in the course of centuries and actually existed.

"In acknowledging that war under existing relations between States is completely inevitable, we affirm, however, at the same time that the law of warfare is not a fantasy but the result of historical experience and the modern state of international life. Being profoundly convinced that the time is coming when war actually will become an exception and when States will find a more feasible means for settling disagreements arising between them, we are persuaded that until that time of greater familiarisation and mutual understanding of peoples the law of warfare is the sole means of removing the brutal character from war and limiting the misfortunes connected with it", Martens wrote.

At the same time, the book stressed that the task of international law is not merely to establish the actual position. It also reflects moral orientators, the ideals of society. Accumulating the past, fixing the present, law simultaneously turns to the future. Therefore the law of warfare also has a certain optimistic side to it: the full development thereof is a matter for the future, and this is not its weakness, but rather its strength, a pledge of its ultimate triumph.

When consolidating the rules for waging war, Martens pointed out, it is necessary to have in view that relations between States are based on the principle of their independence. States have no supreme authority above them - neither legislative, nor executive, nor judicial. It follows that laws of warfare can only be established with the consent of States, by means of concluding an international convention.

A significant part of the book is devoted to an analysis of the actions of Russian and Turkish forces in the Eastern War from the legal point of view. The author drew attention to the fact that the Russian forces were guided by those rules which were contained in the draft convention submitted by Russia to the 1874 Brussels Conference. By Edict of the Senate of 12 May 1877 the rules for the actions of Russian civilian and military authorities were set out with respect to the enemy and his subjects, and also with respect to neutral States and their subjects.[16] Russian forces had been acquainted with the rules for their conduct by means of a distinctive catechism drawn up in the form of questions and answers and printed for the Army in thousands of copies. Using extensive materials Martens compared the behaviour of the Russian and Turkish forces during the War of 1877-78 and drew the conclusion that the use by the Russian Army of the rules for the conducting of warfare contained in the Russian draft for the Brussels Conference made

[16] Martens, ibid., Annex 3.

it more humane and in greater conformity with the concepts of the civilised world of the last quarter of the nineteenth century. Martens had confirmed his thesis concerning the need for the codification of the laws and customs of warfare, in particular the adoption of the respective international convention.

Martens had written his book as a patriot endeavouring to show the noble aims of Russia in the War and the heroism and humanity of the Russian Army. He wrote: "Never had the Russian soldier displayed such selfless courage as in the recent War; never had our forces discovered more moral bravery in the struggle against flammatory passions; never had his moral standard stood so high, and never in any Western European War had the victory of humanity over force, of love for people close to him over a feeling of hatred towards the enemy, and an awareness of his moral duty over the awareness of his power been achieved as in the recent War on the part of the Russian forces".

The work was dedicated to the "valorous Russian Army", and in the preface the author wrote: "If by the present book we add even one stone to the monument being erected to the honour and glory of the Russian soldier and Army, then we consider our labour to be rewarded".[17]

Martens' work furthered a just evaluation of Russia's position in the Eastern War and also strengthened the mood in favour of concluding an international agreement with regard to the laws and customs of warfare. The book in time was translated into French (1901). This is testimony to the fact that the value of Martens' publicist works consisted not only in the popularisation of the idea of adopting an international convention on the laws and customs of warfare. The scholarly conceptions therein with regard to questions of war and peace, the role of international law, and the prospects for its development also attracted attention. Many reflections set out in the work contained to retain their actuality for a long time. They resonated to the mood of our epoch.

---

[17] Martens, ibid., pp. iii-iv.

The *Eastern War and the Brussels Conference* was the first significant publicist experience of Martens, and a very successful experience it was. To the activity of jurist and diplomat was added yet another orientation of work – publicist. One distinctive feature of Martens as a publicist was prominent in the book: the linkage of actual foreign policy events with international law and an elucidation of its scientific problems.

Member of Council of Ministry of Foreign Affairs

The work done by Martens in connection with the 1874 Brussels Conference and his active role in the Institute of International Law were perceived positively by the leadership of the Ministry of Foreign Affairs. In 1879 Councillor of State F. F. Martens was appointed a functionary with special mission, fifth class, attached to Prince A. M. Gorchakov. On this occasion His Grace assigned the functionary on special mission a salary from 1 December 1879 of 2000 rubles per year.[18] The appointment went through Deputy Minister, Councillor of State, N. K. Giers, who subsequently held the post of Minister and who played a large role in the future fate of Martens.

In 1881 Martens received a new appointment in the Ministry of Foreign Affairs: he became a member of the Council attached to the Minister of Foreign Affairs. He remained in this post until his death; this post was indicated on official documents and press communications, Martens used it at international conferences where he represented Russia, and the like. The numerous citations to being a member of the Council of the Ministry of Foreign Affairs may create the impression that it determined the role and place of Martens in diplomatic activity. This was not so.

The Council of the Ministry of Foreign Affairs had in 1832 replaced the Petrine College of Foreign Affairs and was thought of as a consultative organ attached to the Minister. It remained such after the Gorchakov reorganisation of 1869. Formally all matters which the Minister considered necessary to submit for its discussion were subject to its jurisdiction. In reality the

[18] See AVPR, opis 749/1, delo 455, l. 1.

Council did not occupy itself with any foreign policy questions or affairs of the Ministry. From the moment of the appointment of Martens, the Council was convened only once. The Council did not become a consultative organ, and while Martens was there its function consisted of conducting examinations required of diplomats. The participation of Martens in giving examinations was, naturally, rather useful but did not enable a member of the Council to exert any influence on the activity of the Ministry of Foreign Affairs or on the formation of Russian foreign policy. As regards the relationship of the Council to the Ministry of Foreign Affairs, a characteristic episode, entered by Martens in his diary on 3 November 1894, testifies to this. He came to a session of the Council in order to examine diplomats, but none were present because they forgot to notify them. There was not even a table for the session![19]

The position of Martens in the Ministry and in Russian diplomacy was determined not by the fact that he held the post of a member of the Council of the Ministry of Foreign Affairs. His influence on the foreign policy actions of Russia had another basis: Martens was an advisor to all ministers of foreign affairs with whom he had business while a member of the Council: N. K. Giers (1882-95), A. B. Lobanov-Rostovskii (1895-96), M. N. Murav'ev (1897-1900), V. N. Lamzdorf (1900-06), A. P. Izvolskii (1906-10). His advice was used by monarchs and ministers, bankers and publicists. His influence originated not from a "high office in the Ministry of Foreign Affairs", as some authors still continue to assert,[20] but from his personal authority. Nolde, who was closely linked with Martens' work in the Ministry of Foreign Affairs, soon after his death spoke out about the mythical "high office" of his teacher. Pointing to the fact that "Martens possessed a worldwide reputation", Nolde stressed that Martens' authority was secured not by a professorship in the University nor by service in the Ministry of Foreign Affairs. "His official position

[19] AVPR, opis 787, delo 9, ed. khr. 3, l. 101.

[20] See, for example, A. Nussbaum, "Frederic de Martens. Representative Tsarist Writer on International Law," *Nordisk Tidsskrift for International Ret*, XXII (1952), 56.

in and of itself gave him no special rights", Nolde noted. His enormous authority was created by he himself, by his works. "This distinctive role was the personal legacy of Martens", Nolde emphasised.[21]

It is not out of place to recall that the "high office" of a member of the Council of the Ministry of Foreign Affairs brought Martens in 1905, that is, after many years of service, 4,500 rubles per year. The yearly salary of the Russian envoy to Brussels comprised 30,000 rubles, and the Consul General in Shanghai, 15,000 rubles, and so on.

"Russia and England in Central Asia" Immediately after the book on the "Eastern War and Brussels Conference" Martens prepared a new publicist work, this time on one of the most difficult international issues – the Anglo-Russian confrontation in Central Asia. The territorial expansion of both powers in this region had led to direct contact, and the need objectively increased for agreeing and consolidating the boundaries of possessions and spheres of influence. An especially tense situation formed around Afghanistan, which England intended either to occupy or to transform into her vassal. The situation gave rise in the ruling circles of England and among a significant part of English society to an anti-Russian atmosphere caused, in particular, by apprehensions about English domination in India. In 1868 the English diplomat and publicist, Sir Henry Rawlinson (1810-95), submitted a special memorandum to the Government in which he proved that the movement of Russia into Asia had the aim of conquering India and suggested in reaction that a buffer belt be created which would include Afghanistan. The Rawlinson memorandum generated broad consensus in the political circles of England and furthered the growth of anti-Russian feelings. The new splash of an anti-Russian wave in England caused in 1878 the sending of the General N. G. Stoletov (1834-1912) mission to Kabul. Soon afterwards the Anglo-Afghan War commenced. In June 1879 the English Resident was installed in Kabul.

[21] B. E. Nolde, "Ф. Ф. Мартенс" [F.F. Martens], *Русская мысль* [Russian Thought], no. 12 (December 1909), pp. 20-21.

In fact the Tsarist Government had no plans of conquest with respect to British India and was not interested in an exacerbation of relations with England. In 1878-81, that is, during the last years of the reign of Alexander II, the War Minister, D. A. Miliutin, exerted significant influence on the foreign policy of the Russian Empire. He saw the principal task of Russian policy as ensuring a peaceful breathing space for Russia, and in particular commenced to reorganise the army after the 1871 Franco-Prussian War. The greatest military threat Miliutin saw in the newly created German Empire, which had become a powerful military force on the Western frontier of Russia. As the events of 1876-78 showed, this force was far from friendly with respect to Russia. Miliutin relocated a number of military formations from the south and central regions of Russia to the provinces bordering Germany. The incitement of Turkey by English diplomacy to anti-Russian statements angered Miliutin. It furthered the formation of the "alliance of Three Emperors" (Russia, Germany, Austro-Hungary). Miliutin avoided foreign policy conflicts, including conflicts with England.

In England itself changes emerged in favour of a peaceful resolution of the Central Asian confrontation. The conservative cabinet of Benjamin Disraeli (1801-81), Prime Minister since 1874, had fallen. The Liberal Government of William Gladstone came to power with a programme of economising on military expenditure, preservation of peace, and maintenance of the "Concert of Europe", that is, concerted actions of the six Great Powers. Thus, in both countries the political prerequisites for achieving a compromise had been created.

Martens decided in this situation to repeat the experience with his article on the "Policy of Russia in the Eastern Question" and in 1879 published in the same journal a work on "Russia and England in Central Asia" in the French language.[22]

The notion that the "interests of Russia and England in Central Asia are in essence joint and several" occupied a central place in the work. Martens wrote that the ravines and mountains

---

[22] See F. Martens, "La Russie et l'Angleterre dans l'Asie Centrale," *Revue de la droit international*, XI (1879), 227-301.

of Central Asia give sufficient space for both countries to fulfil the "mission of enlightenment" assumed by them, for a "tireless struggle against barbarianism and for the introduction of social institutions which might ensure the success of civilisation". As for India, Martens reassured English public opinion: Russia did not contemplate its conquest; such assertions were the "product of an excitable fantasy". What "would Russia do with those 200 million people who are afraid of and who see Englishmen and Russians as Christians and Europeans?" Martens asked. Already the conquest of the Central Asian Khanates in Central Asia constituted, in his view, "a very grave burden for Russia, and only extreme necessity did not allow the Russian Government to leave at the desired moment". Therefore Russia will not go to India.

Martens was critical in his assessment of English policies in Asia and her anti-Russian actions, writing that "Great Britain herself forced Russia to attempt to create difficulties for her in Asia". However, the existing frictions could not justify a military conflict between the two powers. "Is it conceivably just that a struggle between Russia and England on the shores of the Indus is an absolute necessity and inexorable fate?" Is it possible that these two "great enlightened powers will deliver to the primitive Asiatic tribes the lamentable spectacle of a cruel and useless war?" the author asked.

Martens pointed out that in England there were circles who put the question thus: Russia or England must rule the Asiatic peoples. He proposed that this be done jointly, "to extend to one another a hand at the summit of the Hindu Kush". He opposed any "buffers", suggesting that the "immediate contiguity of Russian and English territories was the sole practical and reasonable basis for perfect harmony between the two great powers".

However, Martens had not taken up his pen to write a political pamphlet. He devoted great attention to the question of how to regulate relations between the European and Asiatic peoples. All are agreed, wrote Martens, that "Europe is becoming too crowded", that it was necessary to develop links with Africa and Asia, that European peoples must carry there the idea of law. But how should this be done? Neither Grotius, nor Vattel, nor G. F. Martens, nor other noted classic writers on international law had written anything about this because the question itself had been raised only at the outset of the nineteenth century. Competent legal scholars said that the relations of Europe with Africa and Asia must be built on the basis of international law. In Bluntschli's notable study of international law set out in the form of a code it was affirmed that the operational domain of international law is the entire world, that it is the law of all mankind. Such views, Martens polemicised, are noble but unrealistic. "How is this law to be applied, a creation of European education and a consequence of the moral and legal ideas of civilised peoples, to peoples who have no decisive awareness of the duties arising from it?" Martens said. Uncivilised peoples may not bear responsibility for their actions which are contrary to international law because they do not understand the foundations on which the community of civilised European peoples is built.

However, the inapplicability of European international law to uncivilised peoples did not mean that a law binding upon Europeans was not to be applied in relations with them at all. This was natural law, that is, a law arising from the very nature of things, from the nature of relations between civilised and uncivilised peoples. In Asia, he pointed out, natural law requires "that a word given is honourably executed so that life and ownership are considered to be sacred and inviolate and so that evil instincts and passions cede place to justness, honour, and noble convictions".

The relations of Europe with Africa and Asia, in the writer's view, would change as the standard of civilisation of African and Asian peoples improved. In Asia there were States already formed, for example, Persia, China, and Japan, which had a solid social organisation and governments capable of conducting normal relations with Europe, in particular, of guaranteeing the inviolability of foreigners and their ownership. "With these States international relations may develop peacefully, and their national independence must be recognised as being as inviolate as that of civilised States", Martens declared. The tribes of Khiva, Bukhara, Eastern Turkestan, and Afghanistan, which had no "solid social structure" and which could not ensure the fulfilment of obligations assumed, were another matter. With them relations were possible on the basis of natural law.

Such was the conception of the international law of civilised peoples which Martens first set out in popular form so fully and which subsequently lent its name to his *cours*.

As regards the principal thoughts of Martens, then he said the following in his book: "In essence they all come down to one idea – the necessity for Russia and England, as enlightened States, to be guided in their mutual relations in Central Asia by European international law – by the law which is incompatible with pursuing exclusive interests, distrust, and enmity towards peoples".

Martens' work enjoyed resounding success. In the form of a substantial pamphlet (91 pages), it was translated into German, English, and then also into Russian.[23] In England the text was reputedly printed in 30,000 copies and even transmitted by telegraph to the United States. The success of the book undoubtedly was facilitated by the fact that its arguments concerning the solidarity of the interests of England and Russia Martens strengthened with scholarly trappings relating to (as M. A Taube, translator of the book into Russian, wrote) "a question virtually untouched in the science of international law concerning the legal relations between the educated and barbaric peoples".[24]

In preceding chapters mention has been made of the fact that by dividing the peoples of the world then into "civilised" and "uncivilised" Martens incurred the reproach of "aiding and abetting colonialism". In this connection it should be said that Martens' adherence to this division originated in the real situation which existed in the world, to objectively existing relations to which international law could not close its eyes. One may remind

[23] See Martens, *Россия и Англия в Средней Азии* [Russia and England in Central Asia] (Spb., 1880).

[24] Ibid., pp. i-iii.

critics of Martens that after the First World War a new era had begun in the history of civilisation, the founders of the League of Nations declaring in its Covenant that the international community was concerned also with peoples "still not capable of governing themselves in the especially difficult conditions of the modern world". The League of Nations considered that the "well-being and development of these peoples comprise the sacred mission of civilisation". It proposed that the best method of giving practical effect to the said aim is that "the tutelage of such peoples should be entrusted to advanced nations ..." (Article 22). As we see, underlying the activity of the League of Nations was the principle of the division of peoples which in his day Martens had followed.

There are no materials at our disposition which would enable us to assess the role of Martens' work in ameliorating Anglo-Russian contradictions in Central Asia. However, its undoubted success is testimony to the fact that Martens was sagacious and timely, even before the fall of the Disraeli Cabinet, in guessing the mood of the governments and society in both countries. In Autumn 1881 Emir Abdurrahman with the assistance of the English established power in Afghanistan. The country remained a protectorate of England, and the Tsarist Govern-ment became reconciled to this, endeavouring only not to allow the English farther north than Afghanistan. The Anglo-Russian rivalry in Central Asia did not grow into a war of the two powers.

Although Martens' book was restrained in the spirit of the solidarity of Russia and England, a search for a compromise, it was greeted with hostility in certain English circles. Legal forces also were mobilised for polemics against Martens, especially with respect to certain accusations addressed against English diplomacy. The English international lawyer J. Westlake published in the same journal his own article following that of Martens which was a refutation of Martens' assertions relative to a violation by England of its international obligations.[25] Soon thereafter, in 1881, a pamphlet which had an analogous purpose

[25] Cited in Nussbaum, note 20 above, p. 56.

by the Kharkov professor, V. P. Danevskii, was published in the French language.[26]

"Russia and China" Meanwhile in 1880 Martens had published yet another work in the French language devoted to a current issue, namely, Chinese-Russian relations.[27] The work was published in the Russian language the following year.[28]

China at the time had survived the expansion of foreign States. Whereas in Central Asia there were two principal competitors – England and Russia, there were many more pretenders in attempts against the possessions of the Chinese emperors. The 1876 Treaty of Kiakhta laid the groundwork for Japanese penetration into Korea, then a vassal of the Chinese Emperor. England already had a large naval base in Chinese waters – Hong Kong. An Englishman headed Chinese Maritime Customs from 1859. The importation of opium to China brought enormous revenues to the English. From the 1870s active efforts were undertaken by them to penetrate into the internal regions of China, through Burma into Yunan Province and along the Yangtze River to Kashgar and Sinkiang, now known as the Sinkiang-Uighur Autonomous Region of China. France had seized Indo-China (which included modern Vietnam, Cambodia, and Laos), also considered to be a vassal of the Chinese Emperor.

In Kashgar and Sinkiang, Russia and China resisted English expansion jointly. In 1879 they signed the Treaty of Livadia under which Russia returned the Ilii territory to China, which had been temporarily occupied by Russian forces. The Treaty opened vast areas of China to Russian trade, and seven Russian consulates were established in the cities of Western China and in Mongolia. However, the Chinese Government refused to ratify the Treaty of Livadia, demanding a new territorial demarcation. On 24 February 1881 a new Russo-Chinese Treaty was signed

---

[26] See V. P. Danewski, *La Russie et l'Angleterre dans l'Asie Centrale. Observations critique sur "La Russie et l'Angleterre dans l'Asie Centrale" par F. Martens* (London, 1881).

[27] F. de Martens, "Le conflit entre la Russie et la Chine, son developpement et sa portee universelle", *Revue de la droit international*, XII (1880).

[28] See F. Martens, *Россия и Китай* (Spb., 1881).

in St. Petersburg which made certain changes in the previous agreement. The diplomatic reversals of fortune were accompanied by anti-Russian commentary in part of the European press, especially the English press.

In the interval between the signature of the Livadia and Petersburg treaties Martens' publicist work appeared. In it he substantiated his central idea: Russia and China had long since lived in peace and were good neighbours; they were friendly powers. Martens resolutely favoured respect for the territorial integrity of China and her sovereign rights. He cautioned that various kinds of privileges for foreigners, attempts to sow Christianity, and territorial seizures inevitably would lead to being repulsed by the Chinese and to conflicts between China and foreign States. Martens appealed to all the powers, including Russia, to be guided in their relations with China by the principles and norms of international law.

The timeliness of the question raised by Martens and the correctness of the position which he took was confirmed rather rapidly by subsequent events. In August 1900 he prepared a confidential memorandum with regard to China for the Minister of Foreign Affairs in connection with the so-called "boxer uprising" in China (published in 1927).[29]

The boxer rebellion in China commenced in May 1900 and was of an anti-imperialist character. A secret society led it, called "Ikhetsyuan" ("the fist in the name of peace and justness"). This provided an occasion for the Western European and American press to christen the uprising as a "boxer" rebellion. The ideology of the rebels, basically peasants, was based to a considerable extent on traditional concepts of the feudal era. The principal slogan of the rebels was "Death to foreigners!" On 20 June 1900 the German envoy was killed on a Peking street. The foreign powers concentrated their warships in the mouth of the River Pei-ho and two-thousand marines landed. In reply the Government of the Tsiang Dynasty declared war. England, Germany, Russia, the United States, France, and Japan prepared to send an expeditionary corps.

---

[29] See *Красный архив* [Red Archive], (1927), I, pp. 177-185.

The solidarity of the powers in suppressing the uprising did not eliminate the contradictions among them. Their interests with respect to China were significantly at variance. It was necessary for the Tsarist Government in this situation to determine its long-term policy in this region. The memorandum by Martens was devoted to this.

Unlike the noisy propagandistic campaign in the European and American press, Martens saw the true reason for the uprising in the "unscrupulous exploitation of the Chinese on the part of Europeans". Germany, for example, for the massacre of two missionaries seized the Shan Dung Peninsula; England, which had concentrated two-thirds of all trade with China in her hands, received twelve million pounds sterling annually from the sale of opium. As Martens noted, "with respect to this State everything is considered to be permissible". Martens cautioned against underestimating the movement: "The present rebellion or uprising is a people's war of the Chinese in which the Peking Government was forced to take the side of the people". He wrote that the "final victory of the European armies over the Chinese forces is beyond doubt", but this victory will not eliminate the "internal reasons for the present disorders in China". He drew the following conclusion: "And thus so long as the European powers do not change the form of their actions with respect to China, so long as opium is a legal means for the inculcation in the Chinese of the elevated ideals of European civilisation, and the propaganda of the Christian religion is a convenient means for undermining the foundations of the Chinese State, and so long, finally, as the inviolability of Chinese territory and supreme power are not obligatory for the European States and the United States, there will be no peace in China and new uprisings and wars with the Chinese are inevitable". These realistic and prophetic conclusions do honour to Martens.

As regards the position of Russia with respect to China, Martens stressed the difference between Russian interests and the interests of the other powers. "For the last China is a colony which must be exploited by all means. For Russia, China is a great neighbouring State which has the right to autonomous life". In accordance with this position of principle, Martens suggested that the division of China be opposed and the initiative be taken urgently for the signature by the great powers of an act "confirming the inviolability of Chinese territory and renunciation of any territorial acquisitions". Only in the event of the failure of England and Germany to agree did Martens advise that Manchuria be temporarily occupied.

Concerning "material remuneration" for damage caused to the foreign States, Martens pointed to the disarray of Chinese finances and recommended the situation be avoided under which each foreign State would itself present demands to the Chinese Government. He was especially disturbed by the speech of the Emperor of Germany, Wilhelm II, which was imbued with a "spirit of merciless revenge and unchristian enmity". Martens proposed that the question of determining the amount of compensation to each power be transferred to the Permanent Court of International Arbitration at The Hague.

Martens' memorandum was used by Count Lamzdorf as the basis of a demarche undertaken on 25 August 1900. The Minister of Foreign Affairs charged Russian ambassadors to communicate to the governments of foreign powers that Russia had introduced forces into Manchuria only to render assistance to the Chinese Government. As soon as the disorders had ceased, the Russian forces would leave China; "unless, however, the actions of other powers serve as an obstacle to this". Martens felt satisfaction from the fact that his memorandum had become a document which had determined Russian foreign policy on the issue. He merely was slighted that Lamzdorf, having received the memorandum, circulated it as a circular "without a word about me". He suspected that the Count had not even named the author of the memorandum to the Tsar.[30]

It should be noted that Martens' advice was not always realised sufficiently by Russian diplomacy. Often it turned out to be unimplemented.

In 1900 the Government of Russia was guided it seemed by a programme set out by Martens in his memorandum: it

[30] See AVPR, op. 787, delo 9, ed. khr. 5, l. 99-100.

proclaimed the course for preserving the territorial integrity of China and cooperation with the Ching monarchy. Martens, however, was justly disturbed by those conditions which bound China to foreign States, including Russia, in the concluding protocol. First, compensation of damage in the amount equivalent to 650 million rubles was placed on China, which had paid merely six years previously an enormous contribution to Japan after the war of 1895-96. The protocol provided for specific items of State revenues to compensate the damage, which further tied the hands of the Peking Government. China, including the Imperial House, was subjected to grave humiliation: a number of State officials were punished, "expiatory monuments" were erected to the European diplomats who perished, and the like. In Peking the quarter occupied by foreign missions was placed under the protection of foreign armed forces. Chinese were prohibited from living in the quarter.

In evaluating the protocol Martens wrote in his diary: "In this act there is not a single condition which would be acceptable to the Chinese without the strongest protest. If they sign, then it will be violated at the first opportunity". He saw the protocol as a manifestation of the lack of talent of the Russian envoy, the son of N. K. Giers. To erect monuments at sites where Christians were murdered and to maintain garrisons in embassies? How can one speak of the establishment of peace and good-neighbourliness with China?"[31]

As in his work on Russia and China, Martens proceeded from respect for the sovereignty and territorial integrity of China. But Nicholas II fell into the hands of groups who frustrated even the evacuation of Russian forces from Manchuria which had been promised in the demarche of Lamzdorf. A palace clique of adventurists headed by A. M. Bezobrazov, who managed to get treasury money for his dubious affairs, incited the Tsar to further expansion. The Bezobrazov group acquired, for example, a forestry concession in the basin of the Yalu River which extended for 800 kilometres along the Chinese-Korean and the Russian-Korean boundaries. They began to introduce Russian

---

[31] AVPR, op. 787, delo 9, ed. khr. 5, l. 110-111.

soldiers on the territory of the concession under the pretext of forest guards. All this intensified annoyance with Russia, especially in Japan. As Martens noted in his diary: "in China disgraceful things and a stupid policy".[32] Martens at an audience in 1898 had warned Nicholas II about the dangers of expansion in China. He prophetically said that the acquisition by Germany, England, Japan, Russia, and certain other powers of their own zones in that country inevitably would lead to a conflict among them. He spoke of the possibility of an anti-Russian coalition, and then "our Port Arthur would fall". But the Tsar followed Bezobrazov and the Minister of Internal Affairs, Phleve, who counted on coping with the revolutionary fermentation in the Empire with the assistance of a little triumphal war. Russia moved forward to war against Japan, and the voices of Councillor Martens (and likewise of Vitte, Lamzdorf, and certain others) were drowned out by other more sonorous voices.

"The Egyptian Question and International Law"

In 1882 Martens wrote an article on the Egyptian question.[33] In the same year the work appeared in a translation from French into Russian under the same title.[34]

A sharp struggle between England and France was being waged for the possession of Egypt, then a nominal dependency of the Sultan of Turkey. Special piquancy and international resonance to the struggle was imparted by the affiliation of the Suez Canal to Egypt – one of the vital water arteries of the world. In 1876 financial control was established over the country which was headed by one Frenchman and one Englishman. The foreign trusteeship was eliminated in 1879 by Egyptian officers taking the field, but the joint pressure of the European powers rapidly forced the Egyptian ruler – the Hediv Ismail – to be removed from the throne. His son Tevfik returned the foreign controllers. The result was an uprising in September 1881 under

[32] ABPR, op. 787, delo 9, ed. khr. 5, l. 127.

[33] See F. de Martens, "La question Egyptienne et la droit international," *Revue de la droit international*, XIV (1882).

[34] See Martens, *Египетский вопрос и международное право* [The Egyptian Question and International Law] (Spb., 1882).

the leadership of Colonel Ahmet-Araby and the creation of a national government. England and France could not reconcile themselves to the loss of Egypt, and since the French Government by reason of tense relations with Germany could not risk diverting her armed forces from Europe, the English in the second half of 1882 occupied the country alone.

Martens' publicist work was actually directed against the monopolistic management of the English and French in Egypt. The principal idea of the author lay in the proposal to consolidate the independence of Egypt by an international agreement against the Sultan of Turkey and foreign States and to neutralise her territory, including the Suez Canal.

Martens fortified his scheme with an abundance of international legal argumentation. He proved, in particular, that the establishment of the Anglo-French condominium (joint possession) in Egypt violated the rights of other powers.

"The African Conference in Berlin" To complete the survey of Martens' publicist works one must mention his article about the Berlin Conference on Africa of 1884-85.[35] Martens' involvement in the work of the Conference will be related below. Here it is more interesting to trace by way of the article the attitude of Martens towards colonial policy.

It should first be said that Martens did not count Russia among the colonial powers. By colonies he had in view various kinds of "overseas" possessions, and the expansion of the territories of the States themselves (for example the Central Asian part of Russia) did not fall within the concept of "colonial policy". Therefore the Berlin Conference was regarded by the author solely in the light of the "colonial policy of modern Western European powers". From the very first lines one discovers in Martens a rather negative attitude towards such policies. He wrote: "During the last twenty years the policies of

---

[35] See Martens, "Африканская конференция в Берлине. Колониальная политика современных государств" [African Converence in Berlin, Colonial Policy of Contemporary States], *Вестник Европы* [Herald of Europe], no. 11-12 (1885).

these powers had turned in a direction which could be regarded as entirely distracted and condemned both by experience and scholarship. The occupation of newly-discovered lands and islands, the founding of new factories and colonies in the most remote parts of the globe, and finally, the protection of those new acquisitions by force of arms – all this obliged one to think that at the end of the nineteenth century events must be repeated with which the history of the sixteenth and seventeenth centuries is so rich. One may suppose that again wars will break out because of dominion over lands which are important as markets or to sell products of European industry, or the purchase of raw materials to be brought to Europe for processing".

Martens noted that in Germany, England, France, and certain other countries the view predominates that the "acquisition of colonies is urgently essential for the progressive development of domestic trade and industry". However, as Martens stated, there also are opponents of colonial acquisitions there who suppose that there is no reason for the metropolitans to bring in such victims since the colonies, having achieved a determined level of economic and social development, will separate and become competitors of the metropolians.

It is noteworthy that neither Martens nor those whom he quotes had any doubt of the right of European States to occupy "free lands". Such was the predominant world outlook at the time, and it was reflected in international law. According to Martens, the Berlin Conference should take a "leading place in the history of the world dissemination of European culture and civilisation among semi-primitive peoples".

As a jurist and proponent of the rule of law in international relations, Martens welcomed the intention of the European powers to establish agreed rules for the founding of colonies and the administration thereof. He saw the sense of those rules especially in that they helped to avoid armed conflicts among the civilised States. Agreed rules, in Martens' view, also should ensure "respect for the rights of the original inhabitants of the territories being occupied" because "civilised peoples rarely treat with respect the undoubted rights of indigenous primitive or semi-primitive tribes". To be sure, Martens had no special illusions about the success of his scheme. He expressed doubt that the colonisation of Africa by the Europeans would have a peaceful future. "The colonial policy of modern States, and in particular of France and Germany, contains the embryo of the most serious dangers for these States themselves and for international peace. It seems to me personally a very doubtful benefit is to be anticipated from the colonies newly founded in Africa and other tropical countries", he observed.

Martens' articles on colonial policies in Africa were known chiefly to the Russian public. They were not disseminated abroad.

"The Nationality Policy of Prince Bismarck"

Martens' publicist works for understandable reasons treated international topics. His essay on the nationality policy of Prince Bismarck, devoted to a domestic political issue, deserves greater attention.[36]

In substance the essay was an historical and legal analysis of 564 acts which were published in 1882 by instruction of Chancellor Otto von Bismarck and which should have traced the process of creating the German Empire proclaimed in 1871. But Martens made the essay a polemic against the propagators of national originality in Russia.

Above all Martens expressed an attitude of scepticism towards the very concepts of "nationality" and "nationality policy". He wrote that the attraction of these "talismans" in Western Europe and in Russia would lead to the "utter misunderstanding of the laws of historical development", to a "frivolous attitude toward the most burning questions", to the "most foolhardy measures". In recent years, he noted, "the view was widely entertained that the aim of Russian nationality policy consisted of a return to the pre-Petrine epoch and the exclusive development of those indigenous Russian features which distinguish the Russian people from other peoples of the world. In this was seen the basis for the success of Russia within the country and on the international plane".

---

[36] See F. F. Martens, "Национальная политика князя Бисамрка" [Nationality Policy of Prince Bismarck], *Вестник Европы* [Herald of Europe], no. 6 (June 1883), pp. 694-753.

Martens protested against such views, especially against attempts to isolate Russia from the European cultural and historical community. In his view the stable basis of the State and its foreign policy was not "historical legends", but common socio-political ideals, cultural and other interests. He stressed the importance of an "identical respect for the highest good of human civilisation". Martens' principal idea was the community of Russia and Europe, of Russia and the entire civilised world. Any partition would be ruinous for the country.

Although names were not named in the essay, the orientation of the polemic was more or less transparent: against the Slavophile camp. The flower of Slavophilism was based on the original path of the development of Russia, distinct from that of Western Europe, during the 1840-50s when the names of A. S. Khomiakov, K. S. Aksakov, P. V. Kireevskii, and others were well-known. The peak of the struggle of their ideas against the Westernisers occurred in those years: A. I. Herzen, T. N. Granovskii, V. G. Belinskii, I. S. Turgenev, K. D. Kavelin, and other noted representatives of Russian social thought. After the Reforms of 1861 the influence of the Slavophiles waned, but certain of their conceptions continued to be developed by N. Ia. Danilevskii, K. A. Leont'ev, and others. The ideas of Slavophilism at the end of the nineteenth century and beginning of the twentieth century were reflected in works of the religious philosopher, poet, and publicist, V. S. Solov'ev, son of the noted Russian historian. In the period when Martens' essay appeared Slavophile ideas were far from predominant, but all the same were noticeable in Russian society and polemics against them were topical.

The Special Characteristics of Martens' Publicist Activity

The success of Martens' appearances in the press were to a considerable extent connected with his exceptional abilities as a publicist. To be noted above all is his remarkable responsiveness to various issues of international politics and law which at that moment disturbed politicians, jurists, and general public. He reacted quickly to actual events and was ready to comment on them.

Those mentioned above were his major works. As for the entire body of Martens' publicist works, they await identification and investigation.

In 1879 his fundamental study on the Eastern War and Brussels Conference appeared; in 1880 his work on Russia and England in Central Asia; in 1881, Russia and China; and in 1882, the Egyptian question and international law. If one bears in mind that in 1882-83 his two-volume treatise on international law was published, that he continued to lecture, participated in international conferences and international arbitrations, and wrote articles, then one must be astonished at his capacity to work and his productivity. Martens wrote for Russian and foreign newspapers, for Russian and foreign journals, for publications intended for a narrow group of specialists, mostly on international law, and for publications for the general reader. "His pamphlets, notes, journal articles on issues of this nature printed in various languages and individually, and in general and specialised journals and newspapers, both in the Old and in the New World, were enormous in quantity", wrote Taube.[37]

Against the general background of publicist works of the time, Martens' submissions were distinctive for combining vital problems of current politics with scholarly conceptions, most, of course, in the domain of international law. In his book on the Eastern War and the Brussels Conference a significant portion was allotted to establishing the rules of land warfare. The book on Russia and England in Central Asia would have become a small pamphlet or even a newspaper article if Martens' substantiation of the various international legal approaches to civilised and noncivilised peoples were removed. The essay on the nationality policy of Prince Bismarck would have been a dry historical and legal analysis if there had not been theoretical propositions concerning the essence of nationality policy and the interlinkage of the domestic and foreign policies of States. Without excursions into the theory of international law, without corresponding historical and normative materials, the colour of

---

[37] M. A. Taube, *Ф. Ф. Мартенс(1845-1909). Некролог* [F.F. Martens (1845-1909). Obituary] (Spb., 1909), p. 13.

Martens' works would have paled in the books on Russia and China and on the Egyptian question and international law.

The great distinctiveness of Martens' publicist works lay in the fact that he viewed events and policies from the standpoint of international law. When he assessed the actions of English or Russian diplomacy, he correlated them not with national interests, but with international law. This approach was rare in publicist works of the day.

Another peculiarity of Martens' publicist works was that many of his submissions to the press were based on materials prepared by him for the Institute of International Law.

Founded in 1873, the Institute played for nearly twenty years a leading role in working out the principles and norms of international law. Objective conditions then required intensive law-creation, and an established mechanism for international norm-formation still did not exist. Whereas these days the United Nations and its International Law Commission and other committees and commissions, and the General Assembly are concerned with this, international conferences did not assemble so frequently then. In the unfolding situation the Institute, which acted as a social, nongovernmental organisation and gathered within its walls the leading jurists from various countries, became the expressor of public legal consciousness, the creator of legal principles and norms. The significance of the Institute began to decline at the end of the century, when States engaged more systematically in the codification of international law at regularly convened conferences.

Martens was the author or co-author of a number of documents prepared by the Institute of International Law. Among them were the Resolution on a protectorate over the Suez Canal (Brussels Session, 1879), a manual on the laws and customs of warfare (Oxford Session, 1880), a draft Reglament on navigation along international rivers (Heidelberg Session, 1887), the draft Convention on an international union for the publication of treaties (Geneva Session, 1892), draft procedural rules for mixed cases in the Orient (Munich Session, 1892), a draft Reglament on trade in negroes (Paris Session, 1894), and others.[38]

The journal in which Martens published the aforesaid articles extensively covered the activity of the Institute, and its chief editor, the noted international lawyer H. Rolin-Jaequemyns, was one of the most active members of the Institute. The linkage of Martens' publicist works with the activity of the Institute of International Law gave additional authority to them.

Some of Martens' works were connected with memoranda which he prepared for the Ministry of Foreign Affairs and which more than once determined the position of Russian diplomacy on a specific issue (for example, the Berlin Conference on Africa). This, of course, increased the interest in Martens' works.

We turn to certain conjectures about Martens' publicist writings which to this day continue to wander about the media. It is asserted, for example, that Martens wrote his articles and pamphlets to order for the Tsarist Government in support of its various foreign policy actions. The works were supposedly written in Russian and then translated into foreign languages and extensively propagandised.[39]

Such assertions do not correspond to reality.

The view that the pamphlets on Russia and England in Central Asia, on Russia and China, and certain other works were written in Russian and only then translated into French is not only contrary to the facts but also casts a shadow on Martens. It would follow that he could not set out his ideas in French. And this was said of a Martens who participated in many international conferences where work was traditionally conducted in the French language and where he not only spoke, but did so with an orator's skill! Martens wrote dozens of drafts, resolutions, memoranda, and other documents in French. One may recall that in the Russian Ministry of Foreign Affairs all foreign correspondence until 1832 was conducted in the French language. At the time when Martens enrolled in the Ministry of Foreign Affairs, documents were already being drawn up in

[38] See Nolde, note 21 above, p. 26.
[39] See Nussbaum, note 20 above, p. 56.

Russian, but the French language was being used very widely still and Martens spoke French with the leading bureaucrats of the Ministry and with Russian and foreign diplomats.

Also untrue is the assertion that Martens supposedly wrote his publicist works to order. The archives of the Ministry of Foreign Affairs disclose nothing to confirm this. There is much direct and indirect evidence that the initiative to write them emanated from the author himself. Support for this is seen, in particular, in the readily traceable link between many publicist utterances by Martens and his work on resolutions of the Institute of International Law, preparation for conferences, and the like. Sometimes the Minister of Foreign Affairs or his deputy learned about Martens' publications from outside and even after publication. In March 1898, for example, the Deputy Minister Count Lamzdorf told Martens that he was interested in his pamphlet about Afghanistan, completely agreed with his notion that Afghanistan was an independent State, and that it was necessary to adhere firmly to this position. Martens said with irony: one should have understood this long since and notified the English.[40]

It also is untrue that Martens set out the position of the Tsarist Government in his publicist works. Actually in his work on Russia and England in Central Asia he relied on the view of A. M. Gorchakov, who considered the Central Asian acquisitions to be a "heavy burden" for Russia. His successor, Giers, the War Minister, Miliutin, and certain other Russian leaders held analogous views. But there also existed in Russia influential circles who opposed that view, and it remains an historical fact that after Martens' pamphlet appeared, where he had called for Anglo-Russian solidarity, the movement of Russian military detachments to Central Asia continued. In Russia matters were very much as they were in England, where there was a split in ruling circles and public opinion: there were stalwart opponents of the seizure of Afghanistan at the price of war and warm proponents of such actions.

[40] See AVPR, op. 787, delo 9, ed. khr. 4, l. 35.

Martens' proposal concerning the neutralisation of Egypt found no support among the leadership of the Russian Ministry of Foreign Affairs. Later, in 1887, Martens wrote in his diary that Minister Giers, the head of the Asian Department, N. A. Zinov'ev, and the noted diplomat, Baron A. G. Zhomini, considered his scheme to be utterly unrealistic. When in a conversation with the former Egyptian leader, Numat-Pasha, Martens received support for his idea he celebrated: "I immediately reported this conversation to Giers! What will Baron Zhomini say?!"[41]

Martens' idea about Russia and England being direct neighbours in Central Asia was never realised. British India was separated from Russia by a territorial buffer.

Finally, the assertion that Martens in his publications supposedly defended the views of the Tsarist Government is destroyed by the negative attitude towards many of his works by the powerful Katkov press.

M. N. Katkov (1818-87) edited the newspaper *Московские ведомости* [Moscow Gazette], where for nearly twenty years with-out interruption he wrote the lead editorial on what were, in his view, urgent issues of the day. He also published *Санкт-Петербургские ведомости* [St. Petersburg Gazette], the journal *Русский вестник* [Russian Herald], and, most important, imparted the tenor of the day to a number of noted newspapers and journals.

Katkov became renowned for his coarse attacks against Alexander Herzen and other leading writers and journalists. In the 1870-80s his name was a symbol of reaction. At the same time he permitted himself sharp attacks against highly-placed officials, up to and including ministers, and unceremoniously wrote about Russian diplomacy.

Katkov's free behaviour can be explained by Alexander IIIs constant favour towards him. Katkov received significant subsidies from the Tsarist treasury and considered himself to be beyond the reach of his opponents. M. E. Saltykov-Shchedrin allegorically portrayed Katkov's behaviour: "'I have', he says, 'in

[41] AVPR, opis 787, delo 9, ed. khr. 4, l. 86.

the rear – power, and if my rear is secured, then I can dare to do much'. Such confidence encourages a feeling of self-satisfaction, but at the same time one's intellectual powers dim. To the extent they dim, then he with impertinence declares war directly in his own name, concludes alliances, and grants peace".[42]

A publicist who himself "declares war and concludes alliances" inevitably experiences frictions with the foreign policy department. These frictions were exacerbated when Katkov changed his foreign policy orientation. Prior to about 1884-85 he favoured an alliance with Germany, and anyone who supported a rapprochement with France or England he called nothing less than a "traitor". In this situation Martens' appeals for joint and several actions with England were guardedly received in the Katkov camp. The situation became more complicated when Katkov did a turnabout and began to inveigh in favour of an alliance of Russia with the Franco-English Entente. Now the "traitors" became proponents of an orientation towards Germany, for example, the Minister of Foreign Affairs, Giers. So did the attitude towards Martens, as an associate of Giers, change, although for Katkov, Martens was a minor figure.

On 11 October 1884 Martens attracted the attention of the newspaper *Санкт-Петербургские ведомости* [St. Petersburg Gazette]. The occasion was his article in the October issue of a leading journal relating to the fiftieth anniversary of the University of Bern (Switzerland), to which he had been invited.

Setting out his impressions, Martens expressed admiration for the fact that Switzerland, a small country, had seven universities, that the university anniversary was a holiday in the City of Bern and the canton, and that the small canton maintained and equipped its university better than Russia did its own universities. "For us Russians," he wrote, "the history of the small cantonal University of Bern is in any event instructive since a familiarisation with the experience and sufferings of the cultural life of other peoples is instructive in general". And Martens, transparently reproaching Russia, continued: "The

---

[42] M. E. Saltykov-Shchedrin, *Собрание сочинений* [Collected Works] VII (1988), p. 445.

Swiss have long since understood what in our century constitutes the real, fundamental, and inevitable power of every nation. This is not millions of bayonets, not the immensity of State territory, and not a multi-million population. This power, before whom all bow and which conquers all, is the power of a high culture, intelligence, and talent". In confirmation of his thoughts Martens quoted the words of the "patriarch of the Slavophiles", A. S. Khomiakov, uttered at the height of the Crimean War (1854-56), which Russia lost: "we will be defeated not by force (we have this), nor by valour (we do not need to seek this); we will be defeated, and decisively so, by thought and intelligence".[43]

Санкт-Петербургские ведомости [St. Petersburg Gazette] was upset by Martens' criticism of Russian customs. As a result, as Martens wrote in his diary, the "most scandalous lampoon about me" ensued. They called him the "golden intermediary" who skated about international congresses at treasury expense. Martens was indignant, went to protest to his superiors, and even handed in his resignation to the rector of the University, but achieved nothing: no one risked communicating with Katkov. On 24 October Martens summed up his efforts: "we are living through a remarkable time. An autocratic sovereign, government, which without trial or investigation can dismiss, banish. And Katkov is higher than the government". Subsequently Martens repeated more than once that "Katkov is higher than the law and the government".[44]

Finally, it should be stressed that Martens developed views in his publicist works which corresponded to his internal convictions. He opposed the territorial expansion of Russia in Central Asia and on this basis favoured peaceful cooperation with England in the region, and this was his own view and not a defence of the government's position. This conclusion is fortified by his diary entries in, for example, 1885. We recall that in 1884, encouraged by the English, the Afghan authorities sent

---

[43] See Martens, "Пятидесятилетний юбилей Бернского университета" [Fiftieth Anniversary of Bern University], *Вестник Европы* [Herald of Europe], no. 10 (1884), pp. 862-863.

[44] AVPR, opis 787, delo 9, ed. khr. 1, l. 21-23.

their detachments to the Turkmen oasis of Pendzhde and occupied it. In March 1885 Russian forces approached the oasis and advanced southward into Turkmen territories. The English Government demanded that Russia in the forthcoming demarcation leave Pendzhde and certain other Turkmen territories to Afghanistan. Petersburg did not agree. War was in the air. Martens was indignant. On 27 March he wrote: "We are on the verge of war with England because of the famous Pendzhde, that is, hamlets consisting of 5-6 huts in Central Asia! It is difficult to imagine what is going on and that the fate and well-being of the 100 million population of Russia depend upon this!" Soon he learned that the envoy of Russia to Copenhagen proposed that in the event of war the Bosphorus and Dardanelles be occupied. "This is stupidity!", Martens exclaimed. With sarcasm he described his impressions from a conversation with the head of the Asian Department of the Ministry of Foreign Affairs, Zinov'ev: he is convinced that he is a marvellous politician and statesman, and by his policies himself has brought Russia to the verge of war for some unknown hamlets. "Misfortunate Russia! An unhappy Russian people, for whom things are passable, but because of some Pendzhde they must sacrifice their lives and blood".[45] Martens' position on this issue, we see, was entirely consistent. He also consistently favoured respect for the territorial integrity of China.

In connection with the publicist activities of Martens it is advisable to dwell briefly on how he was perceived in English-language, and especially English, literature. The historical conditions of the time were such that many of Martens' publicist works touched, to some extent, upon Anglo-Russian contradictions, and therefore his reflections and arguments inevitably generated a polemical reaction on the part of the English. It is not surprising that the greatest number of critical remarks with respect to Martens are contained in English-language publications. An example is Nussbaum's article. The choice of materials and comments in the article were intended to persuade that Martens was not a "man of law" and acted

[45] AVPR, opis 787, delo 9, ed. khr. 1, l. 10-11.

tendentiously in the interests of the Tsarist Government. Nussbaum suggested that all of Martens' activities relating to strengthening international peace emanated from a "desire to serve his sovereign".[46]

Especially unfounded in Nussbaum's article, together with other absurdities, is the proposition concerning the "desire to serve his sovereign". Martens himself never wrote (and deliberately did not write) about his "true feelings as a subject". His diary evaluations of Nicholas II and especially the palace camarilla were rather unflattering. Where is the "desire to serve his sovereign"?

The polemical attacks against Martens scattered about English-language writings and the absence of a translation of his *cours* on international law into the English language should not create the impression that an anti-Martens spirit existed therein. Rather we speak of certain writers and individual publicists. As a whole Martens enjoyed in England, including among English jurists, no less authority than in other countries. We recall the honorary doctorates from Oxford and Cambridge, the gratitude of Queen Victoria, and the fact that the English Government repeatedly requested Martens to be an arbitrator in international disputes.

As regards Martens himself, then one may speak of his undoubted sympathies towards England. As a scholar and a jurist he was attracted by the comparatively high legal protection of the individual in that country, the democratic traditions of parliamentarianism, and the entire "spirit of the laws" lacking in his own motherland. He valued highly, including in diary entries, many English public figures. And he did not do this very often. On the pages of the diary many Tsarist officials, and some foreign ones too, he called nothing other than "rogues" and "scoundrels". His sympathies towards England were certainly no secret to those around him. In any event, in 1905 Martens learned to his surprise that in the Ministry of Foreign Affairs and in "high spheres" he was considered to be an "anglophile". His "anglophilism" supposedly prevented his appointment to the post of envoy at the Hague.[47]

[46] Nussbaum, note 20 above, p. 62.
[47] See AVPR, opis 787, delo 9, ed. khr. 6, l. 14-16.

At International Conferences After successful work at the 1874 Brussels Conference, Martens travelled more often to international conferences as the representative of Russia and was involved in preparing documents which determined the position of Russia at one or another forum. From 1884 he became the permanent representative of Russia at the conferences of the Red Cross. He took an active part, in particular, at the 1906 Geneva Conference which reviewed the 1864 Convention on the Red Cross. For services to the Society, Privy Councillor F. F. Martens was awarded in 1902 a badge of distinction by the Red Cross. In 1893 he was sent to the First Hague Conference on Private International Law, and then he represented Russia at the second, third, and fourth conferences (1904).

Martens played an active role in preparing the Russian Ministry of Foreign Affairs for the Berlin Conference on Africa (November 1884-February 1885).

The convocation of the Conference was caused by the conflicts of interests of the European States in Central Africa. In the summer of 1884 King Leopold II, of Belgium, who had enlisted in his service the noted American journalist and explorer, Henry Stanley, established control over a large part of the Congo River basin. France had created its own bases there, and England had supported the claims of Portugal to the mouth of that River. A conflict situation arose in which the German Chancellor Bismarck in a Circular Note of 24 September 1884 proposed that a conference be held in Berlin to discuss the following questions:

- the establishment of freedom of navigation on the Congo River;
- the extending to the Congo and Niger rivers of the rules of free trade proclaimed by the 1815 Congress of Vienna;
- determining the rules for occupying free lands in Africa.

In October 1884 Giers charged Martens with preparing a memorandum on the forthcoming conference. Martens performed this commission rapidly and thoroughly. He proved the importance of Russia's participation in the Conference since Giers considered the African continent to be too remote. Martens, inter alia, pointed to two circumstances which, in his view, had undoubted significance for Russia:

(1) the international legal principles for occupying new lands which it was proposed to agree in Berlin would find application not only in Africa, but also, for example, in Asia. They would prove to be exceedingly important when consolidating Russian possessions in Central Asia;

(2) the agreeing of rules for free navigation along the Congo and Niger would not only open them to Russian vessels, but as a whole would affect the regime for the use of international rivers, which for Russia was extremely important.

The memorandum was approved by Giers, sent on to the Tsar, and underlay the instructions for the Russian delegation at the Conference. Having regard to his authorship and the abundance of international legal questions at the Conference, Martens reckoned that they would send him to Berlin. But it turned out completely otherwise: Count P. A. Kapnist, the Russian envoy at The Hague, was appointed as first plenipotentiary, and the second plenipotentiary was a naval officer. Martens was indignant, expressed his feelings in his diary, but all that was promised to him was to summon him to Berlin if a lawyer was required there. The summons was withheld, and Martens worried: "The Berlin Conference is in session for the third day, and Giers does not think to send me to Berlin".[48] Martens came to the Conference in December and was able to take part in working out the rules for the occupation of new lands and certain other questions. In Berlin he again was upset: Count Kapnist sets out his arguments in good faith, receives widespread approval, and no one knows who is the author of the arguments.

But many laurels came to Martens too. For him the Brussels Conference on African affairs of 1889-90 proceeded satisfactorily. He acted there as the second plenipotentiary of Russia and became a leading figure in drafting the central portion of the General Act devoted to international measures against trade in negroes at sea. When a conflict situation arose because

[48] AVPR, opis 787, delo 9, ed. khr. 1, l. 25-32.

of contradictions between England and France with regard to the inspection of ships, Martens quickly drew up a "memoire" which brilliantly settled the dispute. Later he recalled how on 27 November 1890 "all members of the Conference bowed low to me" for this memorandum. In March 1906 at a luncheon with Minister of Foreign Affairs, Count Lamzdorf the English chargé d'affaires related that the participants of the Conference extolled the resolution of so complex a question by Martens. Lord Salisbury (1830-1903), British diplomat, prime minister, and foreign secretary, called the Martens memorandum a "masterpiece".[49] Participation in the work of the Conference gained wide recognition and authority for Martens. Queen Victoria of England and Leopold II, King of Belgium, expressed their gratitude to the Tsar, and the English branch of the Order of Malta admitted him as an honorary member with the right to wear the Grand Cross of Malta.[50] The King of Belgium appointed him a life member of the State Council of the Independent State of the Congo. A letter of the Belgian Mission in St. Petersburg is preserved in the archive, dated 12 September 1889, in which it is said that Leopold II, King of Belgium and Sovereign of the Independent State of the Congo, wishes to appoint privy councillor F. de Martens a member of the Supreme Council for the independent State of the Congo. Of seventeen members of the Council, fifteen were Belgians, all except an English lawyer and Martens. The task of the members of the Council was to give opinions on questions affecting the Independent State of the Congo. The Belgian envoy requested the Russian Government to authorise Martens to join the Council.[51] The authorisation was given, but later Martens was not able to be truly engaged with the affairs of the African colony.

Martens' successful activities at international conferences were greatly facilitated by his rare quality – a combination of the gifts of a jurist, diplomat, and publicist. It was this combination and his fluency in French, English, and German which made him one of the most notable figures at international forums.

---

[49] AVPR, opis 787, delo 9, ed. khr. 2, l. 4-5.
[50] AVPR, opis 787, delo 9, ed. khr. 6, l. 101-102.
[51] AVPR, op. 749/1, del 852, l. 66-69.

CHAPTER VI
THE FIRST HAGUE PEACE CONFERENCE

The end of the nineteenth century was marked for Martens by great ordeals as a jurist and diplomat. We refer to his participation in the preparation and conducting of the First Peace Conference convoked at The Hague in 1899.

On 12 August 1898 the Minister of Foreign Affairs, M. N. Murav'ev, sent to foreign representatives in Petersburg a Note in which it was proposed to convene an international conference for the purposes of ensuring a "true and stable peace, and above all to put an end to the progressing development of armaments". The Note was drawn up without preliminary consultations with other governments and therefore was unexpected. It is not surprising that it gave rise to wide and sundry reactions. Illustrative is the entry in the diary of the then War Minister, A. N. Kuropatkin, on 22 September 1898: "The unexpectedness of the circular took us unawares". As regards the general reaction, Kuropatkin summarised it as follows: "(1) the peoples are enthusiastic; (2) the governments, mistrustful. The enthusiasm of the peoples is premature. Expectation of rapid results. They push disarmament. There will be disenchantment and reaction. It is necessary to avert this".

Kuropatkin himself did not believe in the success of disarmament, the more so rapid and effective disarmament. But he did not exclude the possibility of negotiating with Germany and Austro-Hungary, whose armies particularly worried him, about freezing or even a short-term moratorium on further armaments. He attached great significance to the fact that Russia had acted as the initiator of the international discussion of the problem: "A step of historical importance has been made (communication of 12 August). Profound respect of peoples forever has been secured to the Autocrat who has taken upon himself to inform the world about the possibility of another world other than the so-called armed world now destroying us".[1]

[1] "Из дневник А. Н. Куропатнина" [From the Diary of A. N. Kuropatkin], *Красный архив* [Red Archive] (1932), IV-V, pp. 60, 62.

Who was the originator of the idea in Russia it is now very difficult to ascertain. When the draft received support, this "infant" found many "fathers". In his memoirs S. Iu. Vitte declared himself to be one of them.[2]

The press notices about the circular note of the Russian Ministry of Foreign Affairs of 12 August reached Martens on holiday in Lifland. He had no relationship either with the idea of an international conference on disarmament or with drawing up the respective Note. Murav'ev's Note fell on him like "snow on the head", and Martens' first reaction was one of annoyance. In his diary he from the outset wrote about the "extravagant project" and called Murav'ev a "conjurer".[3]

Martens' position requires explanation. In preceding chapters we have spoken about his impassioned publicist works in favour of universal peace and have set out his theoretical propositions concerning the fact that the highest aim of international law is peace between peoples. Martens always reacted to the arms race negatively, considering it to be incompatible with the establishment of a stable world. We recall his ideas on the occasion of the anniversary of the University of Bern: in our century the power of a State is culture, and not millions of bayonets.

However, as a scholar with an analytical turn of mind and a realistic diplomat Martens was convinced that the project to persuade the powers to proceed towards a reduction of their armed forces was utopian. For many centuries attempts had been undertaken to expunge war from international relations and to establish perpetual peace. Martens had cited in his *cours* on international law the proposals of the Abbé Saint-Pierre, Rousseau, Jeremy Bentham, and other thinkers. They all had remained utopians. Could one expect another fate for the Russian disarmament proposal? On 17 August 1898 Martens wrote in his diary: "I do not know and have not found the means for eradicating war or for disarmament".[4] When the peace

---

[2] S. Iu. Vitte, *Воспоминания* [Memoirs] (1960), II, pp. 159-161.

[3] See AVPR, opis 787, delo 9, ed. khr. 4, l. 53.

[4] AVPR, opis 787, delo 9, ed. khr. 4, l. 56.

movements and international congresses of social forces demand peace and disarmament, this is understandable. But Murav'ev proposes to convene a conference of States, and that is another matter completely. Here a well thought-out programme, preliminary agreement, is necessary. Otherwise the result of a noble initiative may turn out to be not universal pacification, but an exacerbation of relations among the great powers.

Martens, evidently recalling the experience of the 1874 Brussels Conference, analysed the position of the great powers. England in all likelihood would completely refuse to participate. The United States would follow her. The similarity of positions would promote an Anglo-American rapprochement. France would seek the return of Alsace and Lorraine, removed from her by Germany as a result of the war of 1870-71. She was interested in strengthening her military might and reacted with extreme distrust to the plans for disarmament. The Emperor of Germany to be sure expressed satisfaction publicly with the initiative of Nicholas II, his fellow crowned-head. But would he reduce the magnificent German army? In exchange for disarmament Germany would demand guarantees of the inviolability of her frontiers, that is, guarantees of the retention of the recently annexed Alsace and Lorraine. Could Russia do this? Moreover, if the improbable happened and one supposed that the powers would sign a treaty to reduce their armies, for example, commensurately with the size of population, who will oversee the execution of the treaty?

Martens studied the world press, and newspaper clippings are preserved in his diary. *Новое время* [New Times] of 23 August 1898 contained a selection of reactions from French publications. The semi-official newspaper of the French Ministry of Foreign Affairs, *Le Temps*, wrote of the unpreparedness of the world, including Russia, for the noble task of disarmament. Would it not be better to confine oneself to a solemn proclamation of the common aspiration? The newspaper *La libre parole*, which recently had greeted the Russian project with enthusiasm, did an about-turn and called it a "Slavic strategem" and even a "German product". *Le Matin* expressed dissatisfaction strongest of all. It pointed out that France had for fifteen years rejected all disarmament schemes since they obstructed the restoration of her might after the defeat of 1870. And what is this? An ally of France displays such an initiative! *Le Figaro* wrote ironically that the French could only extol the wisdom of the Russian projects. But should not Russia have consulted with France in advance? There is a clipping from a German newspaper at the beginning of September with the speech of the Kaiser. Wilhelm II said: "Peace can not be better secured than by a combat-ready German army ready to strike ..." The press reports intensified Martens' pessimism. "The more I think it over," he wrote in his diary, "the more I come to the conclusion that the Russian initiative will be a fiasco". He always was profoundly upset by the successes and failures of Russian foreign policy, and in this situation he could draw the sole conclusion: "The great cause of disarmament increasingly is taking the form of an enormous failure of Russian diplomacy".[5]

It is not superfluous to dwell on the divergence of opinion concerning the fact that the general public of all countries warmly supported the Russian initiative, and only narrow ruling circles resisted it behind the scenes. In reality the situation in society was much more complex. It is not possible here to analyse this in detail. Therefore we confine ourselves to several examples of the mood among the most eminent jurists.

In 1887 at the session of the Institute of International Law in Heidelberg one of the authoritative members, H. Rolin-Jaequemyns urged that the great powers commence negotiations to limit armaments. He noted that in Europe seventeen States maintained three million soldiers and expended on them and on the navies more than four billion francs a year, or 25% of their revenues. In addition to the heavy burden for the population, the armed forces themselves represented a threat to international peace. However, Rolin-Jaequemeyns' initiative received no support. As Professor Kamarovskii wrote, the members of the Institute reacted to the speech of their colleague with "incomprehensible timidity".[6]

---

[5] AVPR, opis 787, delo 9, ed. khr. 4, l. 68.

[6] See L. A. Kamarovskii, "О съезде Института международного права в

The information published by Kamarovskii in connection with the convocation of the Hague Peace Conference and the attitude towards it of leading jurists from various countries is curious.

Lammasch (Austria-Hungary) saw in the Conference a useful beginning but emphasised the impossibility of both disarmament and of control over it. Stoerk (Germany) rejected the Russian project in principle. In his view both full and partial disarmament were undesirable because as a result the State would lost its capacity to act, would be rendered powerless. Lapradelle (France) sharply criticised the very idea of limiting the implements of war because such limitation would obstruct technological progress. Despagnet (France) believed that before disarmament justness must be restored and the Alsace and Lorraine must be returned to France. Vesnich (Serbia) suggested that the great powers might reduce their armaments since they had resolved the task of national unification. The small peoples were still striving for this. Could they disarm? In Vesnich's view, "justness" must triumph first, and then "peace".

In making this survey and analysing the mood in society, Kamarovskii stated with sorrow that the idea of peace is a "great idea, but has penetrated into public awareness but little and only dimly". He cautioned: "Defenders of war are many".[7] Kamarovskii's conclusions are valuable for their competence: he was a passionate advocate of peace and in Russia acquired wide popularity for his pacifist activities.

Martens' pessimism was reinforced by apprehensions relative to the substantive preparations for the Conference. Knowing the leadership of the Russian Ministry of Foreign Affairs and the procedure reigning therein, he doubted that any specific programme existed behind the Murav'ev Note of 12 August (there was nothing in the Note itself).

---

cont'd
Гейдельберге в 1887 г." [On the Session of the Institute of International Law at Heidelberg in 1887], *Юридический вестник* [Legal Herald], no. 4 (1888), pp. 636-637.

[7] Kamarovskii, *Гаагская конференция 1899 г.* [The Hague Peace Conference of 1899] (1905), pp. 6-11.

Martens' gloomy predictions were justified when in mid-September he returned to Petersburg and could speak with colleagues at the Ministry. Except for the Note, there was nothing in the Ministry of Foreign Affairs: no analysis of the situation, no general programme for the Conference, no proposals with respect to individual questions, no reflections about the place and periods for holding it. There was merely the bare idea to hold an international conference on disarmament.

When Martens went to the Deputy Minister Lamzdorf, the latter optimistically informed him that France, Germany, the United States, China, and Japan had accepted the initiative of Russia "with enthusiasm". Only England had not yet replied. Therefore it was a complete success for Russian diplomacy. To be sure, there was as yet no programme for the Conference. This was a "lamentable fact", as Lamzdorf acknowledged.

Programme of Conference Having visited the Ministry of Foreign Affairs, Martens was convinced that the leadership awaited the programme of the future Conference from him. He saw himself as being in an "idiotic situation": on one hand, he could not refuse, and on the other, his labours obviously would bring his downfall. Therefore Martens initially acted "with cunning". When Lamzdorf spoke with him about the programme for the Conference, Martens advised that a special commission be created from among representatives of the Ministry of Foreign Affairs, the war and navy ministries, and the Ministry of Finances. Lamzdorf agreed, but nothing, of course, came from the "cunning" undertaking. The other departments did not even react, and Martens began to bustle about. On 2 October Lamzdorf expressly asked him to prepare a programme for the Conference. Martens submitted the respective memorandum on 11 October 1898.[8]

When one reads the voluminous, integral, rich proposals of the memorandum, one is astonished at the speed with which it was written.[9] Meanwhile in his diary Martens complained that he had never expended such labour on any other memorandum

---

[8] AVPR, opis 787, delo 9, ed. khr. 4, l. 80-86.

[9] AVPR, opis 470, delo 63, l. 93-102.

as he had on this one. This mystery obviously lies not only in the analytical abilities and high capacity for work by Martens, but also in the fact that he, while lamenting the "flippancy" of Murav'ev and Lamzdorf and despite his own pessimism, had long since intensively thought over how to avoid the fiasco of the first experience with a Conference on disarmament ("a question most complex and sacred!") and simultaneously to rescue the initiative of Russian diplomacy from collapse. The diary entries have retained traces of thought and searches. Internally he was ready to plan the Conference programme.

In conversations with the Minister and his deputy Martens attempted to elicit the ideas of the leadership of the Ministry of Foreign Affairs. However, neither Murav'ev nor Lamzdorf, nor other executive officials, could help him. Lamzdorf, for example, rejected the logical proposal of Martens to hold the Conference in Petersburg, the capital of the initiating State. Lamzdorf's arguments came down to the following: if the Conference gives no practical results (which was entirely probable), then the Russian public and press would begin to proclaim its downfall; and in another capital it would be possible to be satisfied with a declaration of the participants of the Conference concerning a renunciation of the use of force. ("And for this an international conference?! How ridiculous!" Martens commented to himself). Murav'ev went even farther, having proposed his own plan: first a very short Conference, virtually a single session of ambassadors and envoys of foreign States in Petersburg, and next a session of the Conference or a commission at the level of specialists ("tea-drinking by envoys" – Martens says ironically). From the conversations with Murav'ev and Lamzdorf, Martens perceived that they did not believe in the success of their undertaking so solemnly set out in the Note of 12 August, and now, after an initial effect beneficial for Russia, were inclined quietly to bury it at sessions of some sort of inconspicuous commission.[10]

Martens rose up against the intentions of the leadership of the Ministry of Foreign Affairs. In his October memorandum he proceeded from the fact that the planned Conference would be

[10] AVPR, opis 787, delo 9, ed. khr. 4, l. 79.

universal and full-fledged, with an extensive agenda and weighty anticipated results. The initial step in this "sacred matter" of disarmament must not suffer collapse. The project of Russian diplomacy should be crowned with tangible and universally recognised success!

Martens idea was, without rejecting the principal idea of the Note of 12 August, to transform the proposed meeting from a Conference on disarmament into a Peace Conference. He proposed to consider the project as a programme with a dual aim: the "preservation of universal peace" and the "possible reduction of excessive armaments". Resolution of the first task, he wrote "seems in general to be possible" if one furthers the strengthening of the foundations for peace in Europe already existing by means of "a precise determination of the *means* which are in a state to maintain the predominant international peace". It would be incomparably more difficult to resolve the second task, on which the general public placed such special hopes. Martens warned: "In no event should one give up the idea of the possibility to force the great European powers immediately and voluntarily to limit their land and naval armed forces". Therefore he proposed to adhere to the course of not a reduction of armaments, but the freezing thereof at a determined level and for a particular period.

In his memorandum Martens pointed to the danger that hopes for resolving various supplementary problems already were linked with the Conference – a review of frontiers, treaties, and the like. He recommended that all these extraneous questions be severed beforehand, the agenda not be treated broadly and in general form, and that the Conference be placed within "the narrowest framework".

Martens' reflections were aimed at outlining the questions of disarmament in to a minimal group of problems, which would enable one to count upon a limited, partial success. He saw a way out in a discussion of the question of freezing armaments. In addition, he proposed to add to the agenda of the Conference those points which would promise the achievement of results on the basis of broad consent of the participant States. The failure of the negotiations with regard to disarmament problems might thus be compensated for by other agreed measures relating to the strengthening of international peace.

In the section devoted to disarmament questions, Martens suggested:

1. To adopt at the Conference a statement that its participants are "obliged in future not to resort to the use of armed force in order to defend their rights and legal interests without having attempted in advance good offices, mediation, or arbitration".
2. To discuss measures relating to the freezing of armaments, to wit:
   - not to increase land and naval forces within three to five years;
   - to agree, even in principle, the maintaining of a certain percentage correlation between the population of a country and the numbers of its armed forces, and between the general State and the military budgets.
3. To unilaterally declare that Russia in future would reduce its recruitment levy by one third to one half.

Another orientation of the work of the Conference must constitute the means for the peaceful settlement of international disputes, in particular, the creation of a mechanism for international arbitration.

Martens pointed to the rather extensive practice of mediation, arbitration, and certain other forms for the settlement of inter-State disputes. Therefore one had in view not the establishment at the Conference of any new rules, but of bringing the existing practices into a system and legally consolidating it. Here no objections of principle were anticipated on the part of the participants. Martens cautioned only against the illusion that the Conference might create an international court binding upon States "always and in all instances".

We recall that in his works, in particular in the *cours* on public international law, Martens had theoretically substantiated the unacceptability of judicial agencies resembling municipal courts for international relations. Who could judge independent sovereign States? And who could guarantee the fulfilment of judicial decisions? An executing army? At the time this had seemed impossible to Martens. Therefore he proposed a careful approach to an international court, recommending that the principle of the voluntariness of recourse to it be taken into account above all. For Martens this was in essence an arbitration court.

Finally, a third orientation of Conference work was sketched out - international consolidation of the laws and customs of warfare. At the 1874 Brussels Conference, Russia had submitted the draft of a respective convention. At the time the draft did not receive the necessary support, whereas now there were real chances of adopting it.

Such was the programme proposed by Martens for the intended Conference and set out in the memorandum for the leadership of the Ministry of Foreign Affairs. This was a programme for a Peace Conference, and it not only pointed to a way out from the deadend which threatened the initiative of Russian diplomacy but also promised to bring weighty results to strengthen relations of peace among peoples and ameliorate those terrors which wars brought. As regards disarmament, then the Martens memorandum in comparison with original statement containing large promises of the Russian Ministry of Foreign Affairs was more well-grounded and directed the negotiations into a channel which promised successes, however modest. Even if the participants of the Conference confined themselves to a solemn statement about the renunciation of the use of military force until the preliminary use of means of peaceful settlement, this modest result would be balanced by progress along the two other orientations of work. The Martens Plan undoubtedly was the fruit of the labour of not only a jurist, but also a diplomat. It created a reliable base for the successful holding of the Conference.

Martens' October memorandum was readily accepted by the Minister and his deputy. The Conference programme acquired not only real configurations but also was augmented by specific content. The memorandum was included in the circular Note of the Ministry of Foreign Affairs of Russia of 30 December 1898. Together with it were points prepared by other officials of the Ministry of Foreign Affairs. Ultimately it was proposed by the circular Note to discuss the following eight questions at the Conference: (1) the freezing of armed forces and armaments; (2) a prohibition against the use by armed forces of new types of firearms and explosives; (3) limitation of the use of explosives in land warfare and a prohibition against the use of projectiles from balloons; (4) a prohibition against torpedo submarines and ships with battering rams; (5) the application to naval warfare of the 1864 Geneva Convention on the wounded and sick; (6) recognition of the neutrality of lifeboats and other rescue craft in naval combat; (7) review of the 1874 Declaration on the Laws and Customs of Warfare; (8) the use by States of good offices, mediation, and voluntary arbitration.

Martens accepted these eight points which distorted his programme with annoyance but could change nothing: it remained only to observe how worried were the French, who had placed great hopes on the construction of new submarines and how other objections rained down. By the end of January 1899 Martens noted that "now the minister is refusing to have anything to do with this programme".[11] Martens' realistic predictions were justified.

In the tense period of preparing the programme for the Conference Murav'ev and Lamzdorf were unstinting in praise and made alluring promises to Martens. They told him that he as the author of the programme naturally would represent Russia at the Conference, and Martens understood the promise to mean that he would head the Russian delegation as first plenipotentiary. Murav'ev and Lamzdorf firmly assured that after the end of the Conference Martens would receive the post of envoy to The Hague, a posting for which he had repeatedly asked. It was suggested that a successful outcome of the Conference would bring lavish rewards to its organisers. Murav'ev authorised Martens to accept the flattering offer to become an umpire in the Anglo-Venezuelan dispute, although the arbitration

[11] AVPR, opis 787, delo 9, ed. khr. 5, l. 7.

could in time have coincided with the Conference. Martens was asked to head the tribunal of two English jurists, Lord Chief Justice Russell and Lord Collins, and two members of the United States Supreme Court, Fuller and Brewer.

However, Martens' hopes were not fated to come true. Nicholas II, after doubts and vacillations, refused to reduce the recruitment levy, as was proposed in the Martens memorandum. On 26 April 1899 the Tsar sealed a final resolution: "I find it difficult to consent to a reduction of the Army".[12] The effective step devised by Martens to strengthen by specific measures the role of Russia in the cause of disarmament and give an example to other States did not happen.

In February the appointment of the head of the delegation of Russia to the Hague Conference was announced: the Russian envoy in London, G. G. Staal. Martens was "completely stunned" and entire pages in the diary were devoted to this "deeply-felt insult". He could not bear it and under the influence of the slight wrote a letter to Lamzdorf. However, the complaints did not help, and Martens had to be satisfied with a promise that he would be included in the Russian delegation to the Conference. As regards the post of envoy at The Hague, Murav'ev said in a conversation that the sovereign had his own candidate. "Again he duped me", said the indignant Martens.[13]

The feeling of offence became more heated by the fact that the foreign press had esteemed the participation of Martens in the Congress more highly than had the Russian Ministry of Foreign Affairs. Martens preserved clippings from several newspapers in his diary. A German newspaper of 1 March 1899, reporting on the composition of the Russian delegation, singled out the inclusion therein of Professor Martens. "Emperor Nicholas by the choice of the last shows his special interest in conducting the great affair of the Conference" said the article. *The Times* (London) of 5 April 1899 contained information in which the importance of the participation in the Conference of experts of a high class, such as Professor Martens, was noted. A Paris

---

[12] AVPR, opis 470, delo 63, l. 450.

[13] AVPR, opis 787, delo 9, ed. khr. 5, l. 7-13.

newspaper wrote that by sending such a noted jurist as Martens, Russia was demonstrating the seriousness of its intentions and the wish to bring the Conference to a "good end".

To the personal affront was mixed disappointment at possible obstacles on the part of Staal: he was far beyond 70 years of age and had never participated in international conferences. Martens was seized by the premonition that at the Conference in which he had invested so much labour he was not able to count on the support of his own delegation. All would be well if there was no interference ...

When Martens met with Staal during April in Petersburg, his premonition proved to be justified. He assessed Staal as the "sweetest Russian diplomat and a complete nonentity". Staal confirmed that he had never been at international conferences and could not imagine how they were conducted. With irony he noted that soon he would be 80 years of age and would return from The Hague as a deceased person.[14] The conversation with Staal left a heavy after-taste in Martens' mouth.

Gloomy thoughts overcame Martens in the spring of 1899. Relations with Murav'ev and Lamzdorf clearly had not been formed. Martens had a low opinion of both. In the course of preparing the Conference he was increasingly disturbed by their "discourtesy and flippancy". Martens supposed that with his October memorandum he had set out a sufficiently precise general programme for the Conference. But in conversation with Murav'ev in February he again was obliged to explain this programme. He set out his reflections to the Minister on the eight points. The Minister approved and commissioned him to draw up a memorandum. Martens submitted it on 1 March.[15] He gave his reflections relative to the Convention on the Laws and Customs of Warfare and extending the 1864 Geneva Convention on the wounded and sick to naval warfare, and made other recommendations relative to conducting the Conference. Martens demonstrated by argument the utopian nature of the proposals to found a "permanent supreme court called upon to

---

[14] AVPR, opis 787, delo 9, ed. khr. 5, l. 32.

[15] AVPR, opis 470, delo 63, l. 386-398.

settle all disputes and conflicts between States". He believed that arbitration to be realistic which is effectuated on "its own grounds and with voluntary consent".

Martens' recommendation concerning the deciding of questions stage-by-stage was of importance: those most acceptable to submit to the forthcoming Conference, and others, more controversial, to carry over to the next one, having established the period for convening it. Thus, consideration of questions of stabilising peace and of disarmament Martens proposed to make a permanent process, and the Conference with regard to these questions a permanent organ.

The Martens memorandum of 1 March was the basis of the instructions of the Ministry of Foreign Affairs of 23 April to the Russian delegation.[16] The instruction contained yet another proposal by Martens: the founding by States of the institution of international commissions of enquiry "from among the best representatives of diplomacy, warfare, and science" in their countries.

The memoranda and the instruction did not come readily to Martens, especially because of the attitudes of Murav'ev and Lamzdorf. On 18 March, Martens entered in his diary: "Was favoured with a conversation with the Minister himself and heard the most unbelievable confusions. The Minister said that 'we will submit nothing to The Hague Conference and will make no proposals'".[17] How could the creator of the extensive programme, the originator of numerous proposals for the Conference, listen to all this? How could a person who has taken part in many international conferences hear this? Was one to expect from such a Conference that it would itself draw up the programme at its sessions and itself decide everything?

On 1 April, that is, after receiving the Martens memorandum, Lamzdorf submitted to him for review the draft instruction for Staal prepared by the Ministry of Foreign Affairs with a request to give an opinion. Martens read the draft with anger. It turned out his last memorandum was not taken into

---

[16] AVPR, opis 470, delo 63, l. 434-444.

[17] ABPR, opis 787, delo 9, ed. khr. 5, l. 17-18.

account in the draft. He submitted eight extensive comments, although he could, in his own words, have done twenty. One may judge the nature of the comments by the following: the proposal concerning the codification of private international law, Martens explained, was not intended for this Conference, because commencing in 1893 special conferences had been held to this end; the proposal of Switzerland and Romania on the codification of international law deserved attention but was not suitable for discussion at this Conference, and the like.[18] Martens took on the task of drawing up the instruction for his delegation.

Martens recalled with bitterness his relations with the former ministers of foreign affairs. Prince Gorchakov treated "my efforts always with good will", Giers "was delighted with my successes", and Prince Lobanov-Rostovskii "displayed sincere respect". And now?[19] Martens did enormous work on the preparation of the Conference, and the attitude towards him on the part of the leadership of the Ministry of Foreign Affairs was rather disdainful. Matters proceeded such that Martens autonomously, actually concealing it from Murav'ev and Lamzdorf ("I am not speaking to the counts"), wrote the draft declaration for the future Conference of 46 articles. He clearly was apprehensive about the "chaotic" instructions and preferred to propose a document already prepared. Murav'ev, having run through the draft, praised it, and A. K. Bazili (1846-19?), appointed together with Staal and Martens as the third plenipotentiary, called it "outstanding" and said that "now we have grounds for a Conference".[20]

Martens did enormous labours for seven months (from October 1898-April 1899). A programme had been drawn up which established a precise framework and orientations for the work of the Conference. Here it should be said that in preparing the Conference Martens never proceeded from any special interests of Russia. In the memoranda and other documents which he wrote there is not a trace of considerations which would have

[18] AVPR, opis 787, delo 9, ed. khr. 5, l. 28.
[19] AVPR, opis 787, delo 9, ed. khr. 5, l. 13.
[20] AVPR, opis 787, delo 9, ed. khr. 5, l. 17-22.

inclined to the advantage of Russia and, moreover, to the prejudice of any other State. Martens supposed the significance of the Conference to be a reduction of the danger of war, amelioration of its terrors, and the strengthening of international legality. The best means along this path he considered to be reaching the very broadest agreement of States.

"Soul of the Conference" On 6 May 1899 the First Peace Conference opened at The Hague. Representatives of twenty-one European and six non-European States (the United States, Mexico, China, Japan, Persia, and Siam) had assembled. By the standards of that time, this was a universal forum. Paying tribute to the respect for the Russian initiative, the Conference elected G. G. Staal as the chairman.

As Martens had feared, Staal experienced great difficulties with presiding and immediately required the assistance of Martens. He wrote for him an outline of the speech to open the Conference. Staal used the outline but forgot to speak about certain organisational questions. Having no experience of participation in Conferences, Staal sat down after the inaugural address and an incomprehensible pause followed at the session. Martens was obliged to approach the chairman and say to him that according to protocol he must officially close the session. Staal hurried to do so.

It became immediately clear that the elected chairman could not take on presiding at the plenary sessions of the Conference. He requested Martens to sit beside him and help in leading the plenary sessions. Martens depicted with irony the work of the two of them in his diary: through the chairman he proposed that three commissions be created: for technical naval questions, for review of the 1874 Brussels Declaration, and for international mediation and arbitration. It was adopted. Rejected as not relevant to the agenda was the question of the Netherlands delegate concerning the inviolability of commercial vessels during wartime. Adopted. And on and on in the same spirit. When Staal decided to display autonomy and read out at the second plenary session on 8 May a speech written for him by Bazili, Martens found it "awful" since, in his view, the participants of the session had gained the impression that Russia had rejected disarmament.

Such "lamentable" instances were many at the Conference. "I was sorry for the good old man", Martens entered in his diary. And his own position, in his assessment, was idiotic.[21]

Saddest of all was the fact that Staal and the other plenipotentiary, Bazili, proved to be incapable of working in the commissions, where the major issues were decided. Martens came to assume this burden as well. He was elected chairman of the second commission, but de facto he had to be engaged with the affairs of the third commission. His indefatigable activity and leading role could not, naturally, be concealed from the delegates, and through them, from the general public. They called Martens the "soul of The Hague Conference".

As draftsman of the programme and draft resolutions, Martens had made a large contribution to preparing the decisions of the Conference. But in order to achieve their adoption he had to use intensively his abilities and experience as a diplomat.

In the second commission the question was the adoption of a Convention on the laws and customs of warfare based on the 1874 Brussels Declaration by means of an article-by-article discussion. It was to discuss about sixty articles.

Having regard to the situation in the second commission, Martens sought to secure the support of the head of the English delegation, Sir J. Pauncefote. To do so he proposed, in particular, to renounce the initiative of Russia in the third commission and support the English proposals relating to arbitration. Personally for Martens this decision meant a sensitive victim: there was a Russian draft, that is, prepared by him, of forty articles. But Martens submitted the victim thanks to strengthened cooperation with the English delegation. To be sure, here too matters did not proceed without "deplorable misunderstandings". When Sir Julian Pauncefote (1828-1902) expressed his delight at the courtesy of the Russian colleagues, it turned out that a Russian draft statute for an international court had been circulated to the members of the third commission. It was ascertained that the author of the draft was Bazili, who had not informed the other Russian plenipotentiaries about his actions. Staal rectified

[21] AVPR, opis 787, delo 9, ed. khr. 5, l. 37-39.

the situation and took back the document which had unexpectedly appeared.

Cooperation with the English bore its own fruits. When in the second commission an English general stated that his government has consented to give necessary instructions to its forces with regard to the rules of conduct but would not sign the respective obligations, Pauncefote hastened to assure that the general was expressing only his personal opinion. For his part, Martens, knowing that the English and French were categorically opposed to a discussion of the inviolability of private property in naval warfare, did not support the respective American proposal as chairman of the commission.

The discussion article-by-article of the draft Convention was a fatiguing procedure, and Martens wrote on 29 May: "I am terribly tired from the plenary speeches". At the beginning of June the examination of the Anglo-Venezuelan dispute was to commence, at which he acted as the umpire. The sessions of the arbitration court proceeded in the building of the French Ministry of Foreign Affairs, and Martens for a month and a half travelled by exhausting night trains from The Hague to Paris, and back. After five hours of a session conducted in the English language, he came out exhausted on to a Paris street greeted by tropical heat. It is entirely understandable that while waiting for the train to The Hague he sought the cool and relief of the uncrowded Paris cathedrals.[22]

However, the great physical load did not reduce Martens' activeness at the Conference. Because of trips to Paris he sometimes was forced to miss sessions of his commission, but if he considered it necessary, he returned to articles already discussed and sought to make the necessary changes in the text of the Convention. The protocols of the sessions and the testimony of contemporaries show that Martens' presentations, prepared and improvised, made as a rule a great impression on those present. The German jurist, H. Wehberg, noted the "vast historical and linguistic knowledge" of Martens. He wrote that

---

[22] See F. F. Martens, "Гаагская конференция мира" [The Hague Peace Conference], *Вестник Европы* [Herald of Europe], no. 2 (1900), p. 24.

Martens had a command of the German, French, and English languages "to perfection" and knew how to cite historical precedents and use a rich legal argumentation. In discussions on the issues of principle Martens spoke "with all of his force" since often he saw farther ahead than his opponents. Underlining the "combative nature" of Martens, Wehberg even wrote about his "ardent eyes" and "enthusiastic words". The Austrian jurist, H. Lammasch, wrote that the "principal burden of work in both commissions (second and third) lay on the broad shoulders of the indefatigible Martens". The Vice President of the Conference, the Dutchman A. P. S. Van Karnebeek, confirmed that the founding of international commissions of enquiry was the exclusive concern of Martens and constituted one of his greatest services. The French jurist, Leon Bourgeois, noted that Martens always knew how to impart to specific problems a universal human significance. Contemporaries agreed that whereas the arguments of Martens could not always persuade opponents to change their position, they "were admired by all associates and inspired them to work on further".[23]

While giving due to Martens' oratorical skills, they do not alone explain all of his successes at the Conference. He achieved much by acting as a diplomat and above all by his realism and by seeking general agreement. Contemporaries noted that while defending his positions ardently, Martens was ready to depart from them when he saw that they did not enjoy the necessary support. An example is Martens' actions in connection with the address to the second commission by the Belgian delegate when discussing the rules for the conduct of an occupying army.

Twenty-five years previously, at the 1874 Brussels Conference, a number of small countries had opposed the articles treating not only the duties, but also the rights, of the occupying army. They demanded de facto the unlimited right of the population of occupied territories to resist. Now Belgium acted for the group of small countries. The Belgian delegate had delivered a substantial speech which, in Martens' view, was

[23] Quoted from H. Wehberg, "Friedrich v. Martens und die Haager Friedenskonferenzen," *Zeitschrift für internationales Recht*, XX (1910).

intended for the general public. Acceptance of the Belgian comments would threaten to overturn the entire principle of combining rights and duties. Martens objected, and objected brilliantly, receiving applause from those present. However, he understood that the rhetorical arts alone were insufficient to achieve agreement. In his diary he wrote: "How can eloquent words force the representatives of the powers to violate their obligations and not perform their instructions! This would be stupid and naive!"[24] Martens knew that the Belgian delegate, in making his speech, acted not spontaneously but in accordance with instructions from Brussels.

As a diplomat having the experience of participating in international conferences, Martens understood that a decisive moment had ensued: if a decision were not found which satisfied the small countries, the entire draft Convention would be under threat.

After thinking it over, Martens decided upon a bold step. He by agreement with the Belgian delegate, whom he knew well and had known for a long time, took a document sent from Brussels, edited it himself and incorporated certain provisions of principle, and proposed that it be adopted in the form of a preamble to the Convention. The text proposed by Brussels provided for the desire of the participants of the Conference to "serve the cause of humanity", the "requirements of civilisation", the aspiration to "reduce the calamities of war", and the like. However, the greatest attention of members of the Commission was attracted by the provision inserted by Martens and formulated by him as follows: "In instances not provided for by provisions adopted by them [States-participants – *V. P.*], the population and the belligerents remain under the protection and operation of the principles of international law insofar as they derive from customs established between civilised nations, from the laws of humanity, and the requirements of the public conscience".

It is difficult to imagine today the situation and the atmosphere in the Commission and at the Conference as a whole.

[24] AVPR, opis 787, delo 9, ed. khr. 5, l. 60.

Therefore it is not easy to understand why the proposal inserted and formulated by Martens was greeted by the delegates so enthusiastically. But decades later (in 1982) the veteran of international humanitarian movement, Jean Pictet, said in a public lecture that "thanks to the genius of Friedrich von Martens" a provision emerged which later became well-known and enabled the Convention on the laws and customs of land warfare to be adopted unanimously.[25]

As frequently happened with Martens, the decision found for a specific issue, to extricate oneself from specific difficulties, acquired great significance for international law as a whole. The provision put forward by Martens became known as the "Martens clause" and entered into common parlance. References to it continue to this day.[26] As regards the formulation proposed by Martens, it proved to be so successful and found such broad recognition that virtually without changes it was passed by the Second Hague Peace Conference, certain later conferences, and almost verbatim was reproduced in Article 1(2) of the Additional Protocol to the 1949 Geneva Conventions on protection of the victims of war. One of the recent instances of the use of the "Martens clause" is the 1980 Convention on the Prohibitions or Restrictions of Use of Certain Conventional Weapons, the preamble to which provides: "Confirming their determination that in cases not covered by this Convention and its annexed Protocols or by other international agreements, the civilian populations and the combatants shall at all times remain under the protection and authority of the principles of international law derived from established custom, from the principles of humanity and from the dictates of public conscience".

Martens' search for mutually acceptable decisions was facilitated to a great extent by the fact that a large number of the most distinguished international lawyers from various

[25] J. Pictet, *Развитие и принципы международного гуманитарного права* [Development and Principles of Humanitarian Law] (Geneva, 1982), p. 78.

[26] See G. S. Starodubtsev, "Ф. Ф. Мартенс в кодификацию международных правил, применяемых в вооруженных конфликтах" [The Contribution of F. F. Martens to the Codification of International Rules Applicable in Armed Conflicts], *Советское государство и право*, no. 7 (1988), pp. 109-110.

countries participated as members of and sometimes as the heads of delegations to the Conference. Martens was acquainted with them from his work at the Institute of International Law. In particular he knew well the Belgian delegate, Descamps. Personal contacts helped avoid many conflicts and find compromises.

Ultimately the jurist and diplomat Martens could celebrate: the entire Brussels Declaration was adopted unanimously by the second commission. On 20 June he wrote in his diary: "I myself did not expect such a brilliant success. The Brussels Declaration – my beloved child – has been adopted".[27]

In final form the draft Convention on the laws and customs of warfare should have been approved at the plenary session of the Conference. There two submerged rocks lay in wait for Martens. The first was the insistent demand of the American delegate, A. D. White, to consider the question of the inviolability of private property in naval warfare. The second was the draft for extending the rules of the Declaration on the bombardment of open cities to naval warfare. Martens knew very well that the White proposal would not pass because England and France were categorically opposed. As regards the second proposal, Martens himself supported the aspiration to extend the agreed rules to naval warfare. But by experience he knew: commence the discussion of a badly prepared draft and you encounter utter disorder. Thus, both proposals, in and of themselves deserving serious attention, threatened for a long time to delay if not frustrate, the adoption of the Convention as a whole. Martens delivered a speech in which he stressed in heartfelt expressions the justness of the American demand. But he proposed to discuss it in substance at the next Conference. His proposal was unanimously approved. An analogous decision was adopted with regard to the second draft. Martens could celebrate: "I won two battles, and the entire draft was adopted by my commission unanimously". His "child", so aggrieved at the 1874 Brussels Conference, "had received brilliant satisfaction".

Here it is instructive to dwell on the special aspiration of Martens to achieve unanimity or, as we now say, consensus.

---

[27] AVPR, opis 787, delo 9, ed. khr. 5, l. 52.

Sometimes the view is encountered that Martens needed success to strengthen his personal authority, that he displayed excessive vanity, and the like. The true reason for Martens' endeavour to achieve unanimity was an understanding that the stability and effectiveness of a legal norm is imparted by its universal recognition. As a scholar, he himself persuasively proved that real relations between States underlie international law and the attainment of unanimity in a world forum served as a certain guarantee that the legal norms adopted reflect the reality of international life and will be complied with.

After the adoption of the Convention on the laws and customs of warfare, Martens concentrated his attentions on the third commission, where the mechanisms for the peaceful settlement of inter-State disputes were being worked out.

The third commission was to consider the voluminous draft Convention of fifty-six articles. The discussion revolved about three issues of principle:

(1) the founding of a permanent court of arbitration;

(2) the bindingness of recourse to the permanent court of arbitration with regard to a certain group of disputes;

(3) the founding of international commissions of enquiry.

In the discussions Martens could rely on a stable basis: of the fifty-six articles of the draft, forty were actually submitted by Russia, that is, by Martens himself. He had allies in the person of eminent jurists from a number of countries. The outcome of the discussions was determined by not legal arguments, but the positions of governments, and here Martens encountered the contradictions among the great powers: at this time England, Russia, and the United States favoured a permanent court of arbitration with binding awards with regard to a certain group of disputed questions, and Germany took a sharply negative position. On 27 May Murav'ev informed de Staal by a secret telegram that Germany had informed Italy of her negative attitude towards the draft for founding a permanent court of arbitration.[28]

---

[28] AVPR, opis 470, delo 63, l. 139.

The position of Germany threatened to topple the entire draft Convention and required much effort to soften it. According to some data, the noted German jurist, Professor P. Zorn, who had participated in the work of the Conference, played a large role in changing the initial German position. Martens was well acquainted with Zorn and, moreover, both jurists had an excellent relationship with one another. Later Martens pointed to the "outstanding role" of Zorn in the cause of founding the permanent court of arbitration since it was Zorn who persuaded his government to agree to this proposal.[29]

Martens was among the most active proponents of the idea of a permanent arbitration tribunal. His passionate speeches in the third commission enjoyed broad support. He could be satisfied with the agreement achieved.

With no less energy Martens advocated the binding nature of awards of the court to be created. At the very commencement of the discussion, the participants of the Conference were of one mind that the questions connected with the vitally important interests of States and their dignity could not become the subject of an arbitral examination. But Martens jointly with his English colleague insisted on the binding nature of arbitration for the less important disputes. However, in this instance eloquent words did not help, nor did solid legal argumentation. On 4 July Zorn in the name of the German delegation rejected the binding nature of an arbitral examination.

It should be noted that the Russian Ministry of Foreign Affairs did not appreciate Martens' energetic interventions in favour of an arbitration court and displayed great vacillations. At first in a telegram to the head of the Russian delegation of 27 May Murav'ev, informing him of German opposition, wrote: "We should adhere to the view of the majority". In a telegram of 30 May Murav'ev was inclined to the view that "despite the objections of Germany, the Conference will find a unanimous solution". Soon after there followed from Petersburg a "retreat". In a new telegram the Ministry of Foreign Affairs indicated that the "dispute with regard to a permanent court of arbitration

---

[29] See Wehberg, note 23 above, p. 356.

may disturb the successful course of the Conference". It was recalled in the telegram that in the initial draft of Russia nothing had been said about a permanent court and that the English representative had advanced this idea. Since the idea was not shared by all of the powers, it was proposed to return to the original draft and find a "conciliatory outcome" from the situation created so as to adopt a "unanimous decision".[30]

The complex situation in the third commission required considerable diplomatic tact from Martens. On one hand, he energetically and insistently strove for the acceptance of his proposals. The participants of the Conference noted the "power and conviction" of his speeches. Many of them remembered the "high flight of thought", the "fervour", and even the poetic spirit in his addresses. On the other hand, he did not persist in his position if he saw that it had no chance of success and merely gave rise to disagreements. He warmly insisted upon the binding nature of arbitration, but conceded when he saw that there was no unanimity and there was no further mention of it.

The above indicates that thanks to cooperation with the English delegation Martens had renounced the role of initiator in the third commission, although he was the author of the extensive draft. He had to survive blows against his vanity on the part of the French delegation. Of the fifty-six articles in the draft Convention on international arbitration the French had proposed only one. But the clever French colleague, Bourgeois, "obscured all this", took the work of the commission in his hands, and one French delegate even turned to Martens with an appeal not to "monopolise" the consideration of the draft. All this from allies! Inside Martens was indignant. But this was not reflected in his cooperation with the French delegation and personally with Bourgeois.

The energetic desire to bring the discussion to a fruitful end sometimes inspired Martens to critical remarks against those who lagged behind or displayed lack of resolution. But never did those criticised have grounds for offence, and if this occurred, it was a misunderstanding. This happened with the Romanian

[30] See AVPR, opis 470, delo 63, l. 139-150.

delegate, who in a defence by Martens of international commissions of enquiry saw a possible insult to his country. The person presiding was forced to explain that this was not so, and the matter ended amicably.[31]

Martens displayed firmness and restraint when defending a position of principle. This happened with his proposal concerning commissions of enquiry, which encountered the opposition of Romania and Serbia (with regard to his proposal, as a result of instigation from Germany). Seeing the extensive support for his proposal, Martens improvised an eloquent speech and finished it with the applause of those present. Martens won the battle for international commissions of enquiry.

As a jurist and diplomat, Martens frequently manifested resourcefulness and ingenuity. At the same time, he clearly was not among those who had a sense of humour. Other participants of the Conference reduced the tension of the situation through an appropriate joke. Martens was too serious for this, and sometimes even pathetic. In his diary entries one finds irony and sarcasm, but one does not encounter humour, especially with respect to himself.

With the adoption of the Convention in the third commission yet another important victory had been gained, and Martens could justifiably consider himself the victor. On the whole, the programme worked out by him in the course of preparing the Conference was fulfilled and brought great fruits.

It should be remembered that while engaged with the Anglo-Venezuelan arbitration Martens could not be present at the closing of the Hague Conference on 17 July 1899. He learned about this in Paris.

The role of Martens at the Conference proved to be so great that, as already has been said, many called him the "soul of The Hague Conference". The view that Martens had been the initiator of convoking The Hague Peace Conference was widely disseminated.[32] He was not in fact the initiator of convoking it,

---

[31] AVPR, opis 787, delo 9, ed. khr. 5, l. 57-61.

[32] See Wehberg, note 23 above, p. 345.

but his indefatigible efforts in the name of the success of the Conference will always link his name with it.

Results of the Conference The participants of the Conference at The Hague adopted a "unanimous decree" which said that for the growth of the material and moral well-being of mankind the limitation of expenditures on military affairs with which the world was burdened would be extremely desirable. Thus was laid the beginning for the international discussion of issues of disarmament and limitation of armaments.

The participants of the Conference (except China, the United States, and Switzerland) signed the Convention on the laws and customs of land warfare. Twenty-three European, American, and Asian States obliged themselves to comply with the rules entered in the Convention. The provisions of the Convention became norms of international law. They laid the basis for the written law of warfare which, while changing and being perfected, remains an integral part of modern international law. The 1899 Hague Convention laid the beginning of this branch of international law.

One should especially underline the humanitarian role of the 1899 Hague conventions. An episode entered by Martens in his diary may serve as one small illustration. In March 1905 he was invited to the General Headquarters of the Russian Army and informed that in Autumn 1904 when sending Japanese prisoners of war home who had been confined in the Far Eastern village of Medved, one of the Japanese military servicemen gave to a Russian officer a petition in which he thanked Russia for humane treatment and requested a gift be accepted of 150 rubles which he had earned while imprisoned. The Japanese serviceman requested that the money be divided as follows: 50 rubles to the village of Medved, 50 rubles to the Russian Red Cross, and 50 rubles to the famous Professor Martens. The latter wish of the prisoner of war was based on the fact that thanks to international law and the labours of Martens in this domain the prisoners of war were treated humanely. In a conversation the prisoner of war explained that he had studied international law according to the *cours* of Martens.[33] This episode was a touching acknowledgement of the role of international law and the services of Martens himself.

The Conference in The Hague also adopted the Convention on the peaceful settlement of international disputes. In accordance with the Convention, the Permanent Chamber of the International Court of Arbitration was founded. The Chamber consisted of jurists singled out by the States-participants (four members each for a term of six years). The name of the organ founded should not mislead relative to its functions. The reference to the permanent status of the Chamber meant in practice that it was prepared at any time to examine inter-State disputes transferred to it by consent of the parties. The Chamber had a prepared list of candidates for the creation of an arbitral tribunal or for the allocation of an individual arbitrator.

The Permanent Chamber of the International Court of Arbitration rather rapidly demonstrated its usefulness. Its vitality was testified to by the fact that it remains healthy to this day. Its significance, however, in this writer's view, goes far beyond the framework of its practical activities. Its creation laid the first stone in the foundation of international justice. Here lies the origin of the entire modern system of international judicial agencies, here lie the sources for the decision to found the Permanent Court of International Justice by the League of Nations (1922-40), and then, the United Nations International Court of Justice (from 1946). The link of time has been consolidated organisationally too: the principal judicial organ of the United Nations is elected from among persons placed on a list by the proposal of national groups of the Permanent Court of International Arbitration (Article 4, Statute of the ICJ).

In accordance with the Convention on the peaceful settlement of international disputes the institution of international commissions of enquiry was founded, which also surprisingly rapidly demonstrated its usefulness.

---

[33] AVPR, opis 787, delo 9, ed. khr. 6, l. 85.

The well-known Hull incident became the first international conflict which was the subject of consideration thereof. The incident occurred with the squadron of Rear Admiral Z. P. Rozhdestvenskii sent during the Russo-Japanese War from the Baltic Sea to the Far East. In Autumn 1904 the commander of the squadron received information from an agent that Japanese destroyers were supposedly awaiting him in the North Sea. In a situation of anxious expectation on the night of 21-22 October 1904, near Dogger Bank not far from the English city of Hull, signal fires of some ships were noticed by the Russian warships. Suspecting Japanese destroyers, Rozhdestvenskii opened fire. It turned out that the shells fell on English fishing boats. The incident took on a rather exacerbated character. English warships approached the Rozhdestvenskii squadron, and the English press called for war against Russia. A proposal to transfer the conflict for the consideration of an international commission of enquiry helped to defuse the situation.

Martens naturally followed attentively the early experience of his child and was satisfied by the result of the concluding session of the Commission on 12 February 1905 in Paris. The Commission came to the conclusion that Rozhdestvenskii could have mistakenly opened fire as the commander of a squadron anticipating an attack of the enemy. Simultaneously, he was deemed to be guilty in that he did not render assistance to the fishermen who suffered when he saw his error and in that he did not immediately report what had happened to the English Government. Russia was obliged to compensate the damage caused. As a whole the conflict was settled by peaceful means. In his diary Martens wrote: "Very happy that the first experience with my commission went well. This commission stopped the beginning of a war on the part of England. And therein was the purpose of my draft submitted to the Hague Conference".[34] The conclusions of Martens relative to the prevention of war against England are somewhat exaggerated, but on the whole he could be satisfied: the new international institution proposed by him had proved to be vital and effective. One may add that M. A.

[34] AVPR, opis 787, del 9, ed. khr. 6, l. 7.

Taube, a pupil and successor of Martens at the Chair of Petersburg University, was the representative of Russia on the international commission of enquiry.

At the Hague Conference a Convention on the application to naval warfare of the principles of the 1864 Geneva Convention on the wounded and sick was signed. In addition three declarations were adopted on the limitation of the means of military actions: a prohibition against dropping explosives from balloons, shells with poisonous gases, and flattening bullets.

The participants of the Conference favoured continuing the work commenced by convoking a new Conference in future.

As a whole the results of the First Hague Conference proved to be weighty. However, they did not receive recognition in Russian doctrinal literature. It was emphasised in a survey placed in the Brockhaus and Efron encyclopaedic dictionary that "the practical results of the Hague Conference so far have not been great". This conclusion was based on the failure of the plans for the limitation of armaments. "The primary and principal aim of the Conference – the reduction of armaments and military budgets or even fixing them at a lower level – was not achieved at all. The Conference expressed the wish for such a reduction, but it was entirely platonic". Further on in the article it was pointed out that the Conference could not prevent the Anglo-Boer War, the Russo-Japanese War, and so on. Martens was not even mentioned in the article.[35]

Soviet doctrinal writings also gave a sharply negative evaluation of the results of the Conference. The 1899 Conference was faulted for the absence of results in the domain of disarmament ("chatter about disarmament"). Moreover, doubt was cast on the significance of the conventions adopted since they were subsequently violated by States.[36]

From the standpoint of today the reproach concerning the lack of progress in disarmament is clearly unjustified. Achievement of the early agreements with regard to disarmament

[35] See *Энциклопедический словарь Брокгауза и Ефрона* [Encyclopedic Dictionary of Bruckhaus and Efron] (1905), II, pp. 481-483.

[36] See *История дипломатии* [History of Diplomacy] (1963), II, pp. 461-462.

(reduction of Soviet and American missile and nuclear potential, reduction of conventional armaments in Europe) required ninety years. Against the background of such historical development the 1898 peace initiative of Russia was the beginning of a long and difficult path and requires adequate assessment. The First Hague Peace Conference opened an entire era of disarmament in international relations, diplomacy, and international law. Today, in a period of intensive disarmament, this must not be forgotten.

When assessing the results of the 1899 (and later the 1907) Hague Peace Conferences, it is commonly said that they created "the law of war". Belligerent States, albeit to a limited degree, were bound by the obligations ameliorating the calamities of war. This traditional view of the "Hague rules" persists to this day, even though somewhat one-sided.

Today it is clear that the Hague Conventions created not merely the "law of war", but laid a solid foundation for modern international humanitarian law. The beginnings of international humanitarian law are justly traced from the 1864 Geneva Convention on Assistance to Wounded in the Field. Modest in content (ten Articles) and number of ratifying parties (sixteen States), the Convention provided that the wounded shall be aided on the field of battle without distinction as to whether they are of the enemy or one's own. Medical personnel are inviolate, neutral, and not subject to being held as prisoners. They wear identifying marks – the Red Cross on a white field (a transformation of the Swiss flag, which is a white cross on a red field).

The Hague Convention on the Laws and Customs of War established rules regulating a considerably larger sphere of military actions. Most importantly, it determined the status of combatants and formulated four conditions (subsequently expanded somewhat) which have passed from one humanitarian convention to another.

The status of a prisoner of war was defined for the first time. It was established in particular that a prisoner of war is not under the authority of individuals or detachments who imprisoned him, but rather of the Government, which is responsible for compliance with the rules on the treatment of prisoners of war. "They must be treated humanely", the Convention stipulates (Article 4). The provisions of the Hague Convention on prisoners of war were incorporated into the humanitarian conventions and further elaborated.

An individual section of the Hague Convention was devoted to the protection of civilians on occupied territories. The substance of the provisions is eloquently expressed in Article 46: "Family honour and rights, the life of individuals, and private property, and likewise religious convictions and rites of faith must be respected. Private property shall not be subject to confiscation." These provisions also have been carried over into humanitarian conventions and elaborated, supplemented, and codified in dozens of articles.

Finally, the noted "Martens clause", virtually unchanged, is to be found in a number of humanitarian articles and protocols of recent times.

At present, when international humanitarian law has been so powerfully developed and taken on such burning urgency, one must not overlook its sources. These were the initiative to create the Red Cross and to convoke the respective international conferences, inspired by Henri Dunant[37] of Switzerland, and the "spirit" of the 1899 Hague Peace Conference, the Russian jurist F. F. Martens.

The 1899 Hague Conventions opened new directions in the development of international law. As regards breaches of them,

---

[37] Henri Dunant was born at Geneva in 1828 in the family of a merchant and judge. Having graduated from college, he became a trainee in a bank. Other pastimes attracted him: in 1855 he founded with friends the World Alliance of Christian Young People. He visited Algiers and Tunis. During the 1859 Franco-Italo-Austrian War he happened upon the field of battle around the village of Solferino and was so distressed that he wrote a volume, "Memoirs of Solferino" in which he put forward two proposals: to create voluntary societies for the care of the wounded and to convoke an international conference to adopt a respective convention. The book was warmly received and in 1863 the first Red Cross Society was established in Switzerland. Other countries followed, and in 1864 the aforementioned Geneva Convention on the Wounded was signed. Dunant was later awarded a Nobel Prize.

it is instructive to ask: is the significance of norms of criminal law reduced by the fact that they are violated by individual citizens? The situation in international law is analogous.

But in stressing the historical importance of the First Hague Peace Conference, one should not lose sight of the shortcomings and omissions in its organisation and work. Contemporaries pointed to them, and a century later they are readily discovered. And Martens himself bears a share of responsibility for some of them.

L. A. Kamarovskii pointed to one shortcoming of the work of the Conference: its closed nature. In truth the questions submitted to the international conference were ones which worried the general public in many countries: limitation of armaments and the peaceful settlement of inter-State disputes. The Conference worked entirely in the spirit of the old diplomatic tradition, that is, behind closed doors. And it should be said that Martens, judging by his rejoinders and diary entries, disapproved of those delegates who "worked in public". Given his own activities as a publicist, such a position is somewhat strange, but Martens evidently was convinced that agreeing complex issues of inter-State relations is best achieved by competent specialists in confidential seclusion rather than in a situation of extensive openness, in the presence of journalists.

Kamarovskii, being an eminent specialist on the international court, welcomed the founding of the Permanent Chamber of the International Court of Arbitration as a major success. He regretted at the same time that the obligatoriness of such a court was not recognised. As Kamarovskii wrote, Martens' memorandum on the question was distinguished by its consistency and clarity. But Martens, in Kamarovskii's view, was guided by the "considerations of practical politics". But the binding nature of an arbitration court would have helped to strengthen universal peace![38] Many shared Kamarovskii's opinion. It evidently seemed to him that had Martens and other delegates displayed greater insistence the Conference might have achieved a decision concerning the obligatoriness of recourse to the judicial

[38] See Kamarovskii, note 7 above, pp. 18, 31-32.

organ being created and the binding nature of its verdict. This view was reinforced apparently by the fact that a majority in favour of such a decision already had been formed at the Conference.

Today the illusory hopes of Kamarovskii and those of like mind are evident, as is the severe realism of Martens and his supporters. An international court with binding judgments with regard to inter-State conflicts, as Kamarovskii imagined it, still has not been created. The reason for such slow progress is not the inactivity of jurists, but the general level of international relations.

Martens personally also encountered criticism of his actions. First, he was reproached because he had permitted an insufficiently careful processing of the documents adopted. It was asserted that in order to rescue the Russian initiative from failure he closed his eyes to the quality of the results achieved. Second, he was criticised because he acted at the Conference as a "Russian politician" and not as an independent jurist, and third, because he acted rather more as a diplomat than as a jurist.[39]

The critical remarks addressed to Martens deserve detailed analysis since they not only affect his activity but also remain of significance for modern legal science and practice.

So, Martens' interest in the success of the Russian initiative. He undoubtedly was interested. But were other countries indifferent to the success or failure of the Hague Conference? In foreign literature to this day the proposition circulates that Russia took the initiative to convoke the Conference because she "badly needed peace".[40] An impression was created of the mercenary nature of Russia's motives when convoking the Conference. But were not other powers interested in the stability of international peace? In achieving success for the Russian scheme Martens thereby rescued the entire Conference from failure. His efforts were in the interests of the participants of

---

[39] See Wehberg, note 23 above, p. 350; A. Nussbaum, "Frederic de Martens. Representative Tsarist Writer on International Law," *Nordisk Tidsskrift for International Ret og jus Gentium*, XXII (1952), p. 60.

[40] Nussbaum, note 39 above, p. 60.

the Conference, and had it concluded unsuccessfully, undoubtedly a serious blow would have been inflicted on the very idea of disarmament and the peaceful settlement of inter-State conflicts. As regards the aspiration of Martens to defer the deciding of certain controversial issues (the inviolability of private property in naval warfare, and others), one should recall his general view of the 1899 Conference. He believed it to be not a one-off measure, but the commencement of regular international congresses as management organs of the world community. Therefore he favoured a stage-by-stage resolution of the questions: first those for which agreement is most achievable, next the more complex. Martens himself saw lack of preparation and omissions. With regard to the Convention on the laws and customs of warfare he wrote that "there are gaps in it, but all foreseeable".[41] The elimination of gaps he considered to be a task of the next Conference.

Nor should one fail to consider Martens' aspiration for consensus. If unanimity required compromise, and compromise inflicted certain damage on the clarity and precision of the provisions, then he went for compromise, understanding that international legal norms are not created automatically by a majority of votes.

What can be said about the comment that Martens supposedly acted at the Conference as a "Russian politician"? The members of all delegations acted at the Conference as the representatives of their countries. Martens was no exception. But if in such a statement there is an allusion that Martens' actions were determined by some sort of mercenary interests of Russia, this must be resolutely refuted. A study of the open and closed materials (memoranda to the minister, instructions, diary entries) discloses not a single instance when Martens singled out some sort of special interests of Russia at the Conference. All his designs were aimed towards achieving real results on the basis of wide agreement. And it is difficult to imagine how Russia could have specific interests when establishing rules called upon

---

[41] Martens, note 22 above, p. 18.

to ameliorate the terrors of warfare and persuade States to settle their conflicts peacefully.

The "Russian politician" is ascribed to Martens when one speaks about the prestige of Russia, his authorship in the development of international law, and his personal authorship as a representative of Russia. In public addresses with regard to the results of the Conference Martens recalled earlier Russian initiatives: the 1868 Petersburg Convention on the prohibition of explosive bullets of less than 400 grammes, the 1874 Brussels Declaration on the laws and customs of warfare. He wrote that "the Hague Conference is merely one and the most recent link in the chain of international efforts undertaken by Russia to establish in international relations a more correct and reasonable order".[42] But one can hardly consider Martens to be guilty of the peace-creating efforts of his country.

Finally, with regard to the reproaches relative to the "jurist" and "diplomat" in Martens. One should first note that Martens was criticised for his qualities as a "diplomat" almost exclusively by his fellow jurists, as a rule those who did not participate in forums which adopted international legal acts. This relates to Professor Kamarovskii, who suggested that the qualities and experience of a diplomat in Martens created a certain scepticism with respect to the idea of peace;[43] to Professor Holland (Oxford), who considered that Martens sometimes acted more as a diplomat in constant touch with his Foreign Office, than a jurist teaching international law at Petersburg University,[44] and certain others. In our times when a unification of the efforts of diplomats and jurists at international conferences has become a reasonable rule, such criticism is an anachronism. In acting as a jurist and diplomat, Martens anticipated the future.

There were certain flaws in the work of the First Hague Conference. However, they did not determine its results. The 1899 Hague Conference became an important landmark in the development of international relations and international law,

---

[42] Martens, note 22 above, p. 24.

[43] See the *Annuaire de l'Institut de droit international*, XXIII (1910), 540.

[44] See Nussbaum, note 39 above, p. 61.

and the central figure of the Conference was the Russian jurist and diplomat, F. F. Martens.

CHAPTER VII
INTERNATIONAL ARBITRATOR

In international relations the arbitration court as a legal institution has roots in remote antiquity. The essence is that the parties in dispute agree to entrust the examination of their dispute to a third person, from whom they expect an impartial and just award. The consent of the parties to submit to an arbitration court presupposes their readiness beforehand to recognise the judgment rendered, and it is entirely understandable that the parties to the dispute would seek a mutually-acceptable candidate. The candidate is expected to have such qualities as independence in adopting a decision, no prior connection with the dispute, and is a widely recognised authority. It is not surprising that initially international arbitrators were, as a rule, Roman high priests, emperors, and kings.

In thirteenth-century Europe King Louis IX of France was praised for his arbitrations, earning the reputation of an "impartial judge". His consideration of the dispute in the City of Amiens in 1264 between King Henry III of England and a coalition of rebellious English barons headed by Simon de Montfort was widely regarded at the time.

In 1493 Pope Alexander IV rendered an award in the dispute between Spain and Portugal relative to their colonial possessions. In a special Bull, the Pope divided the world between the two powers along a meridian for a distance of one hundred leagues westward of the Cape Verde Islands. The King of Spain was granted the right to lands westward of this line, and the King of Portugal, eastward.

In the second half of the nineteenth century international arbitration had become a common phenomenon. The procedures had changed, and States more often invited as arbitrators not the Pope of Rome or a monarch, but other authorities, especially distinguished jurists.

A benchmark in this process was the *Alabama* arbitration. The *Alabama* was one of the cruisers built in English shipyards and sold to the Confederate southern states in the United States. During the American Civil War (1861-65), the Confederacy used the *Alabama* for privateering, and the cruiser destroyed more than sixty Union ships. The Government of the United States accused London of illegally arming the rebellious southerners and demanded compensation for damage caused.

After prolonged diplomatic negotiations, England and the United States created a mixed commission to consider the *Alabama* claims and in 1871 concluded a treaty which settled many issues in dispute. The claims of American citizens who suffered were transferred by the parties to an arbitration court composed of English and American representatives. The court ordered England to pay $15.5 million, and this was done by the British Government.

It was in the nineteenth century that the basic principles and traditions of modern arbitration were formulated. An important role in their formation was played by the major cases such as the *Alabama*, which came to serve as precedents. Martens acted as an arbitrator in certain of them and made a noteworthy contribution to the development of international arbitration.

"Chief Judge of the Christian World" In 1891 England and France decided to transfer for the consideration of the French jurist, A.P.O. Rivier, the English lawyer Grahame, and the Russian jurist, F. F. Martens, their dispute concerning the right to fish in the coastal waters of Newfoundland. The examination of the case did not proceed, but the invitation to Martens testified to his international authority.

In 1893 Martens participated in an arbitration between Great Britain and the United States relating to fishing in the Bering Sea. He managed his role successfully.

The arbitration which brought fame to Martens was the case concerning the arrest by the Dutch authorities of the master of an English whaling ship, the *Costa Rica Packet.* The dispute in the case extended over four years, until England and Holland in 1895 agreed to transfer it for consideration by an arbitrator. The choice fell on Martens. In May 1895 both countries applied to the Emperor of Russia in confidence with a request to recommend a respective specialist from among his subjects. In June the Minister of Foreign Affairs, Count Lobanov-Rostovskii, proposed the candidacy of Martens in a report to the Tsar and met no objections. On 31 August 1895 the appointment of Martens as the arbitrator in the dispute was officially communicated.

Martens was gratified by the appointment and worried about the complexity of the case. "I am a bit terrified by the enormous moral responsibility," he wrote in his diary. "I shall do everything possible to be worthy of this honour. But the time has come to work on the case," Martens mused. It is clear from the diary entries that he had long followed the development of the dispute.

We draw attention once again to that which disturbed Martens: the moral responsibility of the arbitrator who autonomously decides a dispute between two States. A conversation which occurred on 13 September 1895 between Martens and Emperor Nicholas II at a reception in Tsarskoe Selo, to which Martens was invited on the occasion of his appointment as arbitrator, is curious. In his diary Martens quotes his conversation with the Tsar:

"Tsar: Did you very much want this work?

Martens: Yes, Your Majesty, because the case is rather confused. It has dragged on for several years.

Tsar: Is that so? I thought that it had arisen recently".

The Tsar then asked how Martens would operate, and the last briefly related the procedure agreed by the parties. Martens mentioned that the arbitration could last for months. Again the Tsar was surprised. Evidently he imagined that international arbitration was something completely different.

"Tsar: Several months?

Martens: Perhaps, or more, about a year because the arbitrator has the right to give to both governments a postponement to submit evidence.

Tsar: But the award is decreed by our government?

Martens: No, Your Majesty, I decree the award as the arbitrator, and both powers have obliged themselves to strictly execute the award.

Tsar (with surprise): I thought that the Government decrees the award".

Then the Tsar shook Martens' hand and wished him success.

We recall: Martens rendered the award himself, independently of his Government. He informed the Russian sovereign of this. Leaping ahead, it should be noted that in his diary entries devoted to official matters he does not once, directly or indirectly, speak of any conversations with the leadership of the Ministry of Foreign Affairs in regard to the Anglo-Dutch arbitration. There was no data discovered by the present writer either in the materials connected with Martens' activity in the Ministry of Foreign Affairs archive. In the diary Martens mentioned two conversations with the Tsar which touched upon the arbitration.

On one occasion Emperor Nicholas II asked Martens about the progress in the arbitration before the yearly session of the Russian Historical Society in February 1896. Martens briefly related this without any additional questions being raised. The Tsar actually manifested attention not in the case, but to Martens, whom he had recommended as the arbitrator. The conversation had no consequences.

On the other occasion the arbitration gave Martens a reason to seek an audience with the Tsar at the end of 1896. At the time Martens had written a memorandum on certain foreign policy issues, particularly the urgent question of the day on the straits linking the Black Sea and the Mediterranean Sea. He sent the memorandum first to K. P. Pobedonostsev, and then passed it to the Tsar. Since Martens clearly had intruded into the sphere of competence of his chief, the Minister of Foreign Affairs, the arbitration served as the formal occasion for the audience. At the reception which occurred on 18 December 1896 Martens briefly informed the Tsar about the award adopted by him in the case. But it was not the award, as one might expect, which became the subject of conversation. The discussion turned to questions raised by Martens in the memorandum. In conclusion Nicholas II said: "Go abroad on your important case, and when you return – give me the memorandum on the straits".

Thus the attitude of the Tsar to the outcome of the Anglo-Dutch arbitration was: this was a personal matter for Martens as an authoritative jurist.

Martens' diaries preserve a report about his conversation in regard to the arbitration with yet another monarch: the German Emperor. En route from Brussels, where he had conducted the hearings, to Petersburg, Martens stopped over in Berlin and on 25 January 1897 was received by Wilhelm II. At the audience Martens spoke of the arbitration, and the Kaiser expressed himself more decisively than his Russian crowned cousin: his sympathies were with the Dutch and against the English. But His Majesty's opinion had no influence on Martens' award.[1]

Martens successfully performed the function of arbitrator in the Anglo-Dutch dispute. Both sides were satisfied. The gift for the arbitrator from the English and Dutch governments was testimony to this: three silver vases for flowers and fruits.[2]

The legal substantiation imparted authority to the award. Having encountered a complex legal situation when considering the case, Martens first formulated the question of the principle of jurisdiction over the master for a violation on the high seas according to the laws of the flag of the vessel. The principle received wide recognition.

In November 1898 Martens' good friend, the former Belgian minister and then advisor to the King of Siam, G. Rolin-Jaequemyns, arrived in St. Petersburg. He met with the Minister of Foreign Affairs, Count Murav'ev, and asked his permission for Martens to be the umpire in a Franco-Siamese dispute. Murav'ev refused. In conversation with Martens, Rolin-Jaequemyns disclosed that England wanted to invite Martens to be an arbitrator in a dispute with Siam, and Persia, in a dispute with England.[3]

---

[1] See AVPR, op. 787, delo 9, ed. khr. 3, l. 114-116, 122, 130, 135-136.

[2] AVPR, op.787, delo 9, ed. khr. 3, l. 10.

[3] AVPR, op. 787, delo 9, ed. khr. 3, l. 95.

Martens was appointed umpire in 1897 in the Anglo-Venezuelan dispute over territories along the Orinoco River. The hearings in the case took place in 1899.

In 1902 Martens, already on the list of the Permanent Court of International Arbitration in The Hague, became a member of the tribunal in the dispute between Mexico and the United States concerning California theological foundations, and in 1904, a member of the arbitral tribunal considering a dispute between Venezuela and certain European countries.

Other international disputes began to occupy Martens. In 1892 the Greek chargé d'affaires in St. Petersburg requested Martens to write an opinion in the Zappa case (Zappa, a Greek who after his death in Romania had left a rich estate to which Greece laid claim). The Greek Government hoped that the opinion of such an authoritative specialist as Martens would force Romania to transfer the estate to Greece. In February 1893 Martens completed his opinion. He did not share the hopes of Greece and noted with surprise that the Greek Government ascribed to his opinion "some sort of miraculous influence". It supposed that the opinion would convince Romania to release the "booty".[4] Martens did not doubt the legal substantiation of his opinion, but he saw no real power which would force Romania to comply with the judgment of the jurist (the Romanian Government had not agreed to an arbitration). The Greek Government evidently counted upon the influence of world public opinion. Martens' opinion was, therefore, published in the French language.[5]

Here it is instructive to return to the relations between Martens as arbitrator and his Government. The Memorandum in the Zappa Case Martens had showed in its finished form to N. K. Shishkin, appointed to head the Ministry of Foreign Affairs in connection with the illness of the Minister, N. K. Giers. Shishkin liked the Memorandum, and he decided to show it to the Tsar. Having seen the length of the Memorandum (22 pages),

---

[4] AVPR, op. 787, delo 9, ed. khr. 3, l. 34.

[5] See *Memoire sur le conflit entre la Grece et la Romanie concernant l'affaire Zappa* (Athens, 1893).

the Tsar declined to read it but consented to hear the essence. The Report was finished with the observation of the Tsar: "However, what impudence the Romanians!" – and it had no consequences.

Martens prepared legal opinions for the King of Belgium with regard to the Congo (end of 1892) and the dispute of the Chinese Government with the Northern Telegraph Society in Copenhagen (1883). The last was published.[6]

Virtually unknown was Martens' involvement in the granting of foreign loans to Russia in 1906.

The defeat in the war with Japan and revolutionary shocks increased the need of the Tsarist Government for foreign credits. Count Vitte could organise an impressive loan abroad. The situation for receiving the loan was favourable. It was in those years that the Entente was formed. England and France were interested in supporting their ally, Russia. The concerns of the Russian Government about the loan found understanding in London and Paris. The political instability in Russia, however, gave rise to political apprehensions among the bankers. When representatives of the largest banks arrived at Petersburg in October 1905, they were forced to sit at the Hotel Europa in candlelight because the city had been paralysed by a general strike. By Spring 1906 the situation in Russia had stabilised. The governments and the bankers began to be reassured. In this situation Martens went to Vitte. According to the diary entries of Martens, Vitte said that the French bankers were ready to give a loan but feared that the State Duma would not agree to it. Therefore they requested Martens' opinion on the matter. Vitte added: Nicholas II suggested that Martens himself should give the opinion since he enjoyed "enormous authority" abroad.[7] The flattered Martens accepted the task.

In his memoirs Vitte described the episode somewhat differently. He said nothing about Nicholas II, the concerns of the bankers, and their request to turn to Martens. Vitte evidently consciously roused the self-esteem of the last. In his view it was

[6] See *Memoire sur la telegraphe en China* (Copenhagen, 1883).

[7] AVPR, op. 787, delo 9, ed. khr. 7, l. 88.

not the bankers who insisted upon the legal opinion, but the French Minister of Finances, R. Poincaré, who needed this document.[8]

Whatever the case, Martens drew up the opinion in the French language and it was sent to Paris. In the spring of 1906 the loan negotiations ended with the signature of an agreement. Russia received the enormous sum of 2250 million French francs. The granting of loans to the Tsarist Government was conditioned by vital interests of the creditor States and the interest of the banks in profit and in the Russian market. But Martens' opinion made its own contribution.

The frequent recourse to Martens as an international arbitrator testified to his high and stable reputation. The personality of Martens soon became so notable that the English correspondent William T. Stead (1849-1912) called him the "Chief Judge of the Christian World" in an article for the *Daily News* in October 1898. Baron Taube did not find this evaluation too exaggerated and repeated it in the obituary of his late teacher.[9]

Anglo-Venezuelan Arbitration (1899) Martens' success as an international arbitrator, his high authority as a jurist and specialist in international law did not ward off criticism, nor even sharp attacks. The discussion surrounding the 1899 Anglo-Venezuelan arbitration, revived in 1949, is a clear example.

On 3 October 1897 the newspapers brought Martens a "pleasant surprise": England and Venezuela had chosen him as the umpire and chairman of the arbitral tribunal to consider their dispute regarding the territorial boundaries in the Orinoco River basin. The newspaper report said that the name of Professor Martens had proved to be the sole name acceptable to both governments. Martens accepted the news as a "great honour". He noted that there was no previous example in history (neither in the 1873 *Alabama* case nor in the 1893 dispute concerning

---

[8] See S. Iu. Vitte, *Воспоминания* [Memoirs] (1960), III, p. 241.

[9] M. A. Taube, *Ф. Ф. Мартенс (1845-1909) Некролог* [F. F. Martens (1845-1909). Obituary] (1909), pp. 8-9.

the Bering Sea) of such an international tribunal in which in accordance with the agreement of the parties he was not only the chairman, but also the umpire with the right to render an award without an appeal. He wrote in his diary: "I am even afraid, but hope to cope with the honour of my Dear Fatherland and the honour to me and to my family".

The official petition of England and Venezuela was delivered to the Tsar in November 1897, who placed his "C" (the cyrillic letter to indicate Consent). This was notified in the press on 13 December 1897. Martens overflowed with pride. He stated that this was the third time he had been elected an international arbitrator, a judge above States. On 14 January 1898 Martens presented himself to Nicholas II on the occasion of his election as umpire. The reception was "rather lengthy and gracious". Martens briefly set out the essence of the dispute, the Tsar expressed his confidence that he as a "well-known specialist" would cope with the case.[10]

The dispute between England and Venezuela had a long history: the establishment of the boundary between Venezuela and British Guiana. The territory in dispute extended to 50,000 square miles, that is, was somewhat smaller than England itself. This was a little-explored and even a wild place. At one time it had belonged to the King of Spain. Dutch colonists had settled there in compact communities, and the King of Spain had granted them various privileges which were consolidated in a 1648 Treaty of Peace. The French Revolution of 1789 brought great changes to the region. In 1810 the independent State of Venezuela was born. In turn England during the Napoleonic wars occupied extensive territories in the Orinoco River basin principally colonised by the Dutch settlers. Under the 1814 Treaty of Peace England consolidated this territory as its own. However, the boundaries of the Venezuelan and English possessions were determined in these immense and sparsely settled regions very approximately. The English Government in 1834 sent a German natural scientist, R. H. Schomburgk, to the region and charged him to determine the boundary of the English possessions on

[10] See AVPR, op. 787, delo 9, ed. khr. 4, l. 8, 10-13.

site. In 1840 England declared the "Schomburgk Line" to be the boundary of British Guiana. Thereafter English claims grew. Venezuela, for its part, did not recognise the "Schomburgk Line" and demanded that as the successor to the rights of the King of Spain the territories claimed to be an English possession accede to it. The case led to a rupture of diplomatic relations and armed conflicts. Passions burned hotly in the area around the mouth of the Orinoco River, possession of which enabled navigation along the River to be controlled.

The United States Government supported Venezuela in its territorial dispute with England. In January 1896 President Grover Cleveland created with the consent of Congress a special commission to study the dispute. The secretary of the Commission, composed of eminent Americans, was a young Spaniard, Severo Mallet-Prevost, a specialist on Latin America.

Taking into account the situation, England and Venezuela signed an agreement in February 1897 concerning an international arbitration. The materials of the American commission were transferred to it. American jurists were appointed as members of the tribunal for Venezuela.

The following membership of the international tribunal was determined: chairman (president) F. F. Martens; members of the tribunal: Lord Chief Justice C. A. Russell (1832-1900), Lord Justice Collins (1842-1911), M. V. Fuller (1833-1910), Chief Justice of the Supreme Court of the United States, and David J. Brewer (1837-1910), associate justice of the Supreme Court of the United States.

The interests of England before the tribunal were defended by four English jurists headed by the Attorney General, Sir Richard E. Webster, and the interests of Venezuela, by four Americans headed by the former President of the United States, Benjamin Harrison. Mallet-Prevost was part of this group.

Paris was chosen as the site of the hearings, and it was intended to commence the work of the tribunal at the end of 1898. However, the parties submitted their voluminous materials late and the hearings were postponed. Having arrived at the Hague Peace Conference in early May 1899, Martens learned that work was to commence in June. He faced the prospect of combining the intense work at the Hague Peace Conference with hearings of the tribunal in Paris.

The hearings of the tribunal, which began in mid-June (dates now according to the European calendar), took place in the French Ministry of Foreign Affairs. At the opening several words of welcome were uttered by the French Minister of Foreign Affairs, T. Delcassé (1852-1923). He was answered by the President of the Tribunal, Martens. The hearings were dull and tedious. Even Martens was disappointed by the little interest shown by the general public. As he noted in his diary, about a dozen people came to the opening, but the public was not represented in the hall. Martens found that the French arranged the work of the Tribunal "miserly and republicanish".[11]

In all there were 54 sessions of the Tribunal of four hours each. The submissions of the English side took 13 days, and the Venezuelan side received the same amount of time. Webster and Harrison delivered the concluding arguments. The hearing concluded on 27 September 1899. On 3 October 1899 the Tribunal announced its award.

All sessions of the Tribunal were minuted. Later the transcripts were published in eleven volumes. The Foreign Office attentively followed the work of the Tribunal. The Foreign Office archive contains fifteen volumes of materials connected with the arbitration in Paris.[12] The course of the arbitration was publicised in the press.

The award of the Tribunal gave 90% of the disputed territory to England, and 10% to Venezuela. However, Venezuela received the strategically important area at the mouth of the Orinoco River.

The award was unusual in form. It was brief and did not contain a legal substantiation. In addition, it was without names. Whereas the awards of other arbitration courts were adopted by a majority of votes, the position of each member of the court

[11] AVPR, op. 787, delo 9, ed. khr. 5, l. 52.

[12] See Clifton J. Child, "The Venezuela-British Guiana Boundary Arbitration of 1899," *American Journal of International Law*, XLIV (1950), 682-693.

being indicated, the award of 3 October was rendered by the tribunal as a whole. Since there was no division into a majority and a minority, there were no dissenting opinions of the minority.

In the concluding remarks to the Tribunal, an interview with Reuters, and other articles in the press Martens set out his reflections on the results of the arbitration.

He above all stressed the significance of the arbitration for the development of international law. He emphasised that the Tribunal for the first time had issued an award while being guided by the rules adopted by the Hague Peace Conference.

Martens pointed out that the boundary established by the Tribunal was a "line based on equity and law". At the same time, he stated that the award rendered was a compromise between the demands of the parties. The complexity of the question, whose roots went back to the sixteenth century, inspired the compromise.

Martens acknowledged the novelty of the form of the award. He assessed it positively, noting that the award of the Tribunal as a single whole had greater moral force than an award adopted by a majority vote.

The reaction of the parties and the general public of other countries to the award of the Arbitral Tribunal headed by Martens was quite positive. In an interview in *The Times* of 4 October 1899 Harrison and Mallet-Prevost spoke of the "victory" of Venezuela. The English representative in the Venezuelan capital reported to Lord Salisbury about the indifference of the local populace to the Paris award (despatches of 7 and 19 October 1899). In his State of the Union message to the United States Congress, President William McKinley on 5 December 1899 pointed to the importance of the arbitral settlement of the dispute, which had lasted throughout much of the century. The award of the Tribunal was assessed as being "satisfactory to both parties".[13] One should recall that in 1901 Yale University conferred an honorary doctorate on Martens. In October 1899 Queen Victoria had sent a message of gratitude to Martens.[14]

---

[13] Child, note 12 above, pp. 691-693.

[14] AVPR, op. 787, delo 9, ed. khr. 5, l. 87.

The press of those days emphasised that the arbitral award put an end to the dispute between the two countries and opened the prospects for the development of peaceful relations between them. It was especially noted that the expenditures for the rather prolonged arbitral award proved to be lower than the expenses for one day of war between England and Venezuela.

Sensation a Half-Century Later A great sensation was caused by a "Memorandum" written by the American lawyer Otto Schoenrich and dictated by Severo Mallet-Prevost in February 1944 and published after the latter's death in December 1948 by the *American Journal of International Law* (July 1949). Mallet-Prevost later had become a partner in the New York law firm Curtis Mallet-Prevost, Colt & Mosle.

The principal content of the Memorandum and accompanying article came down to the fact that the award of the 1899 arbitral tribunal was unjust and unlawful. Supposedly it was the result of a covert behind the scenes transaction between Great Britain and Russia, and the American members of the Tribunal accepted it on the basis of an ultimatum from the President of the Tribunal, Martens.

In confirmation of these sensational assertions, the following information was cited: according to the recollections of Mallet-Prevost, at a luncheon arranged by the American chargé d'affaires in London, Henry White, for the American representatives travelling to Paris, he happened to sit next to Lord Russell, a member of the Tribunal. When he told Russell that the Tribunal should act exclusively on legal grounds, Russell supposedly objected that the establishment of the boundary should take into consideration international policy. Mallet-Prevost already had drawn the conclusion that on the Tribunal, Lord Russell would not establish the line of demarcation "on the basis of strict rights".

In the course of the hearings the character of the questions from Lord Collins persuaded Mallet-Prevost that he was critical of the English demands and well disposed towards the Venezuelan. When during an adjournment Lord Collins travelled to London, upon returning he took an entirely different position. In London he evidently received proper instructions from his Government.

During the adjournment in the middle of August, Lord Russell and Lord Collins took Martens to London with them. In England a transaction occurred which determined the award of the Tribunal. For support in the Venezuelan matter, England rewarded Russia evidently on some other question.

At the beginning of September 1899, when the hearings had been completed and the award was awaited, Mallet-Prevost, in his own words, was invited by a member of the Tribunal, Brewer (USA), to his hotel. Brewer assured Mallet-Prevost that he and his colleague Fuller were ready to continue to insist upon the interests of Venezuela, but that the President of the Tribunal, Martens, had conversed with them and declared that if they did not agree with the line proposed by him, he would join the English side. If the Americans agreed with the proposed variant, Martens promised to issue the award of the Tribunal without names. Brewer declared that in this situation he and Fuller had decided to speak with Mallet-Prevost. They would act as he decided. Brewer added that he and Fuller were prepared to be a minority and write a dissenting opinion in the award. But this would not influence the award since it was adopted by a majority vote.

With the consent of Brewer and Fuller, Mallet-Prevost hurried to Harrison with the news communicated to him. Harrison, recalled Mallet-Prevost, rose in indignation, pacing the floor, argued, was annoyed with Martens. However, ultimately he considered it best to concur with the compromise.[15]

This "disclosure" brought a surprisingly rapid, carefully argued, and unusually sharp refutation in the same journal (October 1950 issue) by an English jurist and formerly a Commonwealth Fund Fellow at the University of Wisconsin, Clifton J. Child.

Child's concern was easy to understand. Mallet-Prevost and Schoenrich attempted to sully the reputation not only of Martens,

---

[15] See O. Schoenrich, "The Venezuela-British Guiana Boundary Dispute," *American Journal of International Law,* XLIII (1949), 529-530.

but of all members of the Tribunal. According to their version, Lord Russell from the very outset rejected an award based on strict rights. Lord Collins received an instruction in London and immediately changed his initial position. Both brought the President of the Tribunal to England and concluded a secret deal with him there. Fuller and Brewer conducted themselves no better. Instead of acting independently, they secretly sent a courier to Harrison in order to receive his instructions. It transpires that the Tribunal did not consist of independent judges who were guided by law in their award, and only by law, but of spent political dealmakers. Poor Venezuela!

Child took upon himself the great labour of refuting Mallet-Prevost and Schoenrich by using archival and other materials. He accused the authors of the "exposé" of distorting the facts. The distortions and inventions were so many that he confined himself only to certain of them.

Child established that in January 1899, when Mallet-Prevost supposedly spoke with him, Lord Chief Justice Russell not only was not a member of the Tribunal, but he had no relationship whatever to the case. He became a member of the Tribunal unexpectedly, having replaced Lord Herschell, who died unexpectedly in March 1899.

Mallet-Prevost's impression of Lord Collins having undergone a radical change in position after the August adjournment was not confirmed. Child studied the questions of Lord Collins at the hearings before and after the adjournment and established that they did not differ either in number or in character.

As regards the note in *The Times*, Child established that Lord Russell actually was during the adjournment in England at his country estate. No information was discovered either in the press or in the archives of the Foreign Office about Martens' trip to England.

As for the "deal" between England and Russia, Child found not the slightest trace of such being concluded or performed in the fifteen volumes of archival materials in the Foreign Office relating to the arbitration or in the diplomatic correspondence of the day between London and Petersburg. Moreover, Child set out convincing arguments that the worsening relations between England and Russia left no objective place for such a deal.[16]

Child destroyed the impression of two camps in the Tribunal: English and American. He in particular recalled the statements of Brewer, that each judge on the Tribunal had his own view which diverged from the views of the others, and the demarcation line established by the award of the Tribunal passed "between" these four views. Child suggested that if Martens had exerted pressure on the members of the Tribunal, it was on all of them, and not only the Americans.

Child refuted the assertion of Schoenrich that the award of the Tribunal caused "general surprise", that the friends of Venezuela were "shocked". He recalled the interview of Harrison and Mallet-Prevost concerning the "victory" in the Venezuelan case, and the like.

As a whole, Child left no stone unturned against the conjectures of Mallet-Prevost and Schoenrich.

A certain misunderstanding arose in this connection in that in his critical assessment Child seems to circumvent the episode of the meeting among Mallet-Prevost, Brewer, and Harrison. If such a large number of other facts were distorted, why should this part of the Memorandum merit trust? If so many fabrications were discovered with regard to Lord Chief Justice Russell, why should the assertions relative to Martens' "pressure of an ultimatum" on the American members of the Tribunal be believed?

To strengthen Child's devastating criticism, the present writer can add that in working with the archival materials of the Russian Ministry of Foreign Affairs connected with Martens' activity, not the slightest trace was discovered of a "deal" between England and Russia or that Martens, the President of the Tribunal, received instructions regarding the case from his own Government. On the contrary, the diary entries of Martens testify that he acted in the arbitral tribunal autonomously and

---

[16] Child, note 12 above, pp. 684, 686-688.

independently. They contain no indications at all of the "deal" ascribed to him.

In reading Martens' diary for the period from 16-25 August 1899 (in the diary the period was 4-13 August, old-style calendar), it is clear that he was in Paris. He was worried not so much about the Tribunal as about the results of the Hague Conference and the attitude in Russia towards his services to the Conference. Melancholy thoughts preoccupied him. Here is the entry for 27 August, when the Tribunal should have assembled after the adjournment: "Today is my birthday. I am 54 years old. Never have I celebrated it without my wife, my children, my friends. To be sure, *Figaro* and other French newspapers praise me for the Conference, but this is small consolation. There is no praise from my Motherland". There is not a word about the work of the Tribunal in the diary entries. Nor is there any indication of a trip to London or any kind of "deal".

Finally, on 2 October (for Martens, 20 September) 1899 an entry appears in the diary about the completion of the Tribunal's work. The entry was extremely brief and depicted the situation as follows: "Finally the Anglo-American arbitration has ended. I am very tired. Tomorrow I travel to Baden-Baden. I have succeeded in convincing the members of the Tribunal to compromise. Fuller likes me very much. British greed. As a result the award of the arbitral tribunal was adopted unanimously. Hurrah!!!"

Thus, Martens convinced the members of the Tribunal to reach a compromise for the purposes of adopting a unanimous award. His entry is fully consistent with the views of Brewer, the opinion of Child, but not with the inventions of Mallet-Prevost and Schoenrich. As regards the attitude of the members of the Tribunal to the compromise, Martens evidently spoke more readily with the American arbitrators (good attitude of Fuller) than with the English ("British greed"). Where is the "deal"!

In the diary entries mentioned and subsequent ones there is nothing to suggest that Martens would report on the arbitration to the Ministry of Foreign Affairs or to the Russian Embassy in Paris, and the like. He acted autonomously and independently in the arbitration, including independently of his own Government.

En route to Russia Martens was received by Tsar Nicholas II in Darmstadt. Their conversation revolved around the Hague Conference. The arbitration is not even mentioned in the diary entry of Martens.[17]

As regards a "deal", one may add certain details characterising the state of Anglo-Russian relations of those years and the position of Martens himself.

In March 1898 Martens entered in his diary: "Our official newspaper *Novoe Vremia* [New Times] aims supplications against England. An appeal to take Afghanistan and move into India! The scoundrels from *Novoe Vremia* [New Times] rejoiced over the conquest of Port Arthur by Russia and mocked the English. How stupid this is!"[18]

At a time when *Novoe Vremia* [New Times], subsidised by the Tsarist Government, called for Afghanistan to be seized, Martens published a pamphlet in which from the standpoint of international law he called for the independence of that country to be respected.

The behaviour of Professor Martens evidently did not go unnoticed, and in November 1900 *Novoe Vremia* [New Times] published two vicious articles about Martens, including on the occasion of his article in an English journal[19] and his participation in the Anglo-Venezuelan arbitration. In a fit of temper Martens called the semi-official press organ of the Tsarist Government "a cesspit".[20]

In November 1899, soon after the completion of the arbitration, Martens wrote at the request of Count Lamzdorf (as a jurist with an "authoritative name") an article for *Pravitel' stvennyi vestnik* [Governmental Gazette] on "The Hague Peace

[17] AVPR, opis 787, delo 9, ed. khr. 5, l. 63-66, 72-73, 79-80.

[18] AVPR, opis 787, delo 9, ed. khr. 5, l. 32.

[19] See F. Martens, "The Peace Conference, Europe and China," *The Monthly Review* (November, 1900).

[20] See AVPR, op. 787, delo 9, ed. khr. 5, l. 113.

Conference and the Anglo-Boer War in the Transvaal". Count Lamzdorf based his request on the fact that in Russia and abroad many asked why the Peace Conference had not stopped that War. Martens thought to himself: "How could the Conference make war impossible?" But he wrote the article and in it, without expressly naming England or Transvaal, condemned the actions of the English Government. The condemnation he gave readily, as he considered the war of England against the Boers to be "scandalous".[21]

In his article Child was able to restore the historical truth. However, speculation around the 1899 Anglo-Venezuelan arbitration and Martens personally as President of the arbitral tribunal did not cease. The article mentioned previously by Arthur Nussbaum (1952), notwithstanding the refutation of Child, reiterated the full range of conjectures of Mallet-Prevost and Schoenrich. There he spoke of the "unexpectedness" of the award of the Tribunal, and the "secret agreement" of Martens with "one group", and his "ultimatum" to the other group, and the exasperation of Harrison, and the like. Moreover, the Nussbaum article attempts to totally compromise Martens as a scholar, as an international lawyer, and as a person. The article speaks of Martens' unseemly actions in the Tribunal as deriving from his doctrine of international arbitration, which supposedly for him was a political institution and not an instrument of law. Martens is called a politician and diplomat in the article, and not a "man of law". His doctrine is juxtaposed to the "conception of the majority of countries of Western civilisation", according to which an arbitrator must be neutral in a dispute and independent in his awards. According to Nussbaum, Martens was not such an independent arbitrator, nor independent of his Government. As Nussbaum writes pathetically, the entire institution of international arbitration would be compromised if it followed Martens.[22]

---

[21] See AVPR, op. 787, delo 9, ed. khr. 5, l. 83-84.

[22] A. Nussbaum, "Frederic de Martens. Representative Tsarist Writer on International Law," *Nordisk Tidsskrift for International Ret og jus Gentium*, XXII (1952),p. 59.

The position of Martens in the 1899 international arbitration, as in other analogous instances, actually met his scholarly understanding of the nature and role of international arbitration. His practical actions accorded with his theoretical views, and such concordance predetermined his position of principle in the changes of the international situation.

In his works and his addresses at the Hague Peace Conference Martens consistently opposed mixing international arbitration with a municipal court. He himself often called arbitration a "supranational court", but he saw the principal aim of international arbitration not to simply render a "legal judgment" but the final settlement of an inter-State conflict on the basis of law. On the whole he relegated arbitration to the means for the peaceful settlement of international disputes and thereby to the means of preventing war.

In this writer's view, one should single out this as a characteristic feature of Martens' scholarly conception: on one hand, he passionately opposed the subordination of international law to international politics, and on the other hand, cautioned against divorcing international legal principles and norms from the international relations which actually exist. Even the admirers of Martens, as for example H. Wehberg, regarded his aspiration to link legal and political principles as an unresolvable contradiction.[23] To many jurists Martens' proposal to introduce representatives of the parties in dispute on to an arbitration court, his objections against a procedure to appeal the award rendered, and the endeavour to reach a unanimous award were incomprehensible. To Martens these means facilitated achievement of the principal aim: final and irreversible settlement of the dispute between States. For his opponents such means seemed contradictory to the principal task of justice: the rendering of a judgment strictly following legal norms.

However, this entirely scholarly discussion has nothing in common with the assessments by Nussbaum and Schoenrich and based on data which, when verified, proves to be false or doubtful.

---

[23] H. Wehberg, "Friedrich v. Martens und die Haager Friedenskonferenzen," *Zeitschrift für internationales Recht*, XX (1910), 349.

They collapse on the basis of the refutation of the data on which they were based.

Only the stubbornly maintained conjecture about Martens as an obedient executor of the instructions of the Tsarist Government (a "Tsarist writer on international law") motivates one to stress once again that in reality Martens was for his ministerial leadership and for Tsarist bureaucrats a very obstinate specialist. The provisions of the science of international law so dear to him he frequently insisted upon without respect of person. Already noted above have been his publicist addresses and his significant independence in preparing and conducting the 1899 Hague Peace Conference. In addition one may cite certain other curious examples.

In January 1887 a draft Law was being discussed in the State Council which provided for the right of the Minister of Justice to declare sessions of a court to be closed. Martens spoke against this, referring to the international obligations of Russia. The Minister of Justice withdrew the draft law. The members of the Council supported Martens, but the mighty Pobedonostsev "was enraged" and the Tsar in the next report told Giers that "Martens should be given a dressing down". Martens was taken aback by the reaction of Pobedonostsev, but did not change his opinion on the draft law.[24]

In 1893 a dispute arose between Russia and England over whaling. Within two months Russian naval vessels had detained eleven English schooners. An interdepartmental commission was created in St. Petersburg under the chairmanship of M. N. Kapustin, who was appointed personally by the Tsar (he taught the Tsarevich international law). The commission was disposed to support the actions of the naval officers. Only Martens, representing the Ministry of Foreign Affairs on the commission, sharply (and "unpatriotically") spoke against. He pointed to the international rules prohibiting the stopping and confiscation of foreign vessels beyond the 30-mile coastal zone. The remarks of an admiral who was present made no impression on him, and he wrote a dissenting opinion. When Martens saw that he could not

[24] See AVPR, op. 787, delo 9, ed. khr. 2, l. 46-50.

control the naval personnel, he moved away from the "whaling" problem and refused decisively to represent Russia at an international conference on this question in Washington D. C. during 1897.

In 1898 the all-powerful Minister of Finances, Vitte, submitted a draft for the creation of a free port (free trade zone) near the acquired Port Arthur. Martens objected, and when Vitte sent a "secret letter" to the Ministry of Foreign Affairs relative to one "Professor Martens", Martens entered into a polemic with him.[25]

No, Martens was no blind follower of the will of the leadership when one spoke of international law so dear to him. The high professionalism, erudition, and free command of many foreign languages, independence of judgment resting on scholarly international legal conceptions, and understanding of the linkage between law and policy were indeed those qualities of Martens which gave him authority as an international arbitrator.

The interminable discussions around Martens' activity as an arbitrator merely confirms that the key, most complex, issues of international justice give rise to polemics in modern times too. Martens' view with regard to these problems deserves attention because it reflects his enormous international experience.

---

[25] AVPR, op. 787, delo 9, ed. khr. 3, l. 38-45, 163; ed. khr. 4, l. 10, 36.

CHAPTER VIII
COUNSELLOR OF MONARCHS AND MINISTERS

The legend of the "high office" of Martens in the Russian Ministry of Foreign Affairs was to a great extent created by a misunderstanding relative to the influence which an ordinary University professor enjoyed in foreign policy of the country and in international affairs in general. The secret of the influence was that Martens in time had become a valuable counsellor to the leadership of the Ministry, to certain Tsarist nobility, and to the Tsar himself.

N. K. Giers Martens initially performed the role of counsellor to Nikolai Karlovich Giers, a deputy of the aging Prince Gorchakov, and then his successor in the post of Ministry of Foreign Affairs. Martens formed good relations with Giers which went beyond official subordination. Judging from the diaries of Martens, the Minister conversed with him rather frequently and for long periods, speaking of his reports to the Tsar and palace intrigues and sharing reflections about the foreign policy of Russia and international events.

On 19 November 1886 Martens met Giers while on a walk. They strolled together along the entire Bol'shaia Morskaia Street and then in the Aleksandrov Garden. They spoke of the Bulgarian debts.[1] Martens on 14 May 1887 recorded in his diary that he and Giers again took an extended stroll about the Aleksandrov Garden. They spoke about Katkov's attacks on Giers' political policies.[2] Never again did Martens have such close relations with ministers and their deputies. Nor did he stroll with them about the Aleksandrov Garden. But he saw a good bit of them while serving in the Ministry of Foreign Affairs.

To be sure, there was a fatal obstacle between Giers and Martens. Giers' wife, Olga Egorevna, did not look with favour on the professor; she preferred Giers to be among the officials of

---

[1] AVPR, opis 787, delo 9, ed. khr. 1, l. 42.
[2] AVPR, opis 787, delo 9, ed. khr. 1, l. 79.

the Ministry, Count Lamzdorf and Prince Obolenskii, who had a career ahead: the first was elevated to Minister, and the second, to among the senior counsellors of the Ministry of Foreign Affairs. The goodwill of a lady such as Olga Egorevna meant a great deal in Petersburg society of that day.

The coming together of Giers and Martens was facilitated by a danger threatening both of them – the attacks of Katkov and his press. Until 1884 Katkov had been a fervent defender of the alliance with Germany and applied the epithets "traitor" and "betrayer" to all who disagreed. When Katkov's orientation did an about-face, Giers submitted to Emperor Alexander III a collection of Katkov's articles from *Московские ведомости* [Moscow Gazette] for 1882-83 written in this spirit. But the Tsar did not reign in his protégé, who zealously continued to propagandise an alliance with France against Germany and fulminated against all who thought differently. Since Giers was the personification of the Russo-German alliance, he turned out to be the central target of Katkov's attacks. This afforded an opportunity to be at one with Martens, as the unofficial counsellor of the Minister.

On 24 April 1884 Martens, while in Berlin, was received in private audience by Wilhelm II. Regrettably, Martens does not write who assisted in achieving such an honour for the Petersburg professor. Possibly the matter had gone through Giers, who counted upon conveying by such means friendly assurances of the German Emperor to the Russian Autocrat. Wilhelm II did indeed say at the audience that so long as Giers remains Minister of Foreign Affairs he would be content to have friendly relations with Russia. Having returned from the reception to the Zentral-Hotel, Martens recorded the conversation, but did not include these words in the Report for the Ministry of Foreign Affairs which, as he knew, would be brought to Alexander III. Upon returning on 27 April to Petersburg, he consulted with Giers, who naturally did not authorise the inclusion of so flattering an appreciation by the German Emperor. According to Martens, though, he was more than satisfied. And evidently under the influence of intense feelings, he told Martens about the intrigues of the palace cliques, about his efforts to consolidate peaceful relations with Germany, and the like. According to him, the Tsar was experiencing the influence of General Skobelev, Katkov, and other persons who opposed rapprochement with Germany, whereas he, Giers, was assured of full support and confidence. Only he, Giers, did the Tsar choose from all the Ministers after the Report at Gatchina to remain for breakfast in the family circle, and the like.

On 4 May 1884 Giers obtained an audience for Martens with Alexander III. The Tsar courteously shook hands, asked about the visit to Europe, and said that he had read Martens' Report with satisfaction. However, many other people were present at the audience, and this did not enable the flattering words of Wilhelm II concerning Giers to be conveyed to the Tsar. Martens noted in his diary that the "audience was extremely brief and of slight interest." The breakfast which followed the audience for those invited was in this respect even less interesting. For the novice Martens it became an incident: he wore the ribbon of his Order across his left shoulder, though it should have been worn on the right, and the nobility present were in shock. One general even made an unpleasant remark to him. The incident was reported higher up. However, the Tsar noticed nothing, and it all passed over.[3]

The activities of Giers and Martens did not pass unnoticed by Katkov. In particular, on 11 October 1884 the *Санктпетербургские ведомости* [St. Petersburg Gazette] printed the "most scandalous lampoon" about Martens. The newspaper *Гражданин* [Citizen] of Prince Meshcherskii aligned itself with the attacks by Katkov against Giers, which also received annually a subsidy of 40,000 rubles from the Government, and in the diary entries of Martens for 1884-87 the evaluation is fleetingly glimpsed that the "position of Giers is unstable."

Giers took measures against the Katkov campaign. In November 1886 he invited Martens in to ask what arguments might crush Katkov, who was agitating on behalf of Russia

[3] AVPR, opis 787, delo 9, ed. khr. 2, l. 14-18.

renouncing the 1856 Paris Declaration and in favour of introducing privateering at sea. Giers informed him that Katkov had received from the Tsar the high Order of Vladimir, second degree, and had become completely unrestrained. Martens refused to get mixed up in a newspaper polemic, where they already had declared him to be a criminal, and took it upon himself merely to write a memorandum for the Minister.[4]

In January 1887 Martens learned from Baron Zhomini that Katkov had submitted a memorandum to the Tsar opposing Giers' policies. In the press the campaign against Giers in spring 1887 unfolded with new force. Katkov demonstrated that Bismarck had "duped" the Tsar, that Germany was Russia's most pernicious enemy. In the polemics he used secret diplomatic correspondence which an employee of the Russian Embassy in Vienna, S. S. Tatishchev, took away with him before his dismissal from the Ministry of Foreign Affairs. Giers requested an urgent audience with Tsar Alexander III and began to rush out to Gatchina. He demanded Katkov be punished for having published secret State documents. The Tsar suggested, however, that Katkov as a journalist naturally printed interesting materials and that one should attempt to find out who transferred the secret despatches to him. Ultimately the Tsar promised to "take measures". With this promise, Giers left. As Martens wrote, Giers returned from Gatchina as a Minister, but "his authority he had irretrievably lost". Martens wrote emotionally under the circumstances that it would have been better to appoint another Minister, even Katkov, in order to put an end to "governmental anarchy". He pined for the "solid times" of Nicholas I and Alexander II.[5] He still did not suspect that the reign of Alexander III would become for him a pleasing memory during the "governmental anarchy" of Nicholas II.

Giers' anti-Katkov démarche did little to help. The anti-German campaign in the newspapers subsidised by the Government continued. Giers requested that he might resign, but the Tsar did not concur. As Martens noted, the Tsar and

[4] AVPR, opis 787, delo 9, ed. khr. 1, l. 40.
[5] AVPR, opis 787, delo 9, ed. khr. 1, l. 75-77.

Tsaritsa "constantly charmed Giers with courtesy". The Tsar as before had breakfast with him and assured him of his "unlimited confidence." At the same time Katkov publicly called the Minister of Foreign Affairs a "traitor".[6]

Martens' sympathies were on the side of Giers at the time and his policy of rapprochement with Germany. He began in Spring 1887 to gather materials for a pamphlet against the "miscreant Katkov". Although the pamphlet was written in defence of the Tsar's foreign policy and his Minister of Foreign Affairs, Martens was apprehensive of the consequences and took exceptional measures of care. Privy Councillor Martens decided to print the pamphlet anonymously abroad "because in Russia nothing can be said against Katkov since he is higher than the government and the law". But it was necessary to print abroad in the "utmost secrecy" since Delianov and Count Tolstoi and other ruling figures will "not allow me to live" Martens entered in his diary.[7] Therefore the text of the "Open Letter to M. N. Katkov" he requested that his wife copy so as not to leave any trace of his handwriting in the printing house. Through a close acquaintance in the Prussian legation, D. Gessner, the pamphlet was sent to the Berlin printing house, Stankevich, where it was printed in 25 copies. Martens intended to circulate them in sealed envelopes to the most influential persons in Petersburg. However, on the eve of the pamphlet's appearance, Katkov unexpectedly died on 21 July. Appealing by an open letter to a "deceased miscreant" made no sense, so Martens confined himself to sending one copy to Giers.[8]

The well-disposed attitude of the Minister, whom he sincerely respected and whose position he shared, helped Martens to strengthen his role as an advisor on foreign policy issues. After the 1874 Brussels Conference, Martens prepared a conception for the Russian delegation at the 1884-85 Berlin

---

[6] AVPR, opis 787, delo 9, ed. khr. 1, l. 79-80.

[7] Martens refers to N. D. Delianov (1818-97), who was Minister of Public Enlightenment during 1882-97, and to D. A. Tolstoi (1823-89), Minister of Internal Affairs from 1882-89.

[8] AVPR, opis 787, delo 9, ed. khr. 1, l. 87-89.

Conference on Africa and after overcoming obstacles in his own Ministry of Foreign Affairs, participated in its work. It was Giers who obtained from the Tsar special authorisation for Martens' trip to Berlin. During the 1880s, Martens took part in international conferences virtually every year. He had become a sort of permanent representative of Russia, especially when a specialist on international law was required – on the law of the sea, private international law, the Red Cross, and others.

The Swiss Project In 1892 the Swiss Government officially requested Martens to prepare a draft convention on founding in Bern a bureau for the publication of international treaties. Martens was one of the originators of this idea and did not confine himself merely to drawing up the draft document. For two years, he wrote in 1894, I used my personal connections in Brussels, Berlin, and Paris to eliminate the obstacles. In Russia I attempted to persuade Baron Osten-Sacken and Shishkin, leading officials in the Russian Ministry of Foreign Affairs.[9] Martens submitted a respective initiative to the Institute of International Law and received from it a commission to draw up a draft.

The idea of collecting in one place all international treaties for the purpose of publishing them for general information had emanated from international lawyers. The procedure for the collecting and publication would further the strengthening of the international legal order and limit secret diplomacy. It was a qualitatively new element in the formation of the world community of States and was appealing to Martens with his theory of international administration. The organisation of the bureau would be responsive to the new level of international relations being formed at the end of the nineteenth and beginning of the twentieth centuries and therefore proved to have vitality. The procedure worked out by Martens in the draft convention became the predecessor to the registration of international treaties at the Secretariat of the League of Nations and then the United Nations Secretariat.

---

[9] AVPR, opis 787, delo 9, ed. khr. 1, l. 32, 84.

For convenience in using international rules Martens included in the draft convention a point about the publication of collections of international acts. Such collections were called upon to promote the codification of international law.

On 4 October 1892 the Swiss Government by a circular note distributed a draft prepared by Martens to all States, and on 13 October 1894 an international conference was opened in Bern to adopt the respective convention. As the author of the draft Martens reckoned on representing Russia at the conference. However, the ministerial bureaucracy determined otherwise, and no one could help: Giers was ill, the "sincere friend" Zhomini had died, and other influential friends had departed. Martens remained at home. He learned with indignation that Russia would be represented at the Bern Conference not even by the Russian envoy, but by a young first secretary of the mission. It was good that the Ministry of Finance insisted on the appointment of its own delegate, A. Rafalovich (1853-19?), in whom Martens saw a "capable and intelligent young man". It was another matter that Martens, having given so much of his strength and energy to that which in his eyes was of enormous significance for a more precise organisation of international relations, turned out to be kept away. It seemed to Martens that the Ministry of Foreign Affairs should in any event support the founding of the bureau as a Russian initiative, but it was met with incomprehension and no attention. "I will not soon forget the matter of the Bern Conference", he wrote with sorrow in his diary.[10]

The 1894 Bern Conference showed the actual lack of strength of Martens in the Ministry of Foreign Affairs. Giers increasingly had withdrawn from matters. In 1891 Martens wrote about "Nikolai Karlovich constantly burdened with age and fatigue", who complained to him that "everyone forced him to sign". On 15 August 1892 Giers together with his family was sent abroad for extended treatment.

During the Minister's absence, Shishkin – a little-known official of the Ministry of Foreign Affairs – was in charge. "A man very orderly and not stupid – and that is all", Martens

[10] AVPR, opis 787, delo 9, ed. khr. 1, l. 84-89.

wrote of him. People came to the leadership to whom Martens was antipathetic, especially Count Lamzdorf. During 1892-94 Martens did not see Giers. He declared: "I am utterly alone as a penalty", he not have "a single influential person with whom I am friendly".[11] On 14 January 1894 Giers died.

Martens' career as a foreign policy advisor did not end with the death of the Minister. It turned out that his role had a more solid basis than the favour of the Minister. Moreover, his knowledge and experience were essential, and his analytical capabilities and diplomatic skills opened broader opportunities for him.

A. B. Lobanov-Rostovskii The new Minister, Prince A. B. Lobanov-Rostovskii, Martens had not known previously. A "rather mysterious individual", he wrote, having twice visited a ministerial reception. To be sure, one characteristic of the new leader immediately aroused sympathy – a love for "historical investigation". Lobanov-Rostovskii published several works on history and proved to be an erudite conversationalist. When Martens handed him Volume XI of his treaty collection, the Prince discovered "fundamental knowledge", which naturally was pleasing to Martens' soul, for the other Tsarist bureaucrats and officials of the Ministry of Foreign Affairs, like Count Lamzdorf, did not play about with scholarly knowledge. Lobanov-Rostovskii's attitude towards Martens was loyal. He received him with courtesy, listened attentively, immediately formalised his authorisation to be an arbitrator in the Anglo-Dutch dispute. During Easter 1895 Martens received the Order of Vladimir, second degree. The new Minister was progressive. And Martens on the basis of his conversations came to the conclusion that it was unlikely the Ministry of Foreign Affairs would be transformed.[12]

It was no accident that reflections on the abilities of Lobanov-Rostovskii to reform the Ministry of Foreign Affairs disturbed Martens: a memorandum had long lain in his briefcase with respective proposals. Finally, he decided in November 1895

---

[11] AVPR, opis 787, delo 9, ed. khr. 1, l. 83-88.

[12] AVPR, opis 787, delo 9, ed. khr. 1, l. 108-109.

during an ordinary conversation to hand over the memorandum to the Minister. He was thanked, questions put, and a promise made to read it attentively.[13]

In his memorandum[14] Martens set out a brief history of the Ministry of Foreign Affairs from the time of Peter I, critically analysed the structure which existed, compared it with the organisation of the foreign policy departments of other countries, and proposed a reorganisation plan.

In substantiating the need to transform the Ministry of Foreign Affairs, Martens wrote: "The present organisation thereof is an anachronism, the existence of which can be explained only by a stagnation inherent in bureaucratism and an attitude of arrogance towards the legal requirements of life". Take the Council of the Ministry. According to the concept of the 1832 reform, it should have replaced the Petrine collegium but it fails to operate as an advisory agency since it is not endowed with precise functions. A central place in the Ministry of Foreign Affairs is occupied by the chancellery, where political correspondence is concentrated. But the chancellery does not draw up diplomatic notes and instructions! The Asian Department founded by Edict of Paul I of 26 February 1797 was transformed into a "bureaucratic fiefdom" and matters had so proceeded that the chancellery conducts one policy and the department, another. The Department of Internal Relations is also concerned with the consular service (except for the Oriental States), and with trade and industry. In practice it was charged with all questions – political, legal, and economic, which testifies to the "absence of any system and order". The files of the personnel department represent a strange mixture of awards, monetary expenses, personnel appointments, the purchase of wood for heating, and the like. The archives of the Ministry were in a desperate situation.

By an analysis of the structure of the diplomatic services of England, France, Germany, and Italy Martens showed that all political affairs are concentrated in the same department,

[13] AVPR, opis 787, delo 9, ed. khr. 1, l. 118.

[14] AVPR, opis 731, delo 28, l. 3-17.

and the head of the political department also managed the selection of personnel. Everywhere political affairs were separated from economic affairs, and the diplomatic section from the consular service; everywhere personnel matters were separated from economic, and everywhere there was a special legal subdivision.

It was especially stressed in the memorandum that the "policy of a great power should be in essence uniform and indivisible", that under modern conditions it should render greater protection to Russian industry and trade abroad.

In accordance with the "legal designation" of the Ministry of Foreign Affairs the following structure was proposed in the memorandum:

1. Minister
2. Deputy Minister
3. Senior Counsellors
4. Council of the Ministry, to whose jurisdiction was relegated:
   (a) matters subject to discussion by way of legislation;
   (b) matters controversial requiring an interpretation of international law and internal legislation;
   (c) administering of diplomatic examinations
5. Chancellery, engaging in clerical work and courier service
6. Department of Political Affairs
7. Department of Consular Affairs
8. Department of General Affairs, including the legal service of the Ministry of Foreign Affairs
9. Archive Administration[15]

Martens proposed to somewhat expand the leadership of the Ministry of Foreign Affairs through senior counsellors (at the time there was only one senior counsellor); concentrate all foreign policy questions, and also the personnel provision thereof, in one department, which would become the key subdivision of the Ministry; create a special consular department, separating it

[15] AVPR, opis 731, delo 28, l. 16-17.

from foreign policy and other subdivisions; leave chancellery matters to the chancellery, relieving it from foreign policy functions not within its remit; improve the archives by creating a special archive department. Special attention was given by Martens to improving legal work in the Ministry. He provided for the Council of the Ministry to become a permanently working agency which would be much engaged with legal questions (discussion of draft laws, opinions on controversial issues, and the like). In addition it was intended to create a special jurisconsult service. Finally, in proposing to enlarge the number of senior counsellors, Martens assumed that one of them would be in charge of legal matters. This is supported by yet another memorandum by him which he sent to Lobanov-Rostovskii in June 1896 together with a personal letter. In the letter he wrote that he had the honour to submit a "memorandum on reinstating the post of Second Senior Counsellor. Many years of personal experience have led me to the positive conviction that *all* opinions of the Ministry of Foreign Affairs must emanate from one person, and not from individual departments, as at present". Martens assured the Minister that he made his proposal in the interests of business and not personal advantage, that is, he was not proposing an office for himself.[16]

The personal letter to Lobanov-Rostovskii of 7 June 1896 testified to the fact that the Minister was interested in the Martens scheme and evidently discussed it with the author and other officials of the Ministry of Foreign Affairs.

In fact Martens' proposals for reform of the Russian foreign policy department were timely and correctly reflected world developments in this domain. A significant role was played here by Martens' rich personal experience and his knowledge of the situation in analogous departments of foreign States. However, Martens' memorandum had an unhappy fate. In 1896 Prince Lobanov-Rostovskii died. Shishkin again managed the Ministry, and Lamzdorf to a greater degree was concerned with the affairs of the Ministry. Neither favoured reform.

---

[16] AVPR, opis 731, delo 28, l. 2.

It should be said that even Giers had begun to use Martens also during discussions of municipal law. In November 1884 he was invited, for example, to a session of the State Council as an expert on international law. In his brief tenure as Minister, Lobanov-Rostvskii had continued to use Martens as a specialist on international law when discussing various internal decisions. In November 1895 he was involved in considering a draft of the Ministry of Justice to exempt foreigners on the basis of reciprocity from submitting preliminary security for cheques. Martens took part in the discussion of the draft law on naturalisation and withdrawal from Russian citizenship. In 1896 he was invited to serve on the commission for the arrangement of the city of Vladivostok. In particular the question was decided of what kind of port Vladivostok should be: purely commercial, naval, naval-commercial (Martens favoured a purely commercial port).[17]

K. P. Pobedonostsev

Although Martens' memorandum on reorganising the Ministry of Foreign Affairs suffered a sad fate with the death of Lobanov-Rostovskii, in other respects the advisory activities of Martens under that Minister took on new prospects. First, in September 1895 on the occasion of his election as arbitrator in the Anglo-Dutch dispute he was presented to Tsar Nicholas II and had the opportunity, however briefly, to converse with him about business (discussed in a previous Chapter). Second, Martens obtained access to K. P. Pobedonostsev. Under Alexander III he had enormous influence on the affairs of the Russian Empire. He enjoyed the confidence of the Tsar and was constantly with Alexander III, including when in autumn 1894 he died at Yalta from kidney disease. Nicholas II, after the death of his father, inherited the mighty Ober-Procurator of the Holy Synod. The manifestoes connected with the accession of the new Tsar to the throne were drawn up by Pobedonostsev. He stole away after the speech of Nicholas II on 17 January 1895 before the representatives of the zemstvos in which a warning was given about the "senseless dreams" regarding their participation in the affairs of State administration. Liberal reforms were expected

---

[17] AVPR, opis 787, delo 9, ed. khr. 3, l. 124.

from the new Tsar, and he replied with a categorical refusal ("senseless dreams"). This policy line was linked with the name of Pobedonostsev, who was then regarded as the ideologue of reaction and obscurantism. The attitude towards him of the democratic, liberally-minded strata of Russian society was expressed by Alexander Blok in a poem called "Retribution" (composed in 1910):

In those years remote, deaf
Sleep and gloom reigned in hearts
Pobedonostsev over Russia
Extends owlish wings ...

Martens was in a similar mood. When in 1907 Pobedonostsev died, Martens entered in his diary that he always had been an "enemy of any progress and a convinced defender of autocracy".[18] However, Martens enjoyed good relations with him. He treated Martens attentively, and conversations with him proved to be "interesting and instructive".[19] For Martens especially important was the fact that Pobedonostsev had (at least at the beginning of the reign) enormous influence with Nicholas II.

In early 1896 Martens wrote a memorandum on certain questions of foreign policy and took it to Pobedonostsev. He accepted it very courteously and conversed with him long and candidly. Reflections were shared, for example, as to who should be appointed the new Minister of Foreign Affairs. Pobedonostsev asked the opinion of Martens, who suggested Prince Urusov. Pobedonostev mentioned Izvolskii, but agreed that he was very young. Pobedonostsev openly opposed the alliance with France and rapprochement with Germany. "Just what I wish," noted Martens.[20] Evidently the two were of one mind on foreign policy issues.

The consequences of the conversation with Pobedonostsev were not long in coming.

---

[18] AVPR, opis 787, delo 9, ed. khr. 7, l. 16.
[19] AVPR, opis 787, delo 9, ed. khr. l. 16.
[20] AVPR, opis 787, delo 9, ed. khr. 3, l. 126.

Nicholas II On 18 December 1896 Nicholas II received Martens, who wrote in his diary with pride "in a *special* audience" and in his office. The conversation lasted for about an hour and turned principally to "Turkish affairs". The Tsar said that Konstantin Petrovich Pobedonostsev had passed Martens' memorandum to him. He had not read it yet, but would do so immediately. From the conversation with the Tsar, Martens concluded that many ideas coincided. Of special interest to him were the following reflections of the Tsar: the straits between the Black and Mediterranean seas should belong either to Turkey or to Russia. The Black Sea should remain an internal sea. The Tsar "completely agreed" with Martens' view that Russia must protect the Turkish muslims and then the muslims of other countries, India, for example, would turn their eyes to Russia. The Tsar said that the German Emperor was operating at one with him in Asia and that Russia should go hand-in-hand with Germany and France. In his day Nicholas I had believed that he who possesses Constantinople, possesses the sea. But, in the words of Nicholas II, this is stupidity. What is the advantage to us from possessing Constantinople? He who possesses the Suez and Panama isthmuses commands the world. Martens considered "original and accurate" the Tsar's notion that it was essential to apply to the Black Sea straits the approach set out in the Monroe Doctrine of the United States. They also were in accord when discussing the status of Egypt (we recall the favourite plan of Martens concerning neutralisation of Egypt to counterbalance the Anglo-French condominium). In bidding farewell, the Tsar wished Martens success in the arbitration and mentioned "until a meeting in February", that is, after Martens had returned from abroad to Petersburg, and most importantly stated: "Give me your memoranda personally ...". Martens was "utterly delighted".[21] His "delight" with the new Tsar clearly prevented Martens from soberly evaluating his judgments. How, for example, could one proceed hand-in-hand with Germany and France given the implacable Franco-German antagonism?

---

[21] AVPR, opis 787, delo 9, ed. khr. 3, l. 129-130.

After Nicholas II had received Martens it evidently seemed that Martens had been transformed into the personal advisor of the Tsar. Soon he was convinced of the naivety and groundlessness of these hopes. But this happened later. All the same, Martens' weight and authority as an advisor not only on international law, but also foreign policy grew as a result of having been received by Pobedonostsev and the Tsar. He had received the opportunity to express his opinion while by-passing the Minister of Foreign Affairs and the Ministry in general.

On 1 January 1897 there followed an Edict of the Tsar appointing Count M. N. Murav'ev, envoy to Denmark and the youngest of Russian envoys, as head of the Ministry of Foreign Affairs. Martens met with him on the eve of this, in December, and spoke of his project to reorganise the Ministry of Foreign Affairs. Murav'ev agreed. However, after being appointed, doubts emerged. He said to Martens: "it would be possible to introduce peace and quiet in Europe sooner than in the Ministry".[22] Martens' hopes were finally dashed.

The arbitration of the Anglo-Dutch dispute in Brussels proceeded successfully in January 1897. The King of Belgium received him alone and extended other marks of attention. Martens also was able to meet with other legal colleagues who were acquaintances from the world of diplomacy.

Wilhelm II On the way home Martens arrived in Berlin on 25 January and was received there by Emperor Wilhelm II. The audience lasted 45 minutes and proved to be exceedingly interesting for Martens. He was charmed by the German Emperor. "The Emperor himself makes a charming impression ..." he wrote after the conversation. The Emperor's eyes are surprising, they penetrate through a person like x-rays. His head works intensely, and "one grandiose idea comes after another". Having spoken about Martens' arbitration in the Anglo-Dutch dispute and international arbitration in general, they turned to the President of the United States, William McKinley. Wilhelm II set out a "grandiose plan": the creation of an alliance of all the European powers against the United States in economics

[22] AVPR, opis 787, delo 9, ed. khr. 3, l. 133-134.

and trade. Through the charm of the Emperor's personality extended the realism of many years of experience as a diplomat and expert in international relations. Martens recalled the continental blockade of Napoleon I against England, which ended in failure. However, Wilhelm II's enthusiasm was not extinguished. He set out his scheme in greater detail and suggested that Martens work on it. The suggestion of His Majesty flattered Martens' self-esteem, but he decided to undertake nothing without Murav'ev. Evidently the "grandiose plan" seemed to him to be not merely utopian, but also too dangerous to recommend it as Russian foreign policy. In the course of the discussion Japan was touched upon, and Wilhelm II was convinced that a "Japanese-American alliance would be very dangerous for Russia". Martens did not object so as not to be "launched into the labyrinth of political combinations", although inwardly he was sceptical of the arguments of his interlocutor. He only came to the conclusion that Wilhelm II "very much wanted to obtain a port in the Far East". Having promised the Tsar to submit a memorandum on the straits and on Russian policy in general towards Turkey, Martens formed the view that if one supported the aspirations of Wilhelm II in the Far East and America one could count on his assistance to Russia in Turkish matters. From the conversation with the German Emperor, Martens went away with the impression of him as a "very interesting, intelligent, lively and gifted individual".

Martens the diplomat understood that Wilhelm II, in disclosing his plans, counted upon him to inform his fellow crowned head in Petersburg. Therefore he informed Count Osten-Sacken, the Russian ambassador in Berlin, about them. The ambassador convinced him to draw up a memorandum regarding the conversation for the Tsar. Martens did not dispute this, but did not alter his own decision and did not draw up the memorandum. He merely related the conversation with the German Emperor to Murav'ev upon returning to Petersburg on 27 January. The Minister shared the scepticism of his counsellor and noted that let Wilhelm II himself set out his ideas and then he would pass them on to Martens for comments. To cover himself Murav'ev reported to Nicholas II and received approval.[23]

In informing the Minister about the conversation with Wilhelm II, Martens said to him that he had drawn up a memorandum for the Sovereign and requested to hand over the memorandum personally. Martens even passed a fair copy of the Memorandum to the Minister to be handed to the Tsar. He added that the next memorandum would be devoted to the straits. According to Martens' diary, Murav'ev "was surprised and requested to be informed".[24]

M. N. Murav'ev and V. N. Lamzdorf

One can only be astonished at the naivety of Martens. Did he imagine that Murav'ev would be delighted by the news he had heard? A subordinate of the Minister without his knowledge gives foreign policy advice to the Tsar! Murav'ev, naturally, could not prohibit Martens from fulfilling the wish of the Sovereign, nor could he even allude to such and in all likelihood reacted with the greatest courtesy. But the Minister was distressed, and his attitude towards Martens had clearly not improved, which the last was soon to feel. In Martens' diary there is an entry that Murav'ev and Lamzdorf concealed their plans from him and he expressed the apprehension that "Murav'ev would play dirty tricks on him with the Sovereign".[25] In reality the greatest foreign policy initiative of Russia in 1898 – the convocation of a disarmament conference – fell on Martens like "snow on his head".

When on 5 February Martens came to Nicholas II, the courtesy of the reception dispersed the apprehensions. Martens related the conversations with Wilhelm II and evidently expected instructions to write down the plans of the Kaiser. But the Tsar said that at the wish of the German Emperor this could be forgotten. Martens was distressed by his indifference and submitted the memorandum on the straits. It transpired that they both favoured occupation of the Dardanelles. But when?

---

[23] AVPR, opis 787, delo 9, ed. khr. 3, l. 136-138.
[24] AVPR, opis 787, delo 9, ed. khr. 3, l. 138-139.
[25] AVPR, opis 787, delo 9, ed. khr. 3, l. 141.

From the straits the conversation moved to the reforms being conducted in Turkey, and Martens offered to write a memorandum on the Turkish reforms. The Tsar replied: "I would be grateful". The conversation proved to be more restrained and briefer (about 20 minutes) than the previous one. But the instruction for the new memorandum was given formally, and Martens told this to Murav'ev the following day. The Minister was "not very satisfied" by the new instruction and began to prove that one should never write the memorandum on the reforms in Turkey since "this is a very confusing question". Martens, for his part, proved that the memorandum could be written. Since the instruction of the Tsar remained, Martens was not stopped by the objections of the Minister and drew up the memorandum. Inside he boiled: Murav'ev's "thoughtlessness and self-confidence were unlimited".

Ultimately the Minister held sway. When on 23 March 1897 Martens went to him, Murav'ev met Martens with the ill-starred memorandum in his hands. The Tsar had passed it to Murav'ev for report. Moreover, it turned out that neither the Tsar nor the Minister had been able to read it.[26] There were no consequences, and no information has been preserved in Martens' documents, as the author concerned, as to whether his memorandum on the Turkish reforms was read anywhere at all.

"What talentless people surround the Sovereign!", Martens lamented in his intimate diary. He shared these reflections with Pobedonostsev. The last concurred with him, but added that he himself could do nothing.[27] Nicholas II had become increasingly autonomous, new people had been added to his circle, and only certain external indicia remained of Pobedosnostsev's previous influence on State affairs.

Martens' attempt to become a personal counsellor of the Tsar with regard to foreign policy questions ended lamentably. To be sure, he retained access to Nicholas II and used it thereafter. He played the role as advisor in the Ministry of Foreign Affairs more successfully. In March 1897 at Murav'ev's

[26] AVPR, opis 787, delo 9, ed. khr. 3, l. 141-143.

[27] AVPR, opis 787, delo 9, ed. khr. 3, l. 146.

request he wrote a memorandum on an urgent issue of the day – a regime of autonomy for the Island of Crete. The memorandum received the approval of the Minister, and the Tsar, in Pobedonostsev's words, even said that the powers evidently had come to share Martens' idea about the election of a Greek prince as the Cretan prince.[28] True, in April war commenced between Greece and Turkey and the situation sharply changed. Russia, in the spirit of Martens' memorandum, favoured the appointment of a governor-general of Crete, the son of the King of Greece. This appointment ultimately transpired despite the resistance of Germany and Austro-Hungary.

It is appropriate to observe here that the office of a member of the Council of the Ministry of Foreign Affairs had long failed to satisfy Martens by reason of its insignificance, and he dreamed of an appointment as a senior counsellor of the Ministry who represented the Ministry of Foreign Affairs on the State Council, the Committee of Ministers, and the Ruling Senate and who by his status followed immediately after the deputy minister. It should be said at once that Martens did not wish to exchange a university chair for an office in the Ministry of Foreign Affairs. He wished to combine things difficult to combine: the academic freedom of a scholar and the duties of a ministerial bureaucrat. Martens turned to Lobanov-Rostovskii with his wishes. The last reacted favourably, but soon died. Martens renewed the conversation with the new minister in early 1897, and Murav'ev did not refuse. He merely requested that Martens wait: by the spring of that year he would reorganise the Ministry of Foreign Affairs and then he would arrange everything. However, in April the edict appeared which appointed Prince Obolenskii, a friend of Lamzdorf, as the senior counsellor, and Lamzdorf gathered increasing power in the Ministry. It remained for Martens merely to complain that he "again had been duped".[29]

Having failed with the office of senior counsellor, Martens in early 1898 petitioned Murav'ev and Lamzdorf to appoint him as envoy to the capital of one of the smaller European States –

[28] AVPR, opis 787, delo 9, ed. khr. 3, l. 145.

[29] AVPR, opis 787, delo 9, ed. khr. 4, l. 2.

Bern, The Hague, or Brussels. It seemed to him there were more than sufficient grounds for such an appointment. We recall not only his conversations with Nicholas II, but also his election as umpire in the Anglo-Dutch dispute and successful representation at many international conferences, including in Brussels and The Hague. Both leaders reacted sympathetically to Martens' petition. Lamzdorf even said to him that "the question in principle has been decided".[30]

The approved Martens began to perform counsellor functions. In early 1898 he draw up a memorandum on Cyprus, which was circulated as the correct orientation to all embassies and missions of Russia. In March Lamzdorf asked Martens: how should a court and the administration of Port Arthur, newly occupied by Russia, be structured. Martens sat down and drew up his own scheme. The scheme was unsatisfactory to Vitte, who sent a "rather irate letter" to Murav'ev, but Martens, referring to the actions of England in Cyprus and of Austria-Hungary in Bosnia and Herzogovina, recommended that Port Arthur be taken under "administration". He also objected to the creation of porto-franco in Talienvan together with Port Arthur. At Lamzdorf's request, in May 1898 Martens submitted two draft declarations in connection with the Spanish American War between the United States and Spain. The American forces had occupied Puerto Rico in this war, Santiago in Cuba, and Manila in the Philippines. Both of Martens' drafts were restrained in the spirit of Russian neutrality. The provisions of the drafts comprised the basis of the statement of the Russian Government. In addition to the drafts Martens wrote a letter to Lamzdorf in which he recommended to preserve during the war the "most friendly attitude" towards the United States. Martens proposed, in particular, this variant: displaying its self-confidence, Spain cedes Cuba to Russia, which then transfers it to the United States.

In May-June 1898 Martens visited Constantinople. He brought away from there the Order of Medzhlis, first degree, presented by the Sultan and a Memorandum on Contemporary Turkey. In the Memorandum, handed to Lamzdorf, Martens drew

[30] AVPR, opis 787, delo 9, ed. khr. 4, l. 10-11.

special attention to the "peaceful conquest" of the country by Wilhelm II. As regards the Order, Lamzdorf obtained the authorisation of the Tsar to accept it, but the memorandum to him, as Martens observed, "did not especially please him". Also displeasing to Lamzdorf was the reaction of Martens to a memorandum relative to the preparation of the Consular Statute by Osten-Sacken. Martens again was indignant: he was the author of the sole work on consular jurisdiction in the East, his proposal for the consular service of the Ministry of Foreign Affairs lay without movement since 1887, and in Western Europe he was considered the greatest specialist on this question, but the bureaucrats of his own Ministry ignored him and do not read his book![31]

In March 1898 Martens managed to be present at a reception of Nicholas II. The pretext was to bring to the Tsar the just-published volume XII of the *Recueil des traités*. Martens came without a memorandum but was able to set out to the Tsar his view on the situation confronting China, which at the time was the centre of world politics. Martens said that already by virtue of her geographic position Russia played the dominant role in Asia and "by its rash actions" in China (having in view the occupation of Port Arthur by Russian troops) she had merely drawn the other European powers into territorial matters. Consent to the seizure of Kiao-Chao in China by Germany was a mistake. Now England, Germany, and Russia had their own possessions in Peking. In this area Martens was convinced that "conflict is completely inevitable". If Germany, England, and Japan were to unite, then "our Port Arthur would fall".[32]

Martens set out his reflections to Nicholas II, although not so sharply and concisely as he had entered them in his diary. Evidently he used more streamlined and more courtly expressions. However, they did not alter the essence of the matter: Martens actually criticised the entire policy of territorial expansion in the Far East. He prophesied its failure ("our Port Arthur would fall")! It is doubtful that such criticism would be

[31] AVPR, opis 787, delo 9, ed. khr. 4, l. 34-49.
[32] AVPR, opis 787, delo 9, ed. khr. 4, l. 34.

welcome to the Tsar, who had approved the colonial plans in the region, including at the expense of the territory of China. It is remarkable that Martens wrote nothing about the reaction of the Tsar to his reflections. His Majesty's gratitude and other compliments this time evidently did not follow. The counsellor found no understanding in the monarch and the policy of expansion in China continued, leading to war with Japan and defeat in that war.

In Autumn 1898 the Russian proposal to convoke an international conference on disarmament was piled on Martens. His hour to star had come. His mission as counsellor Martens, as noted above, had been performed brilliantly. The activities at the 1899 First Hague Conference brought him world renown.

The successful 1899 Conference had strengthened in Martens the wish to go to The Hague as envoy. However, it soon collapsed, as had his previous wish to be a senior counsellor of the Ministry of Foreign Affairs. First Murav'ev "deceived" him, and he "was duped". The new Minister, Count Lamzdorf, reassured Martens, and the delay with the appointment was explained by the fact that the envoy then in The Hague was supported by Grand Prince Vladimir Aleksandrovich, and other similar reasons. To demonstrate his nonimplication in the delay, Lamzdorf proposed that Martens write a personal letter to the Tsar. On Martens' letter Nicholas II placed the resolution "Appoint Charykov". Martens asked Lamzdorf to explain the reasons for the refusal, and he – in addition to the official version that Martens was more needed in Petersburg – expressed the supposition that the Tsar evidently believed that Martens was an "anglophile". There is "my reward for 37 years of service in the Ministry of Foreign Affairs", agonised Martens, and summing up, wrote: "Count Lamzdorf deceived me utterly".[33]

Leaping forward, it should be said that Martens' third hope also was destroyed – to become a member of the State Council.[34]

---

[33] AVPR, opis 787, delo 9, ed. khr. 6, l. 16-17.

[34] The State Council had been created by Tsar Alexander I in 1810 as the highest consultative organ of the Empire. The Council was engaged with domestic matters, especially the consideration of draft laws. Members of the

At the outset of 1905 Martens wrote in his diary: now they constantly appoint "rogues and scoundrels" to the State Council, and not "orderly people with convictions".[35] Martens all the same continued to try. Taking advantage of a request by Vitte to write an opinion for foreign bankers about a loan, Martens requested support for his candidacy. He also asked the Minister of Finance, Kakovtsev, to whom he brought his opinion, and the Chairman of the State Council, E. V. Frish. All promised, but when at Easter 1906 the newspapers printed the list of newly-appointed members of the State Council, the name of Martens was not included. Martens guessed that this was the intrigue of Lamzdorf and soon received confirmation of his guess. However, a fact remains a fact – he did not join the State Council. In Martens' view, the reason was that they considered him to be "too liberal" for such a senior institution.[36]

Why did Martens despite his service and talents not receive a post higher than a member of the Council of the Ministry of Foreign Affairs? Posts which enabled merely to include him in delegations, travel abroad on business, and send him to various interdepartmental commissions?

Martens himself considered his "liberal views" to be at fault and the machinations of various highly-placed officials, especially Ministers Murav'ev and Lamzdorf. A special chapter was devoted above to the socio-political views of Martens, and in this connection one may merely confirm that in his official memoranda and in his public utterances Martens displayed independence of judgment which frequently was not to the taste of the senior leadership. He strengthened his arguments with references to international law, against which nothing could be expressed. Recalling his numerous protests against impingements on his rights, for example, not sending him to the Berlin Conference of 1889-90, not appointing him as head of the Russian delegation to the 1899 Hague Peace Conference, and

cont'd
Council were experienced, often retired, public officials. In 1905 there were eminent jurists on the Council (A. F. Koni, N. S. Tagantsev, and others).

[35] AVPR, opis 787, delo 9, ed. khr. 6, l. 5.

[36] AVPR, opis 787, delo 9, ed. khr. 6, l. 107, 112.

the like, his obstinacy also should be added to those qualities which caused dissatisfaction in the leadership. His attempt, in by-passing the minister, to become the personal counsellor of the Tsar, did not commend him to Murav'ev and Lamzdorf. As regards the support of Pobedonostsev, then under Nicholas II, his significance had quickly declined to nothing.

Martens was right when he wrote about the intrigues of those who did not wish him well. But there remains one, and in this writer's view, the most important, reason for the dashing of all hopes for a diplomatic career: the class-reservedness of the corps of Russian diplomats and reception of Martens in the upper strata of Petersburg as an alien body. In society Martens was first and foremost a "professor", and this concept in Russia of those days had a completely different resonance than now. In the modern world, where science and technology are inseparable from the progress and well-being of society, a university professor enjoys respect and authority. In Russia of the nobility, the intelligentsia was viewed with suspicion and condescension. In Western Europe of those years the appointment of "Professor Martens" to the Russian delegation was perceived as the aspiration of the Tsarist Government to impart additional weight to the delegation. In aristocratic Petersburg news about the appointment of a "professor" to a delegation could give rise only to ridicule, and Martens had protested to the Minister when in an official communique he was called only a professor and not a member of the Council of the Ministry of Foreign Affairs (he had no post more significant). The difference in social atmosphere determined to a great extent the difference in attitude towards Martens in Europe and Russia. In Europe they placed him together with the outstanding scholars, diplomats, and publicists, and this placed him high. In Russia the world of officials viewed him as a useful specialist whom they used as needed and of which they forgot immediately afterward.

Martens justly supposed that he would cope better than Count Kapnist with the representation of Russia at the Berlin Conference on Africa, that better than de Staal he could preside at the 1899 Hague Conference, that he knew more and was more experienced than Prince Obolenskii, that he had greater knowledge and understanding of international life than did Charykov, and the like. But he was a Russian intellectual not of gentle birth and a professor, whereas his competitors belonged to the upper strata of the nobility and often to the most ancient families. Georg Georgievich (Egor Egorovich) de Staal came from an ancient family of Baltic barons. Obolenskii, held in contempt by Martens, was Prince Obolenskii-Nelidinskii-Maletskii, and his ministerial career was combined with a palace career. Even Bazili, who vexed Martens at the 1899 Hague Conference and then was appointed instead of him as senior counsellor (Obolenskii became a deputy minister), was reliably protected by a noble origin and palace office. At Easter 1901 by Imperial Edict Alexander Bazili, Senior Counsellor of the Ministry of Foreign Affairs with the rank of chamberlain, was appointed to the Ruling Senate and became Steward of the Household of the Court of His Imperial Majesty while retaining his previous office.[37] Martens was far removed from this world. At first he evidently did not understand he was an outcast and was worried and indignant when they passed him over. As years passed the indignation turned into hopeless despondency, although attempts to take a post worthy of his knowledge and experience did not cease until his death.

Russia and China In the 1900s Martens as a counsellor became more engaged with the Far East. An example is his memorandum drawn up in August 1900 in connection with the so-called "Boxer Rebellion" in China (published in 1927).[38]

The uprising in China commenced in May 1900 and was anti-imperialist in character. It was led by a secret society previously called: "a fist in the name of peace and justness". The formulation gave occasion to the Western European and American press to christen it the "Boxer Rebellion". The ideology of the rebels, mostly peasants, was based to a great extent on traditional concepts of the feudal epoch. The principal slogan of

[37] AVPR, opis 749/2, delo 9, l. 21.

[38] *Красный архив*, I(20)(1927).

the rebels was "death to foreigners!" On 20 June the German envoy was murdered on a street in Peking. The foreign powers concentrated their warships in the mouth of the Bei-he River and landed two thousand marines. In response the Government of the Ching Dynasty declared war. England, Germany, Russia, the United States, France, and Japan expanded preparations to land an expeditionary corps.

The solidarity of the powers in the cause of putting down the rebellion did not eliminate the contradictions among them. Their interests with respect to China diverged significantly. In this situation the Tsarist Government found it necessary to determine its long-term policy in the region. Martens' memorandum was devoted to this issue.

In contrast to the noisy propagandistic campaign conducted in the European and American press, Martens saw the true cause of the rebellion in the "unscrupulous exploitation of the Chinese on the part of the Europeans". Germany, for example, for the massacre of two missionaries seized the Shandul peninsula; England, who had concentrated in its hands two-thirds of all the trade with China, received 12 million pounds sterling annually from the sale of opium. As Martens remarked, "with respect to this State, everything is considered to be permissible". Martens cautioned against underestimating the movement. "The present rebellion or uprising is a people's war of the Chinese in which the Peking Government is forced to take the side of the people". He wrote that the "final victory of the European armies over the Chinese forces is not subject to doubt," but this victory will not eliminate the "internal reasons for the present mess in China".[39] He drew the following conclusions: "Thus, so long as the European powers do not change the nature of their actions with respect to China, so long as opium is a legal means for inculcating in the Chinese the elevated ideals of European civilisation, and the propaganda of Christian religion is the most convenient means for subverting the foundations of the Chinese State, and, finally, so long as the inviolability of Chinese territory and supreme power is not obligatory for European States and the United States,

[39] Ibid., pp. 177-180.

there will be no peace in China and new uprisings and wars against the Chinese will be completely inevitable".[40] These realistic and sagacious conclusions do honour to Martens.

As regards the position of Russia with respect to China, Martens stressed the distinction between Russian interests and the interests of other powers. "For the last China is a colony which it is necessary to exploit by all means. For Russia, China is a great neighbouring State which has the right to an autonomous life". In accordance with this position of principle Martens suggested to oppose the division of China and to urgently put forward an initiative of the signature of an act by the great powers "in affirmation of the inviolability of Chinese territory and a renunciation of any territorial acquisitions". In the event of objections by England and Germany, Martens advised the occupation of Manchuria.

Regarding "material remuneration" for the damage caused to foreign States, Martens pointed to the disarray of Chinese finances and recommended to avoid a situation under which each foreign State itself would present its demands to the Chinese Government. He was especially worried about the speech of Emperor Wilhelm II, which was permeated by "a spirit of merciless revenge and un-Christian enmity". Martens suggested transferring the question of determining the amount of contributory compensation for each power to the consideration of the arbitration court in The Hague.[41]

Martens' memorandum was the basis of a démarche by Lamzdorf undertaken on 25 August 1900. The Minister of Foreign Affairs charged Russian ambassadors to communicate to the governments of foreign powers that Russia had introduced forces into Manchuria only in order to assist the Chinese Government. As soon as the disorders ceased, Russian forces would leave China, "if, however, this is not an obstacle to the form of actions of the other powers". Martens felt satisfaction from the fact that his memorandum had become the document which determined the foreign policy of Russia on this issue. He

---

[40] Ibid., p. 185.
[41] Ibid., pp. 184-185.

merely was offended that Lamzdorf, having received the memorandum, circulated it as a circular "but without a word about me". He suspected that the Count did not even name the author of the memorandum to the Tsar.[42]

Martens and Russian Diplomacy

In concluding this chapter about the role of Martens as a counsellor of monarchs and ministers it is appropriate to raise the question: what influence did he exert on Russian foreign policy?

For all of his authority and services, Martens can not be included among the State public figures of Russia. He was not among those persons who under Alexander III and Nicholas II determined the foreign policy of the Empire in a particular region or on a particular question. In this respect even the newspaper owner Katkov possessed greater influence than he, not to mention Rasputin.

It should be noted that Martens' advice was far from always sufficiently realised by Russian diplomacy. Frequently the advice proved to be impossible to implement. We recall the idea of the neutralisation of Egypt. England did not cede control over this country, and English dominance continued there for many decades. Martens opposed the expansion of Russia in Central Asia, but his voice was not heard. Together with the Minister of Foreign Affairs, Giers, Martens long supported a strengthening of the alliance with Germany and was subjected to attack by Katkov for this. But Giers, and Martens with him, lost the campaign against Katkov, and the State ship of Russia sailed towards rapprochement with France and England. In 1900 the Russian Government was guided, it seemed, by a programme set out by Martens in his secret memorandum. It proclaimed a course for the preservation of the territorial integrity of China and cooperation with the Chinese monarchy. Martens, however, was justly indignant about the conditions by which China was bound by foreign States, including Russia, in the final protocol. Above all, there was placed on China, which had paid off only six years ago, after the war of 1895-96, the enormous contribution of

---

[42] AVPR, opis 787, delo 9, ed. khr. 5, l. 99-100.

Japan, compensation in the amount of about 600 million Russian rubles at the time. In so doing the protocol made provision for specific items of State revenues, which additionally tied the hands of the Peking Government. China, including the Imperial House, was subjected to grave humiliation: a number of State officials were punished, exculpatory monuments were erected to the European diplomats who had perished, and the like. In Peking the quarter occupied by foreign missions was placed under the protection of foreign armed forces. It was prohibited for Chinese to live in the quarter.

Martens, assessing the protocol, wrote in his diary: "In this act there is not one condition which would be acceptable to the Chinese without the strongest protest. If they sign, they will violate it at the first opportunity". He saw in the protocol a manifestation of the lack of ability of the son of Giers, a Russian envoy. To place monuments at the sites of the murder of Christians, to maintain garrisons in embassies? What significance did all this have for establishing peace and good-neighbourliness with China?[43]

Martens proceeded from respect for the sovereignty of China. But Nicholas II had fallen into the hands of groupings who interrupted even the evacuation of Russian forces from Manchuria promised in the démarche of Lamzdorf. The Tsar was pushed towards further expansion, in particular, by the palace clique of adventurists headed by Bezobrazov, who arranged his doubtful affairs with treasury money. The Bezobrazov group, for example, acquired a forest concession in the basin of the Yalu River which extended for 800 kilometres along the Chinese-Korean and Chinese-Korean frontier. Under the pretext of a forest guard on the territory of the concession soldiers began to be introduced. All this intensified the anger against Russia, especially in Japan. As Martens noted in his diary, "in China outrages and a stupid policy".[44] Back in 1898 Martens had warned Nicholas II at an audience about the dangers of territorial expansion in China. He prophetically said that the

[43] AVPR, opis 787, delo 9, ed. khr. 5, l. 110-111.
[44] AVPR, opis 787, delo 9, ed. khr. 5, l. 127.

acquisition by Germany, England, Japan, Russia, and certain other powers of their own zones in China inevitably would lead to a conflict among them. He spoke of the possibility of an anti-Russian coalition, and then "we would lose our Port Arthur". But the Tsar followed Bezobrazov, and the Minister of Internal Affairs, Phleve, who reckoned to cope with the revolutionary ferment in the Empire with the assistance of a small victorious war. Russia moved on to war with Japan, and the voice of counsellor Martens (and likewise of Vitte, Lamzdorf, and certain others) was drowned out by other more powerful sounds.

At the same time the abundance of Martens' advice which went into the fabric of Russian foreign policy is astonishing. The 1874 draft convention on the laws and customs of land warfare for the Brussels Conference, the proposals for the Berlin Conference on Africa, the proposal relating to Crete, the draft declaration of Russia in connection with the Spanish-American War, the programme for the 1899 Hague Peace Conference, the circular note of the Russian Ministry of Foreign Affairs relating to China of August 1900, and the like. Martens advised the King of Belgium, Leopold II, with regard to the Congo, objected to the scheme of Wilhelm II relating to the creation of an economic bloc against the United States, and others.

Martens had worked out the draft consular statute for the Ministry of Foreign Affairs and a plan for reforming the Ministry itself. He did not live to see the effectuation of his plans, but they had their influence. The reform of the Ministry did not occur until 1914, but the reforms contained features which Martens had proposed to Lobanov-Rostovskii and Murav'ev. The autonomy of the Asian Department was eliminated and all foreign policy affairs were transferred to regional administrations; the chancellery returned to its functions; and, especially dear to Martens, a special legal section was created. To be sure, the Council of the Ministry of Foreign Affairs was not given an active life, being occupied basically with diplomatic examinations.

Searches in the Archive of Foreign Policy of Russia enabled only some of Martens' memorandums to be discovered, but they give an unexpectedly rich and virtually unknown picture of his activity as a counsellor on foreign policy issues. The memoranda reflect the activeness and vast range of their author: the United States and the Balkans, Turkey and Egypt, China and Afghanistan, the Berlin and Hague conferences, and the like. The contribution of Martens to the formation of Russian foreign policy turns out to be no less than that of many ambassadors and envoys and executive officials of the Ministry of Foreign Affairs. Concealed from the public, the advisory activities of Martens advance him to the ranks of eminent diplomats of Russia at the time. The time has come to remove this aspect of the activity of an outstanding jurist from the shadow of oblivion.

CHAPTER IX
SOCIO-POLITICAL VIEWS OF MARTENS

After graduating from University in 1868 and until his death in 1909 the socio-political views of Martens underwent significant evolution. Of great significance was the fact that many concepts of which in his youth he had knowledge from books (the Tsar, the Autocracy, the Ministry of Foreign Affairs, an embassy, an international conference, and the like) in the course of time were augmented by specific, personally felt, content. Meetings with Tsar Nicholas II or Kaiser Wilhelm II, joint work with the most eminent jurists of the world, participation in conferences, and decades of work in the Ministry of Foreign Affairs enabled him to know real life at close hand and give it adequate due.

In addition, the material and social position of Martens himself had changed substantially. The young docent had been transformed into a venerable professor with a world reputation, a privy councillor awarded many Russian and foreign orders; the debutant at the 1874 Brussels Conference had become a central figure of the 1899 Hague Conference. The complex and for a time contradictory process of the development of Martens' socio-political views had naturally been under the strong influence of the surrounding world. He learned to view it critically, soberly analysing it, but remained part of that world, being part of the Russian Ministry of Foreign Affairs, Tsarist Petersburg, the Russian science of international law, and finally one of the bearers of Russian social thought of the day.

Three factors exerted a strong influence on the formation of Martens' worldview. First was a passionate devotion to the science of international law, which accompanied him until his death. The second factor was his patriotism, his love for Russia. The third factor was constant communion with Western Europe and to a certain extent with the United States of America. Martens saw himself and his scholarly, diplomatic, and publicist activity exclusively within the framework of European culture.

Russia for him belonged among the civilised States, the civilised nature of which had roots in Europe, in European culture.

These must constantly be borne in mind when one speaks of any specific position of Martens. They help us to understand more profoundly the reasons for many of his actions.

Martens' life path began at the very bottom of the social ladder. Climbing up that ladder, step by step, was achieved mostly by persistent labour. Gradually the labour become more qualified, less oppressive, but he continued until the end of his life. The creative character of many types of the work assisted immensely. Martens loved to engage in scholarly analysis of the science of international law in general, loved historical investigations, archival searches, loved to create, to enlarge, the power of his intellect. In this respect he was a true member of the intelligentsia, and he carried an undwindling respect for intellectual labour throughout his life.

His attitude towards labour singled out Martens against the background of the traditions of the nobility and imparted to his figure, even dressed in a cloak and covered with orders, an undoubtedly democratic coloration. When at a reception of the Tsar he arrived with the ribbon of the order not on his shoulder, as it should have been, he, treating this as a curiosity, a petty amusing incident, did not share the panic-stricken reaction which seized certain of the officials present at the reception in view of the breach of the established rules. And when he did not turn out in short trousers specially prescribed for lunch with the King of England, he accepted this as a regrettable inconvenience, and the permission to appear in ordinary dress, with a certain ironic satisfaction.

Martens was a honest toiler, and he remained alien to the world of highly-placed embezzlers of the treasury and the dark deeds connected with them. He also did not know the world of large estate and factory owners. He did not move in the Petersburg world or "demi-world". His diaries are full of anxieties about the abuses and machinations which became known to him.

Official careers obliged for their success to birth or secular contacts frequently distressed him. There were the sons of

Minister Giers: the eldest, Nikolai "a complete dimwit"; the youngest, Mikhail, "a good man, still a youth who has not completed a course of study, completely uneducated". However, they both, "thanks to their better father," successfully made a career in the Ministry of Foreign Affairs.

It is instructive that in his diary entries Martens, when describing a person, did not write about his origin or affiliation to an estate. He valued most of all in people intelligence, order, competence, good-faith fulfilment of employment duties. Nikolai Karlovich Giers, for example, won him over by all this. He noted with respect the rebuff of the Minister to various intrigues of the "palace clique" and his correctness in relations with people.

When rumours reached him about those enormous amounts which the Tsarist officials received or stole from the State treasury, he lamented with indignation: "poor Russia!"

However, one must not fail to see that the situation in which he lived left its imprint. In February 1883 he learned about the appointment of A. D. Mal'tikov as envoy to Persia and was indignant: "My God, a shopkeeper an envoy! What have we come to!"[1] In an indignant comment the voice of the nobility also is heard, dissatisfied by the intrusion into diplomacy – his own preserve – of a merchant from the Gostinnyi Dvor in Petersburg. Having learned about the appointment of S. Iu. Vitte as minister, Martens did not refrain from repeating the gloating commentary which came from the circles of bureaucrats: "a former postmaster" has become a minister! In 1905 Martens accompanied Vitte to the United States for the negotiations with Japan. He already had changed his opinion about Vitte and had great respect for him. But he clearly was disturbed that a Tsarist Minister "shakes the hand of any worker" and "bows left and right", and the like.[2]

Wishing to underscore his status and services to Count Lamzdorf, in June 1905 he appeared before him in the full dress of a privy councillor with all of his orders. And they were many: St. Alexander Nevskii, St. Vladimir, St. Anna. To the

---

[1] AVPR, op. 787, delo 9, ed. khr. 1, l. 7.

[2] AVPR, op. 787, delo 9, ed. khr. 2, l. 31; ed. khr. 6, l. 34.

Russian awards were added foreign ones: the Saviour of Greece, 1st degree; the Turkish Medzhid, 1st degree, and others. The Count himself, accustomed to every possible ceremony with protocol dress, was surprised at the solemn appearance of Martens.[3]

In Russia of that day the belles-lettres played a large role in the formation of public consciousness. Tolstoi and Chekhov, A. I. Kuprin, and Maxim Gorky, other writers, poets, dramatists were dominant influences on the intelligentsia and a significant part of the student youth.

It is exceedingly difficult now to judge this aspect of the spiritual life of Martens. In scholarly and publicist works he never had recourse to the belles-lettres. It is difficult to say whether he read those novels, verses, and tales which moved Russian society, whether he went to the theatre or to musical concerts. His intensive work in his own speciality hardly left time for this. All of the diary entries have preserved only indirect evidence. On 27 September 1887 Martens entered his impressions of the burial of the "greatest Russian writer", Ivan Turgenev. According to his observations, never had Petersburg seen such a solemn event in which the "Government took not the slightest part". With clear disapproval he wrote that officers were given a strict order not to participate in the burial.[4]

Individual allusions enable one to guess that Martens read Saltykov-Shchedrin and his journal, *Отечественные записки* [Fatherland Notes]. Thus, he wrote about the "hack writers of the villainous *Новое время* [New Times]", and called the newspaper itself a "cesspit". But this is what the great satirist himself called the *Новое время* [New Times].[5] Martens recalled Maxim Gorky with respect and was disturbed about his arrest.[6]

It is remarkable that his diary, begun on 5 January 1883, opens with lines from the great English post, Lord Byron.

---

[3] AVPR, op. 787, delo 9, ed. khr. 6, l. 25.

[4] AVPR, op. 787, delo 9, ed. khr. 1, l. 9-10.

[5] See M. E. Saltykov-Shchedrin, *Собрание сочинений* [Collection of Works], VII, p. 440.

[6] See AVPR, op. 787, delo 9, ed. khr. 6, l. 3.

Evidently a poetic bent noted even in the gymnasium did not leave him for a long time.

The international preoccupations of Martens left little place for addresses on domestic political affairs, but all the same the various utterances together suffice to show that he was not to be numbered among the proponents of retaining the socio-political orders which existed in Russia. In the treatise on international law he compared the absence of the right to withdraw from being a Russian subject with being attached to the land, in other words, with serfdom. In Autumn 1883 an article by Martens appeared in the journal *Вестник Европы* [Herald of Europe] in which he allowed himself to express the view that education and culture, and not extensive territory and an army of millions, constitute the power of a modern State. For this he also received abuse in the Katkovs *Санкт-Петербургские Ведомости* [St. Petersburg Gazette]. In early 1887 Martens as a specialist on international law opposed a draft law on granting to the Minister of Justice the right to have closed judicial sessions, which displeased Pobedonostsev and angered the Tsar. *Новое время* [New Times] called him an "ill-starred jurist". Despite this, in March 1887 Martens opposed a draft law to introduce a tax on foreign passports (10 rubles per month, 360 rubles per year).[7] There are other examples which testify to the liberality of Martens' views. His remarks originated in his scholarly conceptions, and he had the courage to uphold them even if they did not coincide with fashionable trends. He, for example, was an opponent of abolishing the death penalty in Russia and was disapproving of the speech in 1906 on this question in the State Council of his friend and noted specialist on criminal law, N. P. Tagantsev.[8]

Jurist and Tsar Just as many in Russia, Martens believed that all misfortunes and sufferings emanated not from the autocracy, but from "evil advisors" who concealed the "truth" from the Tsar. Especially during the reign of Tsar Nicholas II, which commenced in 1894, his diary abounds with

[7] AVPR, op. 787, delo 9, ed. khr. 1, l. 73.
[8] AVPR, op. 787, delo 9, ed. khr. 6, l. 117.

such entries: "The young Sovereign was very gentle and unpretentious in manner but is surrounded by almost exclusively rogues, courtiers who fawn upon him and cheat him" (1900); the Sovereign is not at fault, having such "ungifted and base advisors as Count Lamzdorf, Alekseev,[9] Bezobrazov,[10] and the like" (1905); "Poor, poor Russia! In whose hands is thy fate!" (1908).[11] In conversations with the Tsar and in memoranda for him Martens endeavoured to speak the "truth" – on the policy of Russia in Central Asia, in the Balkans, in the Far East, and the like. He died with unshakeable Tsarist views.

At the same time, his attitude towards the specific bearer of Tsarist power underwent a significant evolution. The diaries offer rich material of this.

Martens was nurtured in a school and in a university in the spirit of the official formula "autocracy, orthodoxy, and national character", and initially the figure of the Russian Autocrat was for him, undoubtedly, surrounded by a halo of the supernatural.

As a youth in February 1861 he saw how Alexander II, the Tsar-Liberator, left the Winter Palace and the crowd which had gathered fell on their knees. The events of those days were deeply etched in the memory, and Martens recalled them with "gratitude" forty years later.[12]

However, communion with living tsars and coming into contact with autocratic procedures gradually dissipated the halo. He did not meet Alexander II, but he was able to make a close acquaintance of Alexander III.

In early 1887 Martens, having regard to the international obligations of Russia, opposed in the State Council closed judicial sessions. The powerful ober-procurator of the Holy Synod and tutor of the tsar, Pobedonostsev "was in a rage", and Giers

[9] The reference is to E. I. Alekseev, Governor-General of the Tsar in the Far East.

[10] The reference is to A. M. Bezobrazov, Secretary of State of Nicholas II from 1903-05 and head of a group of highly-placed adventurists who pushed the Tsar towards territorial annexations in the Far East.

[11] AVPR, op. 787, delo 9, ed. khr. 6, l. 80.

[12] AVPR, op. 787, delo 9, ed. khr. 5, l. 126.

immediately received from Alexander III an instruction to "give Martens a good dressing down". Martens was stunned, for he had not expected "such an effect" from his fervour for the good of Russia.[13]

In February 1892 Martens was present at the annual session of the Russian Imperial Historical Society, as was the Tsar, the patron of the Society. During the two-hour session Alexander III did not utter a word, and Martens wrote: "He makes an impression of an underdeveloped and entirely uninterested youth". A very unflattering assessment of the Russian Autocrat! Subsequently Martens gave a more considered description of his rule, especially in the domain of foreign policy. For this he needed to be acquainted with the successor of Alexander III, Emperor Nicholas II.

Nicholas II succeeded his late father in Autumn 1894. In April 1895 Martens was presented for the first time to the new Tsar, in September conversed briefly with him, and in December 1896 upon the recommendation of Pobedonostsev a detailed conversation occurred on an extensive range of foreign policy problems. Martens was "completely charmed" by the young Tsar.

Martens in February 1897 against visited the office of Nicholas II. The conversation was briefer, with elements of the Tsar's indifference to Martens' opinions. But all the same he juxtaposed the Tsar to the "thoughtless" Minister Murav'ev and wrote: "Excellent that the Tsar so firmly and soberly looks after affairs".[14]

In early 1898 there was yet another audience with Nicholas II. The attitude of the Tsar was, as before, "gracious", but his words that Martens "as a well-known specialist" successfully cope with the role of umpire in the Anglo-Venezuelan dispute already give rise to a certain critical reaction in Martens' soul: he thrice was chosen as an international arbitrator, but could he not bring great benefit to Russia if the Ministry of Foreign Affairs were to use him more actively? To be sure, the principal reproach was directed not at the Tsar, but at the "advisors of the Tsar", Murav'ev and Lamzdorf.

---

[13] AVPR, op. 787, delo 9, ed. khr. 2, l. 35, 47-52.

[14] AVPR, op. 787, delo 9, ed. khr. 3, l. 28, 130, 143.

At a reception in March 1898 Martens attempted to "open the eyes" of Nicholas II to the undistinguished policy of the "two counts" in the Far East, but could write nothing in the diary about the well-disposed reaction of the Tsar.[15] In speaking of these meetings between Martens and Nicholas II, it would be interesting to learn what the impressions of the Tsar were of such meetings and his characterisation of Martens. However, the diary of Nicholas II is noteworthy for its surprising lack of content. From the Tsar's diary one may learn how many crows the Tsar killed, but not a word of impression about those with whom he met. So it was with Martens. The Tsar's diary for 18 December 1896 noted: "Next was the report of old man Delianov, completely recovered from his illness, and then Professor Martens".[16]

In the second half of 1898 and first half of 1899 Martens did enormous work in preparing the First Hague Peace Conference. The Tsar, however (undoubtedly based on Murav'ev's report), appointed as the first Russian plenipotentiary not him, but Staal, and he was designated to "be attached to full privy councillor G. G. Staal". When Murav'ev, in his words, then petitioned to appoint Martens as envoy to The Hague, the Tsar replied that he already had his own candidate for this post. As a result, Martens did not even receive an audience with the Tsar before departing for the Hague Conference, and after it ended was only accorded the Tsar's gratitude through the Ministry. To be sure, upon the petition of Pobedonostsev, Nicholas II received him and graciously thanked him for his labours, but this had no consequences for Martens. This behaviour of the Tsar was attributed by Martens entirely to Murav'ev and Lamzdorf. In March 1899 he wrote in his diary: "It is sad. A Sovereign, young, good, and motivated by the best intentions, but under his sceptre – astonishing things".

In March 1900 Martens heard rumours that the German Emperor Wilhelm supposedly had said about Nicholas II: "One

---

[15] AVPR, op. 787, delo 9, ed. khr. 4, l. 13, 34.

[16] See *Дневник Императора Николая II* [Diary of Emperor Nicholas II] (Moscow, 1991), p. 185.

can never govern Russia by smoking cigarettes, listening to fools, and playing tennis". Martens wrote in his diary: "This is malicious, but rather intelligent!"

This was an attempt to explain the misfortunes of Russia also by the personal qualities of Nicholas II; gradually the assessment of the Tsar is changing. At the end of 1900 Martens wrote: "The Sovereign has the most beneficent of intentions but neither the character, nor the energy, to bring them into being. Would that he had more character and more intelligence ... Then he would not support ministers without talent". When Martens expressed similar thoughts to Pobedonostsev and he agreed with him, Martens immediately posed a perplexing question: "Such a reaction from the mouth of the tutor and closest advisor of Alexander III and Nicholas II. Why did he not try to give them a better education and higher ideals?!"

In May 1901 Martens, noting the second anniversary of the Hague Peace Conference, sadly declared: "The Tsar himself is trying to forget it. My leading role at The Hague had made me at fault".[17] Already claims are felt not only against the Tsarist advisor, but also against the Tsar himself. However, hope for the Tsar's mercy still is alive, and Martens happily wrote that in the report to Nicholas II in February 1901 a surprise awaited Count Lamzdorf: when he spoke about the removal of foreign consuls from Sevastopol, declared a military port, the Tsar said: "Ask for the opinion of Martens". It turned out that the Tsar remembered Professor Martens and valued his opinion!

A meeting of Nicholas II and Wilhelm II took place at Danzig in Autumn 1901. Martens compared both monarchs and concluded: "What an enormous difference between them! One boils with power, energy, and indestructible will; the other is good-natured, agreeable to everything and doing a good turn for all; one is himself the First Minister and constantly around the neck of even such genius ministers as Prince Bismarck ...; the other allows his ministers to do what they wish and always writes on all reports "Съ", that is, "agreed" in the cyrillic alphabet. He compared those accompanying both emperors, Chancellor von

[17] AVPR, op. 787, delo 9, ed.khr. 5, l. 65, 92, 12-113, 116, 139.

Bülow[18] and the Minister of Foreign Affairs of Russia, Count Lamzdorf, and wrote that Count Bülow is a most educated, intelligent, and talented person, whereas Count Lamzdorf achieved his post as a "servile servant".[19] As we see, the initial "charm" of Nicholas II has irretrievably passed on, ceding place to a sober view. The halo of the Russian Autocrat was noticeably tarnished.

The 1905 Revolution had intensified Martens' critical attitude towards Nicholas II. Martens with his own eyes had seen from the window of the Ministry of Foreign Affairs how on the "Bloody Sunday" of 9 January 1905 the horse guards had cut down unarmed people who had come to the Winter Palace for the Tsar's grace. Martens regarded the actions of the Government as a tragic mistake and considered that all of these disturbances could have been avoided by having given attention, and not displayed force, with respect to a peaceful demonstration of loyal subjects. He lamented that the Tsar did not go out to the workers, on which they had counted. In this event "his Tsarist power would have been stronger than ever". He was distressed about the repressions of the capital authorities who arrested without investigation all "liberals". The "police are mindless", he noted. The Moscow City Governor declared that the disorders in Petersburg had been organised by the money of the English and the Japanese. The English Ambassador sent a sharp protest. And what of the Tsar? To the English note he laid down a resolution: "So many lies and slanders are disseminated in the English press!" Martens could not concur with such a position. As a jurist he noted: the Tsar does not understand the difference between the reporting of a free English press not subordinate to the Government and the statements of governmental agencies, in this instance the Moscow City Governor.

Martens survived with distress the "anarchy" caused by revolutionary speeches, was disturbed about the "obscurantism

---

[18] The reference is to Bernhard Heinrich Martin Bülow (1849-1929), Prince, German public figure, and diplomat, and from 1900-09, Reichskantzler of Germany.

[19] AVPR, op. 787, delo 9, ed. krh. 5, l. 127 148.

and lawlessness", wrote about the protests of the workers, and declared that in this stormy, tragic time "only the Tsar and Tsaritsa live peacefully at Tsarskoe Selo". He all the same was aware that the Tsarist court was isolated from society. Terrorists killed Grand Prince Sergei Aleksandrovich. Murder is always a crime, and in this instance it was committed with respect to one of the close relations of the Tsar. And what reaction? "A surprising indifference of society to it". No one expressed condolences, and some of the newspapers did not even print an obituary.

Martens was distressed too about the defeat of the Russian Army in the War against Japan. When information was received about the catastrophe with the squadrons of Rozhdestvenskii and Nebogatov, sent from the Baltic Sea to the Far East, Martens commented in his diary: "Here are the results of the wild arbitrariness and murderous discourtesy predominant among us!" He perceived as a mockery the rumours which reached him that the Governor General in the Far East, Alekseev, received from the Tsar a lump-sum of 500,000 rubles for his arrangements and a salary of 108,000 rubles per year. General Kuropatkin, guilty of the defeats, supposedly had "given offence" to the Tsar: he did not retain the salary of the commander-in-chief of 144,000 rubles; but was left "in all" only 104,000. For a member of the Council of the Ministry of Foreign Affairs with a salary of 4,500 rubles per year, such amounts were astronomical. And to whom were they designated? Those guilty of military defeats! Martens took a special interest in Lamzdorf, who had returned from Tsarskoe Selo with a report about how Nicholas II had reacted to the catastrophe with the Russian squadrons. Lamzdorf replied that he did not completely understand the attitude of the Tsar: "indifference" or "cold-bloodedness". Another time Lamzdorf reported that the Tsar saw the "finger of God" in the defeat of the squadrons.

In May 1905 Martens was received by Nicholas II alone in his working office. The Tsar was silent ("I spoke much more than he"). He said that he had read Martens' letter published in *Новое время* [New Times] and devoted to the neutrality of France in the Russo-Japanese War. Martens reported that *The Times* had attacked him for this letter. The Tsar was consoling: "To your honour". The conversation proceeded sluggishly. The Tsar enlivened and began to listen attentively when Martens related how in his presence at a banquet in New York in 1901 the Russian Tsar has been toasted as the creator of the Hague Peace Conference. "The reception was gracious, but not productive" concluded Martens in his diary. Not a trace remained from the bygone fascination with Tsarist conversations.

The entries of conversations with the Tsar also are abbreviated. Whereas previously Martens had reproduced in the diary a verbatim account of the entire dialogue, now the reports concerning the audiences are extremely brief. Martens drily noted about the reception in July 1905 with regard to the trip as a member of the delegation to the negotiations with Japan in Portsmouth that he reported to Nicholas II that he did not wish to go since he was an opponent of a "shameful peace". The Tsar said that everyone recommended to conclude a peace: both the President of the United States, Theodore Roosevelt, and Wilhelm II, the Emperor of Germany. Therefore he had decided in favour of peace but not under humiliating conditions. That was the entire entry of the conversation.

Made wiser by the experience of communion with Nicholas II and his advisors, Martens nonetheless was disappointed in the Tsar. When in Autumn 1905 he returned from Portsmouth, the Consul General of Russia in Berlin arranged a luncheon. Those present extolled the results achieved by Vitte at the peace negotiations and said that he would receive the "highest awards" from the Tsar. He already knew the Tsar's grace and did not count on awards. And indeed at the reception after the return from Portsmouth Nicholas II confined himself to several words of gratitude and left. "It is terrible to live under such a regime!" Martens wrote in his diary. To be sure, he was more indignant not about the Tsar himself, but his Minister, Lamzdorf. ("Our Sovereign has surrounded himself with such scoundrels!"). However, the person of Nicholas II is more frequently criticised. In Autumn 1906 Martens enters in his diary the results of his observations and reflections: the Tsar is indifferent to everything, and therefore no one loves him. All reforms were "torn away from him by force, circumstances, and the audacity of plotters". Martens was reinforced in this opinion by a conversation with an English journalist, W. T. Stead, who at the time was a correspondent in Petersburg and at the end of 1905 had come to Russia in order to gather materials. He established friendly relations with Martens and said to him candidly, on the basis of meetings during trips about the country: No one believes the Tsar". The Empress made a very unfavourable impression on Stead, and the Grand Princes amazed him by their lack of courtesy. "All are such, except Grand Prince Konstantin Konstantinovich", he confirmed to Martens.[20]

Nicholas II held a regular reception in connection with the preparations for the Second Hague Peace Conference in 1907. Now Martens' attention was riveted to save the convocation of the Conference from the consequences of the "weak character of the Sovereign". After the end of the Conference in Autumn 1907, he again arrived at Tsarskoe Selo. Those presenting themselves were many, and although Martens attempted to converse about his future diplomatic service, nothing came of it. He confined himself to stating that the "Sovereign was gracious".

In January 1909 Nicholas II himself wished to receive Martens. "Surprising", noted Martens. The Tsar was courteous: he was received alone, in the working office, and for the first time was invited to sit in an armchair at his desk, and conversed for a long time. And the results of the conversation? "Everything remained as before", Martens declared.

The January meeting proved for Martens to be the last, but he still succeeded in drawing a conclusion from his many years of communion with the Tsar: "The Sovereign, being one of the perfidious Romanovs ...".[21] The path of cognition commenced with a young, fascinating Tsar and ended with a "perfidious Romanov". Martens did not live to see the shameless merry-

---

[20] AVPR, op. 787, delo 9, ed. khr. 6, l. 1-3, 8, 19-22, 23, 29, 75-79, 81-82, 119.

[21] AVPR, op. 787, delo 9, ed. khr. 7, l. 20-21, 92, 151-153, 155.

making of Grishka Rasputin, by which the last years of the reign of the House of Romanov were marked.

The critical attitude towards Nicholas II may seem incompatible with Tsarist convictions. But in this Martens was far from alone. His evaluation of the Tsar and those around the Tsar was more gentle than those of other better informed contemporaries, including the monarchist camp. Suffice it to read the memoirs of such convinced monarchists as General A. I. Denikin, after the Revolution commander of the Voluntary White Army, V. M. Purishkevich, leader of the extreme right in the last State Duma, and many others. Denikin, for example, also wrote of the Tsarist court: "I will not rummage in the mire which covered the ministerial chambers and intimate Tsarist chambers ...".[22] In emigré monarchist literature the opinion is precisely represented that the pernicious personal qualities of the last Tsar, and especially the Tsaritsa, greatly facilitated the downfall of the dynasty. Against this background the critical remarks of Martens seem quite restrained.

Attitude towards Autocracy The diaries preserve certain traces of the ruminations of Martens about the autocracy. In connection with the visit of the Russian naval squadron to Toulon he compared the social system of Russia and France. The comparison was extremely contrastive: "In Russia there is despotism going to the ultimate limits of senseless arbitrariness; in France there is the freedom of the enlightenment, science, and art taking the forms of systematic unbelief and the fullest shakiness ... of morality and propriety ...".[23] In the eyes of a jurist autocracy gives rise not only to "wild arbitrariness". Yet paradoxically it does not ensure the coordination of State administration, as Martens continuously encountered. Complaints against the "anarchy" in the Ministry of Foreign Affairs, and in general against the "the upper strata" run throughout his diaries, and as time passes more and more examples of "anarchy" are given. During the rule of Alexander

[22] A. I. Denikin, «Очерки русской смуты» [Essays of Russian Sedition], *Вопросы истории* [Questions of History], no. 3 (1990), p. 128.
[23] AVPR, op. 787, delo 9, ed. khr. 3, l. 67.

III, Katkov was "higher than the Government and higher than Law" and conducted his own "foreign policy" in addition to and despite the Minister of Foreign Affairs, Giers. Three times the Tsar ordered the movement of Russian forces in the area of Pendzhde, which threatened a conflict with England, to cease, and three times the order was not executed. In 1887 Alexander III signed a gracious rescript to Giers, and Pobedonostsev by his own power stopped its publication. "We live in an *autocratic* State!" commented Martens with sarcasm. Under Nicholas II the "anarchy" in State administration intensified. According to Martens, in May 1905 the Minister of Foreign Affairs, Lamzdorf, to his surprise, learned that his Ministry was not alone in being engaged with foreign policy in the Far East, together with the Governor General of the Tsar in the Far East, Alekseev, but so too was the head of the chancellery of the Special Committee created for the Far East, A. M. Abaza,[24] who in the name of the Tsar gave consent to the complete renunciation by Russia of her interests in Korea. Widely known was the scandalous episode of the signature by Nicholas II of a Treaty of Alliance with Germany during a meeting with Wilhelm II on the Tsarist yacht in Bjorke in July 1905. Since the treaty was contrary to obligations of Russia to France, the Tsar under the pressure of Vitte and Lamzdorf removed his signature, to the indignation of the German Emperor.

All this led Martens to the idea of the need to limit the autocracy. Judging from various notes and utterances, his greatest sympathy lay with the constitutional monarchy in England. It did not follow from this, however, that he was a proponent of limiting the Russian autocracy by a Constitution. Remarkable was his conversation with the Queen of Wurtemberg, Olga Nikolaevna (formerly a Russian Grand Duchess) which took place in the royal apartments in 1887. Martens related in detail the situation in Russia: "It is in a state of political decay and completely indifferent to everything". He told of Katkov, the Minister of Finances Vyshnegradskii, the Minister of Enlighten-

[24] The reference is to A. M. Abaza, Rear Admiral and Member of the Special Committee for the Far East.

ment Delianov, and the like. The Queen did not object, but merely exclaimed: "God, when will it end?!" How could the Sovereign appoint "such a lout" as Vyshnegradskii? In turn Olga Nikolaevna shared her reflections about what should be done with Russia. In her view, it was necessary to form a solid cabinet with the First Minister at the head. Then quarrels among the ministers would cease. If one were to follow the idea of the Wurtemberg Queen, she proposed to limit not the autocracy of the Tsar, but the chaos arising therefrom by means of forming a "solid" government, the premier of which would receive significant autonomy. We shall not press the reality of such a scheme, but add the judgment in principle of the Queen: "In my view Russia is not mature enough for a Constitution". Martens sincerely supported this view.[25]

In 1891 he repeated this cardinal thought. The occasion was the failure of the French Chamber of Deputies to ratify a General Act signed by the French plenipotentiary representative at the recent international conference in Brussels. And all this, in Martens' view, "thanks to the reckless speeches of two French deputies!" Now other governments might reject the agreed document. Martens was full of sarcasm: "How is one not carried away by the virtue of the representative form of government? How does one not wish for a Russian parliament? God, save Russia from such a misfortune!" With the accession to the throne of Nicholas II in 1894 there were hopes of liberal reforms in Russian society, above all the granting of a constitution, and the address of the new Tsar about "senseless dreams" was met with disappointment. Martens continued to adhere to his former view: a constitution would be "a great calamity in view of the ignorant state of even the leading Russian people". He concluded his reflections: "God save Russia from a constitution!"[26] Under the pressure of revolutionary events, Nicholas II in February 1907 all the same convoked a Duma. But by spring 1907 Martens had published in the *Times* a letter in which he criticised the Duma for an inability to work and proved the need to dissolve it. The

[25] AVPR, op. 787, delo 9, ed. khr. 2, l. 74, 92-93.
[26] AVPR, op. 787, delo 9, ed. khr. 3, l. 28, 106.

Letter caused a great storm in Russia. Premier Stolypin sent an irate letter to the Ministry of Foreign Affairs, and many newspapers came down with criticism. Martens was obliged to endure a "long conversation" with Izvol'skii, his Minister.[27] As we see, the initial experience with Russian parliamentarianism only strengthened Martens' scepticism.

Why the ineradicable sympathies for an autocratic system despite the disappointment with Nicholas II, an understanding of the perniciousness of "wild arbitrariness", and distress with those surrounding the Tsar? One of the principal reasons undoubtedly was faith that it was the autocracy which would ensure the necessary economic, social, and political reforms and save the country from anarchy. It should not be forgotten that Martens had grown up in a situation of "revolution from the top" which had been linked with the name of Alexander II and the greatest manifestation of which was the emancipation of the peasants from serfdom. The autocratic power of the Tsar, capable of overcoming resistance to the reforms at the very apex of the Empire, in the privileged nobility, and not to allow "revolution from below", had played the leading role in implementing the reforms. Therefore the eminent proponents of reforms, for example the future war minister, D. A. Miliutin, objected to a weakening of the autocracy. The resolve personally of Alexander II to assume responsibility for the reforms, for the emancipation of the peasants, was emphasised.[28] Martens saw an enlightened and law-abiding monarch whose firm hand would lead Russia along the path of prosperity and progress. At the time similar feelings were rather widely shared in Russian society.

Legality and Order

What would have been Martens' positive programme? He set it out concisely in the treatise on international law, in certain publicist works, and repeatedly confirmed it in diary entries: respect for the rights of the person, strict compliance with legality, legal order. A State in which the human person is recognised to be a

[27] AVPR, op. 787, delo 9, ed. khr. 6, l. 32-34.

[28] See N. Eidelman, "«Революция сверху» в России" ['Revolution from Above' in Russia], *Наука и жизнь* [Science and Life], no. 1 (1989).

source of civil and political rights, a State in which law is dominant – that is the ideal. In wishing that the Most High save Russia from a constitution, Martens simultaneously wrote: "We need respect for law and the court ...".[29]

The Tsarist Manifesto of 17 October 1905 which promised to limit the autocracy Martens welcomed warmly. "A most happy day!", he wrote, a day which "converts the autocracy and bureaucracy or departmental Russia into a free, new, and constitutional Russia". However, he perceived these changes in his own way, from his own basic position. He wrote: "Hail legal freedom and legal order!".[30] Lex and jus for him had priority.

Such views were guided by his behaviour, which caused among those surrounding him conflicting commentary. When in Autumn 1905 a wave of strikes spread across Petersburg, Martens noted that "hooligans and anarchists are committing excesses". On 19 November *Новое время* [New Times] published his open letter under the headline "It is Necessary Not Only to Speak, but also to Act". In the Letter he called the strike of postal employees an "outrage" which impinged upon the interests of other people and appealed to all readers to come to the post office and by their personal labour restore it to normal work. Martens himself went to the Petersburg Post Office and saw with satisfaction that there (under the protection of the military) about 300 persons came on the first day: Countess Mordvinova, Count Bobrinskii, certain grand princes, students, and other volunteers. The democratic press naturally called Martens a strikebreaker.

In November 1906 Martens entered an analogous episode in his diary. His daughter Edith had married Count A. M. Sollogub. Just as Martens' wife, Edith too was a Lutheran. They were married Russian Orthodox. Earlier in the event of such a marriage the bride should have signed a special document with an obligation to baptise future children in the Russian Orthodox faith. Under a new Statute introduced after the Manifesto of 17 October 1905, such limitation was abolished, and Martens was

---

29 AVPR, op. 787, delo 9, ed. khr. 2, l. 106.
30 AVPR, op. 787, delo 9, ed. khr. 6, l. 69-70.

troubled when he learned of this. For him, naturally, the question was not that he saw future grandchildren as Lutherans, but a violation of the legal rights of the person. He went to the ober-procurator of the Holy Synod, P. P. Izvol'skii. It was explained to him that the old law had been repealed and a new one issued, but its application was a matter for the future. Martens was indignant, but the incident was resolved simply and amicably in a purely Russian manner: the Lyceé priest, the enlightened and dear M. N. Pospelov, performed the wedding rites and simply did not require any obligations from the bride.[31]

Respect for the rights of man, and for law – this was most important, and the form of the State – monarchy or republic – was to Martens a secondary matter. He related similarly to the nationality question. Most important was respect for the nationality peculiarities of man: freedom of communion in the national language, compliance with national customs, not allowing discrimination by reason of nationality. As regards the creation of national autonomy, especially the formation of national States, Martens related to such ideas with profound distrust, supposing that the "principle of nationality ... creates nothing stable but is in a state to disturb very much".[32] He condemned forcible russification and various administrative oppressions of national minorities, but stood for preservation of the integrity of the Russian Empire. Relative to domestic policy under Alexander III he wrote in his diary: "I could not welcome the internal policy of the late Sovereign, which was to a high degree ruinous for the unity of Russia. The systematic persecution of Jews, Finns, and Baltic Germans significantly increased the centrifugal aspirations within the Empire.[33]

Peace and International Legality

Martens' approach to the foreign policy of Russia is of important significance for his socio-political views. Here it should be recalled that the major decisions in this domain

[31] AVPR, op. 787, delo 9, ed. khr. 6, l. 89, 122.

[32] See F. F. Martens, *Современное международное право цивилизованных народов* [Contemporary International Law of Civilised Peoples] (Spb., 1882-83), I, p. 151.

[33] AVPR, op. 787, delo 9, ed. khr. 3, l. 101.

(change from alliance with Germany to alliance with France and England under Alexander III, expansion in the Far East, war against Japan under Nicholas II, and others) were adopted without him and without his influence.

When Giers headed the Ministry of Foreign Affairs, Martens actively favoured the alliance with Germany and was delighted, having learned from a conversation with Pobedonostsev in December 1896, that he was of the same opinion. His enthusiastic reactions to Wilhelm II relate to this and to the later period. Here Martens clearly was lagging behind, for the formation of the Russian-French-English Entente had become irreversible. In 1907 Martens already was writing in his diary: "my political ideal always was the triple alliance: Russia, France, and England! If such an alliance is built, the peace and quiet of Europe will be truly ensured".[34]

At the same time, Martens had certain positions to which he adhered constantly and which to a great extent determined his specific proposals. Thus, he always proceeded from the peaceful development of inter-State relations and never, anywhere, favoured military actions of Russia.

With the nonacceptance of war, the cult of which he endeavoured to spread in his book on "The Eastern War and the Brussels Conference", Martens organically linked a negative attitude towards military preparations and the arms race. He publicly declared that it was not millions of bayonets which comprised the might and glory of the Russian State contemporary to him. Only sober realism did not allow him to make disarmament his political slogan.

Yet another point consolidated his peace-creating position: he always related very negatively to the territorial expansion of Russia. In the colonial policies of England, France, Germany, and other countries he saw the source of inevitable conflicts and wars which would destroy the international community being formed. Even more persuasively he opposed, within the framework of his position, naturally, Russian conquests in Central Asia. The accession of the Central Asian khanates he

---

[34] AVPR, op. 787, delo 9, ed. khr. 6, l. 83.

designated publicly as a "heavy burden" (in his book "Russia and England in Central Asia"). In official memoranda and publicist addresses he proved the importance of respect for the independence, sovereignty, and territorial integrity of Afghanistan and, as noted above, even wrote a pamphlet on this question. He called for respect for the independence, sovereignty, and territorial integrity of China. He condemned adventurist actions which led Russia to war against Japan.

Martens' creative legacy includes only one single article devoted to a Russian Emperor who had reigned at the time. The article set out his remarks to students of the Law Faculty of Petersburg University on the ninth day[35] after the death of Alexander III. Martens called the late Emperor the "creator of peace in Europe" and praised him especially for the fact that during the thirteen years of his reign Russia had not a single military conflict with foreign States.[36]

It is difficult today to guess what motives inspired Martens, besides lectures, to set out his reflections relative to the foreign policy of Russia under Alexander III. It is known that at the time the Tsarist court wished the noted historian, V. O. Kliuchevskii, to write a book on the late Emperor. Kliuchevskii declined to write the book, but was obliged in 1894 to memorialise the deceased Emperor at a session of the Society of Russian History and Antiquities attached to Moscow University.[37] There he too was hissed by the students present. In an analogous address of Martens, the students, according to newspaper reports, reacted favourably. The reason for such a diverse perception was evidently due to the choice of topic. Whereas Martens could speak about foreign policy, where the late Tsar appeared as a creator of peace, Kliuchevskii touched upon internal affairs, where the autocracy seemed completely different.

In portraying Alexander III as the leader of Russian foreign policy, Martens did not make courtier curtsies to the Minister

---

[35] In the Russian Orthodox tradition remembrance of the late departed is held on the ninth day after death.

[36] See *Новости* [News] [Spb.], 3 November 1894.

[37] See V. O. Kliuchevskii, *Сочинения* [Works] (Moscow, 1987), I, p. 15.

of Foreign Affairs, Giers, because he knew very well that "Nikolai Karlovich had not conducted our policy for the last 13 years, but rather the late Sovereign". Attention was attracted to the address by Martens also by the fact that the praise of the "creator of peace in Europe" echoed as a distinctive instruction to his son, Nicholas II.

It is appropriate to note that Martens' publicist addresses were alien to the "loyal subject" spirit accepted in official and right-wing publications. He had dedicated the book "The Eastern War and the Brussels Conference" not to the Tsar-liberator, Alexander II, but to the "valorous Russian Army". Addressing students, Professor Martens spoke of a love for the Motherland, ties with the *alma mater* University, honourable labour, devotion to scholarship, and the "ideals of truth and justness". Completely lacking were such customary references at the time to the "Sovereign Emperor", the "reigning house", "autocracy, orthodoxy, and national character", and "loyalty to Tsar and Fatherland", and the like.

Martens' socio-political views would be easier to classify, especially for the modern reader brought up amongst organised social and political forces, if he had joined any social movement or political party. In the course of the Revolution of 1905 they received a legal foundation for their activity in Russia. But Martens was remote from all of them.

To what party might he all the same be relegated?

Martens categorically rejected revolutionary organisations which had as their aim to overthrow the autocracy or which resorted to forcible actions, among which he numbered strikes. For him they all were "anarchists" and "dynamiters". His attitude towards them he manifested precisely in the question of the extradition of political criminals.

Extradition of Political Criminals For Tsarism this question in the second half of the nineteenth century acquired special urgency because revolutionary centres were constantly being formed abroad which were linked with underground organisations in Russia. The Tsarist Government created a special service which exposed

Russian revolutionaries in foreign States, watched them, and took measures to suppress their activities. One method became a demand to extradite such persons as Russian subjects and criminals who had violated the laws of the Russian Empire. It should be taken into account that Russian legislation did not know the concept of emigration. Martens himself wrote that "all contemporary civilised States are imbued with the conviction that the right of migration is the inalienable right of each citizen and that each citizen is free to withdraw from his citizenship". Russia constituted an exception; the existing legislation stipulated that "Russian subjects may never lawfully withdraw from citizenship".[38] Relying on its own legislation, the Tsarist Government could consider any political emigrant to be a Russian subject and demand of him compliance with Russian laws up to and including return to the country at the order of the authorities.

An example is the case of the noted representative of the raznochinets stage of the revolutionary movement in Russia, S. G. Nechaev (1847-82), who from 1869 took refuge abroad (Switzerland, England, France, Italy, Bulgaria) with the support of local revolutionaries. The Russian Government expended considerable effort and large financial resources to apprehend and deliver him to Russia. Officially he was accused of organising the murder of a student, Ivanov, but the true reason for the activity of the Tsarist Government was the revolutionary activity of Nechaev and his supporters. In 1872 Nechaev was arrested by the Swiss police and extradited to Russia, where he was tried. Nechaev perished in the solitary cell of the Alekseev Ravelin of the Peter and Paul Fortress, where he as a "political criminal" was imprisoned "forever" at the personal instruction of Alexander II with a prohibition to mention his surname (the court sentenced Nechaev to twenty years of forced labour).[39]

The extradition of political criminals, including Nechaev, gave rise to protests against the Tsarist Government by the

---

[38] F. F. Martens, note 32 above, I, pp. 167, 173.

[39] See Iu. A. Ber, "Страницы биографии революционера (С. Г. Нечаев)" [Pages of the Biography of a Revolutionary (S. G. Nechaev)], *Вопросы истории* [Questions of History], no. 4 (1989), pp. 138-146.

general public of European countries. It should be taken into account that in about the 1840s virtually all European States had ceased to extradite emigrants accused of political crimes. The nonextradition of political criminals had become a common practice.

In this situation Martens as an eminent specialist on international law opposed the "predominant view" and substantiated the need for international cooperation in the extradition of all criminals, irrespective of the reasons by which they justified their acts. He wrote that in the past under conditions of monarchical arbitrariness, neglect of the rights of the individual in feudal monarchies, the institution of political asylum had played a positive role. An analogous situation had arisen during the "period of universal reaction which enveloped continental Europe after the 1815 Congress of Vienna" and had defended people "who had sympathised with the principles of freedom and constitutional orders and endeavoured to effectuate them by word and deed". Now, Martens proved, the situation had cardinally changed and States increasingly were aware of the "common danger of those contemporary political criminals who openly favoured the proponents of the entire existing social and State system". Is it doubtful now, Martens wrote, that one can apply the right of asylum to those persons "who call themselves socialists, anarchists, and 'dynamiters' and who have declared war to the death against any Government?" Therefore he opposed the "dominant point of view in international law and called upon the governments of all States to join forces in the struggle against socialists, anarchists, and 'dynamiters'."[40]

In Soviet doctrinal writings of the 1950s Martens' position was evaluated unequivocally as support for the Tsarist Government in its struggle against the revolutionary movement.[41] That assessment is one-sided. Martens' position absolutely was affected by his negative attitude towards the Russian revolutionary movement. One should not suppose that he did

---

[40] Martens, note 38 above, II, pp. 406-408, 410-411.

[41] See, for example, *Большая Советская энциклопедия* [Great Soviet Encyclopedia] (1954), XXVI, p. 394.

not see those reasons which gave rise to political crimes in Russia of the day, namely, the oppression and arbitrariness of the autocracy. But his position on the extradition of political criminals undoubtedly also was dictated by his conceptual approach. He stood on the foundation of compliance with legality, condemning its violation for whatever reasons.

It should be noted in this connection that the obligatoriness of extradition has still not become an imperative norm of international law, that is, a "norm accepted and recognised by the international community of States as a whole as a norm from which no derogation is permitted ..." (Article 53, 1969 Vienna Convention on the Law of Treaties). But a trend in this direction has emerged during recent decades. As example is the extradition of air pirates and other terrorists, which increasingly is taking on the character of a generally-recognised rule. The extradition of criminals (under determined conditions) is an integral part of an international-legal conception which underlies the strengthened cooperation of States, including within the framework of the United Nations, in the struggle against such a global threat as international terrorism. These days the position of Martens is viewed in another light than it was one hundred or fifty years ago.

Martens never publicly said anything with regard to the rapidly spreading socialist ideas in Europe. Some notion of his view is given by a diary entry concerning a conversation with the Duke of Baden in June 1887. The Duke said much about the duty of the State to come to the assistance of workers and the poor peasants in general, in a word, in the spirit of Bismarckian "State socialism". Martens agreed with "this practical theory", but also expressed certain objections. Could a State in its social policy come to a "denial of acquired and legal rights?" The Duke shared Martens' doubts but all the same countered that the rich so often abuse their wealth.[42] As we see, Martens viewed social inequality and the various sorts of oppression arising from it from the standpoint of law and legality. It is noteworthy that the problem of the poor and rich, the mutual

[42] See AVPR, op. 787, del 9, ed. khr. 2, l. 84.

relations of social strata (or, as he wrote, "social circles") was absent in his scientific conceptions. Free possession and disposition of legally acquired material benefits was for him as inalienable a right as the other rights of the individual. The social consequences of the accumulation of wealth did not relate to the domain of law. In any event the idea of social revolutions consisted for him, evidently, in the acquisition of rights and freedoms and not in a change of the relations of ownership.

"A True Conservative" Hostile to the revolutionary camp, Martens distanced himself also from the reactionary camp. His diary entries are replete with indignation against not only the "scoundrels" who surrounded the Tsar, but also the atmosphere of "obscurantism" which had been sown. When in 1907 he read in the official newspaper a discourse concerning the fact that autocracy and popular representation constitute the foundation of Russian Statehood and that as popular representation develops for the better, the stronger will be autocracy, the rejoinder appeared in his diary: "What could be more absurd!"[43] The ideology of "autocracy, orthodoxy, and national character" seemed to him to be unscientific and reactionary. Despite respect for Pobedonostsev, Martens never forgot that he was the "enemy of all progress", and progress in the scholarly conceptions of Martens was the engine of social and international development.

Cast aside in the appointment of the State Council in 1906, Martens saw the reason for this in the fact that he was too "liberal" for the Tsar and his circle. Was he a liberal? In criticising the state of affairs in the Ministry of Foreign Affairs, the court, and the country as a whole, Martens came in despair and exclaimed: "The Russian people will fall unless they take their own future into their hands" (1905).[44] However, one can not only on the basis of this utterance count Martens among the proponents of radical changes in the State structure of Russia. He merely once publicly made an utterance relating to political sympathies, and they were on the side of the conservatives, or

[43] AVPR, op. 787, delo 9, ed. khr. 7, l. 88.
[44] AVPR, op. 787, delo 9, ed. khr. 6, l. 21.

more precisely, the "true conservatives", as he wrote in an article devoted to the fiftieth anniversary of the University of Bern (1884). "A true conservative he there contrasted to "liberalism".[45] In the course of time Martens' political sympathies did not evolve so as to consider him to be a liberal during the last years of his life. He reacted positively to the formation in England of the Liberal cabinet of Campbell-Bannerman (1906). But that was in England, and not in Russia.

If one judges by the enthusiastic acceptance of the Tsarist Manifesto of 17 October 1905 declaring the establishment of a constitutional monarchy in Russia, then Martens should be given a place in that political camp which considered this Manifesto to be its own programme. He could sympathise with the constitutional-democratic party (cadets), one of whose leaders was the noted historian and publicist, P. N. Miliukov, the future Minister of Foreign Affairs of the Provisional Government. He could become a follower of the Union of 17th October, one of the founders of which was A. I. Guchkov, a great industrialist who saw in England an example for Russia. However, Martens not only did not support the activity of these parties, he was rather sceptical of their leaders. In his diary he called Miliukov and Guchkov "undistinguished", notable for the "lack of a State idea". Moreover, as already mentioned, the convocation of the State Duma in February 1907 gave no rise to enthusiasm on his part. This Russian parliament evidently did not meet his notions, and in April 1907 he published a letter in a London newspaper in which he favoured its dissolution. On 3 June 1907 the Tsar dissolved the Duma, retracting the promise given in October 1905 and having in essence committed a State coup d'etat. Martens approved this course of action. But when deputies were brought to trial who had signed the so-called Vyborg Appeal which declared the dissolution of the Duma to be illegal, including people well-known to Martens (S. A. Muromtsev (jurist, specialist on Roman Law at Moscow University, then an advocate

---

[45] See F. F. Martens, "Пятидесятилетний юбилей Вернского университета" [Fiftieth Jubilee of Bern University], *Вестник Европы* [Herald of Europe], no. 10 (October 1884), pp. 852-858.

and Chairman of the Duma), V. D. Nabokov (jurist, professor, specialist in criminal law), L. I. Petrazhitskii (jurist, professor at Petersburg University, legal theorist), I. I. Petrunkevich (one of the senior figures in the Zemstvo Movement), and certain others, he sympathised with them not for political reasons nor party affiliation, but because these were, in his view, "people of talent and knowledge, of whom we have exceedingly few".[46]

The sole State figure who Martens constantly treated with profound respect and on whom he placed hopes of withdrawing the country from the socio-political crisis was S. Iu. Vitte. His indignation in connection with the appointment as minister a "former postmaster" passed rather quickly, and his official encounters with Vitte, including at the peace negotiations with Japan (see Chapter IX), did not change his attitude to the "most intelligent Vitte". In Autumn 1905, after difficult cooperation with Vitte at the peace negotiations, Martens entered in his diary: "Only S. Iu. has a real State mind and is a man with great character and enormous will power. None of our ministers can be compared with him". When the Manifesto of 17 October 1905 appeared, Martens noted in his diary: "Vitte convinced the Tsar to perform this feat. In the entries of that time the words "most wise Vitte" appear fleetingly and the conviction is expressed: if it is possible to rescue Russia, only Vitte is in a state to do so. When Vitte in 1906 was forced to resign and in his place I. L. Goremykin was appointed the head of the Government, Martens summed up his impressions: "Vitte and Goremykin. One – a most able person, the other, utterly without talent ... To Vitte monuments will be erected; Goremykin everyone will forget on the day of his death".[47]

However, one must not judge the socio-political views of Martens by his attitude towards Vitte, much less include him in a specific political camp.

Patriot of Russia

An integral feature of Martens' social position was his patriotism. The works of an outstanding jurist, in particular his publicist works, were

[46] AVPR, op. 787, delo 9, ed. khr. 7, l. 100.
[47] AVPR, op. 787, delo 9, ed. khr. 6, l. 78, 85, 113.

imbued with pride in the role of Russia in international affairs. As already noted, he dedicated his book on "The Eastern War and the Brussels Conference" to the "valorous Russian Army". In the preface he wrote: "If with the present book we add even one stone to the monument erected to the honour and glory of the Russian soldier and the Russian Army, then we consider our labour to be remunerated a hundred times".[48] In that book and in his work on "Russia and England in Central Asia" and other publications he reacted rather sharply against ill-disposed publications with respect to the Russian Army, diplomacy, and foreign policy.

Martens repeatedly pointed in his works to the role of the Russian initiatives in the codification of the laws and customs of warfare and the peaceful settlement of international disputes. In assessing the results of the 1899 Hague Peace Conference, he wrote: "I am unaware of the history of any other civilised people which has made so many attempts for the peaceloving settlement of questions of international order and law".[49]

Although Martens unequivocally expressed his patriotic feelings, he was, it seems to this writer, subjected to the greatest attacks for precisely this. He lived through reproaches for extolling Russia to excess and also for lacking a "truly Russian feeling". Allusions to this are mentioned in the article devoted to the 25th anniversary of his teaching at Petersburg University, and in the obituaries of Nolde, Taube, and others. Wehberg considered it necessary to indicate that while favouring the primacy of *jus* in international relations and striving for the creation of an international court, the decisions of which would be binding upon all, Martens acted as a "Russian politician".[50] In the postwar *Encyclopedia Britannica* the publicist works of Martens were labelled "tendentious" for this reason.[51]

---

[48] F. F. Martens, *Восточная война и Брюссельская конференция* [The Eastern War and the Brussels Conference] (1879), p. iv.

[49] F. F. Martens, "Гаагская конференция мира 1899 г." [The 1899 Hague Peace Conference], *Вестник Европы* [Herald of Europe], no. 2 (February 1900), p. 25.

[50] See H. Wehberg, "Friedrich v. Martens und die Haager Friedens-konferenzen," *Zeitschrift für internationales Recht*, XX (1910), 351.

[51] *Encyclopedia Britannica*, XIV, p. 982.

Martens' diary entries are permeated with alarm about the fate of Russia and surviving the failures of her foreign policy. Martens, for example, lived through with difficulty the defeat of the Russian forces in the War against Japan. "Misfortunate Russia and the long-suffering Russian people are covered with such disgrace and shame!" he wrote in his diary. The peace treaty with Japan he considered until the end of his days to be a "disgrace".

Concerning Murav'ev and Lamzdorf he experienced a feeling of intensifying personal affront over the years. Of Lamzdorf he wrote: "my most malicious enemy" - and even did not attend his funeral in March 1907. But the greatest sufferings were caused by the "talentless actions" of both ministers who "got themselves into a mess" and thereby damaged the foreign policy interests and prestige of Russia. He wrote about Lamzdorf: a minister without talent who brought Russia to war with Japan. Relative to the war with Japan Martens clearly exaggerated because Lamzdorf did not play a decisive role. Martens went on to write: "The wretched state of our Ministry of Foreign Affairs - is down to him".[52] Martens also overestimated the role of the Minister in this respect because the situation in the Ministry of Foreign Affairs reflected the general state of the State apparatus before the 1917 revolution. Of course, Lamzdorf dragged in as deputy minister his friend, Prince Obolenskii, a completely talentless individual; he also strove to appoint Bazili as the director of the Asian Department, who previously was Consul General in Budapest; he facilitated greatly the promotion of other of his personal acquaintances, and the like. But on the whole this was the inevitable result of the entire dominant estate system and of the autocratic arbitrariness which made Goremykin higher than Vitte and Grishka Rasputin higher than all the ministers. Martens' final observations relative to the deteriorating quality of the personnel of the Ministry of Foreign Affairs ("the executive of the Ministry of Foreign Affairs can not be compared with that of 30 years ago under Gorchakov") were on the whole just: no one could write a diplomatic dispatch in French, and the

[52] AVPR, op. 787, delo 9, ed. khr. 6, l. 5, 20.

Asian Department was completely without workers who had been in and knew Asia, and the like.

It seems to the present writer that these moods inspired Martens to judge his Ministry more severely than the foreign policy departments of other countries. Those foreign ministries he knew "from without", superficially, and not "from within" in all the details of official bureaucratism. His diary entry of 27 October 1900 is illustrative: "Today I must repent", Martens wrote, who constantly was indignant about the sway of lack of talent and discourtesy in the Russian Ministry of Foreign Affairs. But it turns out that other countries are no better. In England, Lord Salisbury arranged after the parliamentary elections a "family" cabinet of ministers in which four of his relatives became ministers and their aides. In particular, Lord Lansdowne was appointed as head of the Foreign Office. As Martens noted, two of his qualities are known which make his capable of occupying the armchair of the Foreign Secretary: he is courteous and he speaks French superbly. "Just as with us!", Martens exclaimed. He is consoled only by the fact that Salisbury himself intends to lead foreign policy.[53]

Martens' patriotism had, naturally, its distinctive features which generated his partiality to international affairs. By virtue of his profession he not only was chained to international life, but he also spent a significant part of his time abroad (two to four months annually). Among his friends and acquaintances were many foreign scholars, jurists, diplomats, and publicists. He visited Berlin, Bern, Brussels, The Hague, Dublin, Copenhagen, London, New York, Paris, Rome, Oxford, Istanbul, and other foreign cities. In Russia, except for Petersburg, he knew virtually only one little corner of Lifland. He was never in Moscow or Kiev, not to mention more remote cities.

A diary entry of his son is curious: "Deep love for Motherland – Russia, which seemed to him, however, something abstract as a power".[54]

[53] AVPR, op. 787, delo 9, ed. khr. 5, l. 109.
[54] AVPR, op. 787, delo 8, l. 4.

Whereas determining the socio-political views of Martens leads to great difficulties, an analysis of his attitude towards his mother country is even more complex. Here we are concerned not with rational considerations, but with feelings. An example is the reaction of Martens to Russia's defeat in the War with Japan. The offence felt for the "power" was so strong that it not only came straight on to the pages of the diary as numerous emotional splashes, but also impeded him in soberly viewing events during his participation in working out the peace treaty with Japan. The failure to accept a "disgraceful peace" led to Martens sobbing as he wrote in his diary during the first meeting with the Japanese delegation (diplomat Martens "sobbed", naturally, internally, without external manifestations). At the same time, the disgraceful defeat in the War only intensified Martens' patriotic feelings and did not kill his faith in the future of Russia.

On what "political platform" can Martens be included? The information set out above, in this writer's view, is sufficiently convincing to show how difficult it is to place this multi-faceted and complex person in one of the cubby-holes in the political schemes usual for us. "It is my deep conviction," he wrote in his diary in 1884, "that the State can not exist without order and obesiance to lex".[55] And the measure of order, of the civilisedness of a State, and of social progress for him was respect for the rights of the individual. This was his socio-political "platform", and we should judge Martens by this.

---

[55] AVPR, op. 787, delo 9, ed. khr. 1, l. 27.

CHAPTER X
THE PEACE TREATY WITH JAPAN

In 1905 Martens participated in a major foreign policy event for Russia: the conclusion of the Peace Treaty with Japan.

The diplomatic history of the Russo-Japanese War is rather well-known and has been researched in detail. The archival materials studied by the present writer in connection with Martens' activity do not make any changes of principle in the picture which has formed. However, they do enable us to understand anew certain episodes and, most important, more correctly illuminate the role of Martens himself.

Russia lost the war with Japan, lost on land (the decisive battle at Mukden), and lost at sea (the decisive battle in the Tsushima Strait). The defeat of a mighty military power with rich traditions of victories in Europe and Asia by a country little-known militarily was received in the world with unconcealed astonishment, and in Russian society, as a national disgrace. However, neither the condition of Russia nor the condition of Japan allowed them to consider a continuation of the war. England, France, and Germany, for various reasons, insisted upon the conclusion of a peace. The President of the United States, Theodore Roosevelt, offered his good offices, and an agreement was reached about beginning, in the summer of 1905, Russo-Japanese peace negotiations in the American city of Portsmouth, New Hampshire.

Martens was resting at his dacha in Waldensee when on Sunday, 19 June 1905, he received a telegram from his son: Count Lamzdorf requested him to come to Petersburg. Martens guessed that the matter concerned the peace negotiations, and decided to refuse categorically: first, in store was to conclude a "shameful peace"; and second, again he would play a secondary role, behind the scenes. On Tuesday Martens arrived in Petersburg and read in the newspapers that N. V. Murav'ev[1] was

[1] The reference is to N. V. Murav'ev (1850-1908), State figure and diplomat, from 1894-1905 as Minister of Justice, and then Ambassador to Rome.

contemplated as the first plenipotentiary of Russia, and as the second the Russian Ambassador to Washington, Baron R. R. Rozen. Then, after enumerating the plenipotentiaries comprising the Russian delegation, third was named "Professor F. F. Martens". The newspaper reports strengthened Martens' intention to refuse the trip. "They do not even consider me to be a plenipotentiary, but to be 'attached to' Murav'ev and Rozen. I decided to retire immediately," he wrote in his diary. Martens wore his civil servant uniform with all of the stars which he had and in a combative mood went to the Minister.

Lamzdorf, somewhat puzzled by the emphatically official appearance of Martens, related to him that, having regard to the composition of the Japanese delegation (Ministry of Foreign Affairs, D. Komura, and Envoy to Washington, K. Takahira), the Sovereign had appointed Murav'ev and Rozen as plenipotentiaries to conduct negotiations, and also was disposed to send Martens to the negotiations in view of his international authority and rich international practice. In reply Martens declared his refusal, adding that they had not even asked him in advance, as is usually done. Lamzdorf was beside himself. In a fit of temper he even said that it was all right for Martens to take his leisure in the open air whereas he had to sit in "humid Petersburg". Martens, however, insisted on his position: in Portsmouth there was nothing for him to do. There could be no discussion of international law between the victor and the vanquished. As regards the experience of participation in international conferences, he remained unused because he was behind the scenes and not participating in the negotiations. And here Martens revealed why he was offended: he was not admitted to the negotiations but named "professor", as though he did not serve the Ministry of Foreign Affairs, and so on. Why not appoint Professor Taube instead of him or someone else. Here the Minister raised his voice and threatened that if Martens refused the trip to Portsmouth, then his future career would be finished, he would never receive a post abroad, this would be reported to the Tsar, and the like. Martens held his ground and the conversation ended with Lamzdorf requesting him to think it over and return the following day.

Martens, as he wrote, did not sleep all night, but when in the morning he went to see the Minister he continued to insist upon his refusal. Lamzdorf waxed eloquent. He declared that everything was finished between them, and he had considered Martens to be his best friend! Moreover, he said that he was thinking of suggesting to the Sovereign the candidacy of Martens for the post of envoy to Washington. As regards participation in the negotiations with the Japanese, he had discussed this subject with Murav'ev and all was arranged. Martens left the Minister without giving his clear consent and even departed for Waldensee. But when on 29 June, summoned by a telegram from Lamzdorf, he returned a second time to Petersburg, a pleasant surprise awaited him: Murav'ev, in poor health, refused to travel and S. Iu. Vitte was appointed as the head of the Russian delegation. Martens no longer objected and wrote in his diary: "I was forced by the leadership to participate in this matter so disgraceful for Russia".

Martens was satisfied with the appointment of Vitte, who during 1892-1903 was Minister of Railways and Minister of Finances, and then became Chairman of the Committee of Ministers. He hurried to meet with him. Vitte spoke at once about joint work. He acknowledged that he did not know the English language at all and requested assistance. He also asked Martens to be present at all negotiations with the Japanese. In general he proposed to be candid with him. The conversation made a most favourable impression on Martens. "What an intelligent person", he wrote in his diary. Martens incidentally learned at the Ministry of Foreign Affairs that his conversations with the Minister were not without result: in the new instruction for the Russian delegation he was endowed with the right to participate in all negotiations.[2]

Vitte in his memoirs set out his impression of the conversation with Martens otherwise: "Member of the Council of Ministers of Foreign Affairs Professor Martens is a very good

[2] AVPR, op. 787, delo 9, ed. khr. 6, l. 24-27, 28-29.

man with an enormous baggage of knowledge and a distinguished professor of international law at St. Petersburg University, an honorary member of many foreign universities who enjoys, perhaps incidentally, great renown abroad, is an extremely limited person, not to say more, but with excessive self-esteem".[3]

Notwithstanding this, good contact was established between the head and a member of the delegation.

On 8 July 1905 Martens was received by Nicholas II on the occasion of the departure for Portsmouth. He related to the Tsar that he had not wanted to travel to the negotiations since he was an opponent of a "shameful peace". The Tsar reacted with understanding to the feelings of Martens but said that it was necessary to proceed to the negotiations with the Japanese. President Roosevelt and Emperor Wilhelm also had requested this of him. But he would not agree to humiliating conditions.[4]

On 26 July 1905 (hereinafter in this Chapter dates are given in the new style calendar) the entire Russian delegation numbering twelve persons embarked at Cherbourg (France) on an ocean liner and sailed to New York. The diplomats in the delegation spoiled Martens' mood: in conversations they spread the fact that he was merely "some professor", and that his inclusion in the delegation was incomprehensible since he was a "scholar, and not a diplomat".

Vitte at first displayed a certain reserve, but soon contact with Martens developed: Vitte gave to him his draft speech of greeting in the English and requested that he not only review the text but also read it out during the presentation to the American press. Martens successfully fulfilled the first task of the head of the delegation.

In being sent for negotiations with the Japanese, Vitte was aware of the great complexity of his position. The victors had not assembled to celebrate with vanquished Russia but intended to obtain under the peace treaty maximum advantage. What could the Russian delegation juxtapose to their demands?

---

[3] S. Iu. Vitte, *Воспоминания* [Memoirs] (Moscow, 1960), I, p. 402.

[4] See AVPR, op. 787, delo 9, ed. khr. 6, l. 29.

Vitte devoted attention to world and American public opinion. He energetically sought contacts with the press, especially the American press, and endeavoured to make himself available to the American public. Taking American traditions into account, he behaved in a decidedly democratic way, relying on the fact that he was a man of labour (formerly a engine-driver on a locomotive), a man of the people who had made his own career. Such behaviour from a Tsarist envoy, from whom coldness and pomposity was expected, produced a favourable impression in the United States. In comparison with Vitte, the Japanese plenipotentiaries suffered by reason of their stiffness and reserve.

Martens viewed with disapproval the style of behaviour chosen by Vitte, which he had practised in the ship when communing with the foreign correspondents who travelled along. He had translated conscientiously Vitte's interview with the correspondent of *The Daily Telegraph*, but had seemed "vainglorious and falsely proud". It should be said that Martens did not assess the political significance of Vitte's behaviour. Not understanding inwardly, he observed how "Sergei Iul'evich bowed left and right to any worker who offered his hand". With light irony he commented: "Roosevelt brings us and shows us to the public. Such a show was arranged in Portsmouth on an even grander scale". Outwardly Martens did not discern the favourable consequences of the fact that the President was "attracted" by the personality of Vitte, that the Americans were struck by his being a "man who did things for himself".[5]

Upon arriving in the United States Martens was able to acquaint himself with fresh newspapers and to speak with Russian and foreign diplomats and correspondents and drew for himself the conclusion: "I am convinced that nothing awaits me but unpleasantness and humiliation". His emotional mood manifested itself during the first acquaintanceship with the Japanese (Roosevelt received both delegations on board the Presidential yacht). Martens entered in his diary: "I nearly cried when we were introduced to the Japanese".

---

[5] AVPR, op. 787, delo 9, ed. khr. 6, l. 3032, 43-46.

Martens believed that the head of the Russian delegation did not behave properly and that the entire process of negotiations would be unfamiliar to him. He, for example, was perplexed that the Ministry of Foreign Affairs had not sent any instructions to the Embassy, and that the envoy himself had learned of his appointment to the delegation only from the newspapers. With astonishment he saw that Vitte did not need instructions from the Ministry of Foreign Affairs and devoted little attention to the despatches of Lamzdorf. For the first time Martens was working under the direction of a powerful State figure who thought on a broad scale and was accustomed to take autonomous decisions. Vitte above all endeavoured to elicit the optimal amount of concessions which could be expected from the conclusion of a peace and was must less interested in the details, and even less in questions of protocol. When the Japanese proposed that negotiations be conducted among the plenipotentiaries with the participation of the experts, Vitte agreed without hesitation. And whereas Komura and Takahashi regularly went out to consult Japanese "assistants" in a neighbouring room, Vitte himself spoke and himself immediately answered questions without even thinking to ask the opinion of experts. Even the second plenipotentiary, Rozen, was as a rule silent.

Martens painfully accepted his *de facto* elimination from the negotiations. Initially he understood Vitte to mean that the Japanese categorically opposed his participation in the negotiations, but were not against the participation of all experts. Vitte wrote in his memoirs: "This decision was very annoying to Martens, and he for the entire time could not set his mind at rest".[6] Martens attempted to object, but Vitte repled that one must not spoil relations with the Japanese because of a personal issue which in future might possibly be ameliorated.

The negotiations commenced on 9 August 1905. The procedural questions were agreed at the first session.

At the second session the Japanese representatives communicated to the Russians their peace conditions. They were

---

[6] Vitte, note 3 above, p. 427.

set out in twelve points and seemed exceedingly harsh: recognition of Japanese dominion in Korea, complete evacuation of Russian forces from Manchuria, cession of Sakhalin and lease rights to Port Arthur and the railway leading to it, compensation to Japan for the costs of the war (the amount was not indicated), the transfer to Japan of all Russian warships concealed in neutral waters, limitations on the naval forces of Russia in the Far East, and certain others.

By 12 August Vitte had communicated his reply to the Japanese conditions. Such a surprisingly rapid reaction was possible because Vitte himself, without consultations with Petersburg, took the decisions and Martens was entrusted with drawing up the report. As Martens noted with satisfaction, he fulfilled this commission in one sitting, and the text which he wrote was sent to the Japanese "without the slightest amendments". He suggested in particular the argumentation with respect to the demand to surrender Russian interned ships: the ships were in Chinese ports, and their future fate must not be decided without China.

The Russian side accepted the Japanese conditions (naturally, with reservations intended for future discussion), except for four: the cession of Sakhalin, monetary compensation (that is, virtually an indemnity), limitations on naval forces in the Pacific Ocean, and surrendering the interned ships. Vitte's reply was an entirely satisfactory diplomatic step which exerted a favourable impact on the entire course of the negotiations for Russia. Russia for the sake of achieving peace had agreed with the majority of the Japanese demands and resisted only certain of them which would especially impinge not only her interests, but also her honour and dignity. Reports appeared in the American press that the peace conference was threatened with rupture because of the Japanese claims against Russian territory and exorbitant indemnities. The Japanese delegation was forced to manoeuvre. Komura first removed the demand to limit Russian naval forces and surrender interned ships. Next he proposed a last compromise: Russia would cede Southern Sakhalin to Japan and for the retention of Northern Sakhalin pay to Japan the colossal sum of 1,200,000,000 Japanese yen. A secret session of the plenipotentiaries discussed the Japanese variant for a long time, but Vitte flatly refused to pay. The Conference had reached a dead-end.

Martens remained apart from those tense and dramatic negotiations. He sat in the hotel together with the other experts. Time passed by slowly in this small resort city on the Atlantic coast of the United States, and Martens out of boredom read and played cards. The mood was not improved by the utterance of Rozen which had reached his ears, that he from the very outset had opposed the inclusion of "Professor Martens" as a member of the delegation since "a conference is not a parliament". In a state of idleness and irritation Martens wrote a letter to Lamzdorf in which he not only expressed his offence but also announced his resignation and even threatened to resettle abroad as the fatherland no longer required his services.[7]

The arrival of Sir Donald MacKenzie Wallace (1841-1919), with whom Martens had been acquainted for more than thirty years ("old friend"), served to lessen the tension. He related that he now occupied a very special position attached to the Palace in England and had arrived in order to confidentially report on the course of the Russo-Japanese negotiations. As is evident from Martens' diary, Wallace visited him daily in the hotel ("otherwise I would have fallen into melancholy").[8]

Unlike other members of the Russian delegation who whiled away time in the hotel, Martens was too well-known a figure, so his absence at the negotiations did not pass unnoticed. Commentary appeared in the press. A cutting from *The Times* has been kept in the Martens diary which said that the refusal of the Japanese to admit an experienced specialist to the negotiating table was caused by an aspiration to obtain great freedom of action. Martens was "a man of too high a position" to act merely as a secretary. Under the influence of press reports Martens suggested: "The scandal about me has achieved the scale of a great Japanese victory over the Russians".[9] Here he clearly

[7] AVPR, op. 787, delo 9, ed. khr. 6, l. 29.
[8] AVPR, op. 787, delo 9, ed.khr. 6, l. 55.
[9] AVPR, op.787, delo 9, ed khr. 6, l. 37.

exaggerated. But undoubtedly he could have brought great benefit to the Russian delegation had he participated more actively in the negotiations. An example is the formalisation of the protocols of the negotiations.

The protocols, which are kept by the secretaries of delegations in the French language, set down the arrangements reached among the plenipotentiaries of both sides. When, at the request of Vitte, Martens familiarised himself with the first four, he found them "terrible". He wrote that the "the French language is murderous, the form, unclear, and the exposition, incomprehensible". And to amend the protocols would have been exceedingly complex: on them were the signatures of Vitte and Komura.

President Roosevelt, informed about the deadlock situation, undertook to exert energetic pressure on both parties. As a result Nicholas II agreed to cede Southern Sakhalin. There remained only the question of indemnities. Vitte categorically refused to pay, and to demonstrate his resolve, instructed that on 26 August his account at the hotel be paid. The Russian delegation was preparing to depart. World public opinion would be convinced: Russia had made all possible concessions, but the Japanese for reasons of money broke off the conclusion of a peace. The Japanese Government was in a complicated situation, and Komura requested to postpone the negotiations for two days.

The demonstration of resolve on the part of Vitte was, as is evident from the Martens diary, a diplomatic step. Publicly giving the instruction to prepare for departure, Vitte quietly charged Martens to draw up the draft peace treaty on the basis of the protocols. "I understand nothing!" wondered Martens. Vitte's calculation proved to be correct: on the morning of 29 August Komura reported the consent of Tokyo to half of Sakhalin and renounced the compensation for military expenses. The result of the session was received by the press and the public as a success for Vitte. According to the evidence of Martens, Vitte was greeted with applause after the session. Moreover, they lifted him up as a sign of esteem.

The sudden turn in the course of the negotiations affected the future sojourn of Martens in Portsmouth. As the advisor on legal questions he was invited to the session together with the American, M. Denison, consultant to the Japanese Ministry of Foreign Affairs. The advisors were charged with drawing up the draft peace treaty on the basis of the protocols.

Having been present at the session of plenipotentiaries and familiarised himself with the protocols of the sessions, Martens was rather critical of Vitte's style of work.

At the sessions he noted the difference between the approach of the Japanese and the Russian plenipotentiaries, that is, Vitte, since Rozen was silent. "It was surprising how sound and circumspect were the Japanese", he stated. The Japanese came to a session with prepared drafts of certain articles of the treaty: on prisoners of war, ratification, and others. The Russian side was without its own drafts, and the procedure of the session came down to Vitte hearing the Japanese proposals and immediately giving a reply. "The most confusing questions seemed to be simple to him", Martens wrote in wonder. Soon he ascertained that at the remaining sessions only the Japanese plenipotentiaries offered written drafts. Vitte confined himself to oral statements. As a result, a number of articles, as they were recorded in the protocols, proved textually to be very inconvenient for the Russian side. But when this was ascertained (thanks to the circumspection of Martens) and the Russian side attempted to make corrections, the Japanese protested, referring to the texts signed by the plenipotentiaries. The confusion was intensified by the fact that the protocols were drawn up in "murderous French language".

In his diary Martens cited examples of the "slips" of Vitte. Thus, when discussing a respective article Vitte insisted that the policy of "open doors" also be extended to the Kwantung province being ceded to the Japanese. Komura did not object. But when the Japanese submitted their written draft for the protocol, Vitte and Rozen signed the protocol "without looking". Next it was ascertained that the entry did not reflect the oral arrangement of Vitte and Komura. Vitte demanded a correction.

Martens prepared his own version, Vitte approved it, and even persuaded Komura to agree. But the Japanese waved the protocols signed by the Russian plenipotentiaries, and Vitte was forced to give up.

As another example Martens cited the article concerning Southern Sakhalin. On 16 August Vitte made a statement concerning the cession of Southern Sakhalin with the addition that the Japanese could not place military fortifications thereon. However, he did not provide a written draft of the respective article. ("I would have done so!" exclaimed Martens). As a result in the final editing of the article on demilitarisation Komura said: "On a mutual basis" and immediately handed over a prepared draft. The Russian delegation struggled to "extricate itself" since the mutuality also was suggested for the limitation of Russian defensive measures.[10]

Vitte is a man of great intelligence, wrote Martens, but he does not know diplomatic practice. One may be a great Minister of Finances and all the same understand nothing about the conducting of diplomatic affairs.[11]

Martens' judgments were unjust and biased. They were built solely on the "slips" of Vitte in the discussion of details, editorial clarifications, and the processing of formulas. Here Martens was truly correct. The neglect on the part of Vitte can neither be justified nor excused. It undoubtedly caused certain damage to Russian interests on specific questions. But these particular instances blinded Martens to the principal merits of Vitte's diplomatic activity: the correct strategic calculation, precise assessment of the situation, and possible limits of compromise, the intelligence to separate out that which is important, the ability to adjust relations with allies, and with a recent adversary. Vitte understood and knew how to use the growing role of the press and public opinion.

The conclusion of the Portsmouth Peace Treaty was unequivocally assessed as a success for the Russian State figure and his diplomatic line. As archival documents testify, Vitte

---

[10] AVPR, op. 787, delo 9, ed. khr. 6, l. 52-62, 65-69.

[11] AVPR, op. 787, delo 9, ed. khr. 6, l. 60.

would have succeeded in forcing the Japanese to renounce their claims to Sakhalin if Nicholas II had not conceded prematurely to the pressure of President Roosevelt. In assessing the actions of Vitte it is not Martens who is correct, but the noted Russian jurist, A. F. Koni, who wrote about Vitte: "A powerful and influential State figure and skillful diplomat rendered to his Motherland, in a year of shame and humiliation, an immense service ...".[12]

The diary entries of Martens also contain interesting information about the diplomatic efforts undertaken by him when processing the text of the peace treaty.

One of his "cunning moves" was that he proposed to abbreviate the article being discussed on boundaries and that part thereof which concerned frontier commissions to move to another article (the possibility to make adjustments thereafter would emerge). The Japanese agreed. Another "cunning move" of Martens was to apply with respect to the Tatary Strait and the La Perouse Strait the general rules for freedom of navigation. The Japanese from the outset did not note the "crafty character" of the proposal, but then Komura remembered suddenly and declared that the version of Martens must not limit the right of Japan to military fortifications. They came to an agreement on the formula: both powers renounced the right to military fortifications in the straits. Martens was inwardly satisfied that there was nothing in the formula which spoke of fortifying the coasts of the straits. This meant that the limitations did not extend to the Maritime Province.

In the editorial commission Martens initially encountered distrust on the part of the Japanese. The Japanese reacted with great caution even to the proposals for organising the work of the commission, which Martens had made on the basis of his rich experience (the allocation to him of two secretaries to assist in keeping the entries, preliminary preparation of draft articles, and the like). When at the first session of the commission Martens arrived with ten draft articles of the treaty prepared by him,

---

[12] A. F. Koni, *Сергей Юльевич Витте. Отрывочные воспоминания* [Sergei Iul'evich Vitte. Fragmentary Recollections] (Moscow, 1925), p. 5.

the Japanese were taken unawares. Five articles were agreed with difficulty. Gradually, however, the lack of trust dissipated and soon Martens noted in his diary: "The Japanese side little by little subjected itself to my authority". The Japanese naturally endeavoured to use in the final editing of the text those "slips" which Vitte had permitted during the negotiations, and it was not easy for Martens. His authority as an expert in international law and his knowledge of the history of international relations helped. He entered in his diary: "A stubborn struggle with the Japanese. But closer to the end they were more concessionary".[13]

When the commission completed drawing up the draft peace treaty, the text in the English and French languages was sent by cypher to Petersburg for approval. The Japanese delegation sent their text to Tokyo. Upon receiving consent from the capitals, the plenipotentiaries of Russia and Japan signed the treaty on 5 September 1905.

According to the Peace of Portsmouth, Russia renounced any influence in Korea and recognised there the predominant interests of Japan. Both parties obliged themselves simultaneously to evacuate their forces from Manchuria and to return them to administration by China (except the Liao Dong Peninsula). Russia ceded to Japan lease rights to the Liao Dong Peninsula from Port Arthur and Dal'nyi, and to the South Korean railway, from Chanchun to Port Arthur. Russia ceded Southern Sakhalin along the 50th parallel, both parties obliging themselves not to erect fortifications on the island and not to obstruct freedom of navigation along both straits washing the islands. Russia should conclude a fisheries convention with Japan granting to Japanese subjects the right to catch fish in the Sea of Japan, Sea of Okhotsk, and Bering Sea. The parties returned prisoners of war and compensated expenses for their maintenance.[14]

For Martens the treaty, to which he also had made his contribution, remained a "peace of shame". More than once he

---

[13] AVPR, op. 787, delo 9, ed. khr. 6, l. 70, 74.

[14] See *Сборник договоров России с другими государствами 1856-1917* [Collection of Treaties of Russia with Other States 1856-1917] (Spb., 1955), pp. 338-339.

declared subsequently that he bore no responsibility for the text thereof. Nonetheless, the moral nonacceptance of the treaty and the criticism of individual "slips" by Vitte did not prevent him from giving in the end his due to the head of the delegation. He wrote in his diary: "Only he could bring the cause of the peace treaty to such an end".

Martens was in a grave spiritual state during the peace negotiations. The conclusion of the "peace of shame" caused an inner protest in himself. His own position at the negotiations seemed to him to be "stupid", damaging to his prestige. His health had cracked. Because of illness he was not present when the treaty was signed, for which he was glad. "When does my forced punishment end?" he wrote. In this mood Martens celebrated his sixtieth birthday on 15 August. "My season of life has ended ... never have I spent such an awful day, even remembering childhood, far from my wife, children, a people beloved!" – he wrote in his diary. Evidently his mood was caused by Martens' wish to return home as soon as possible. Vitte had warned him to stay until the departure of the entire delegation, intended for the 12 September, but Martens was adamant, and on 30 August he already had set sail on the Atlantic Ocean by a French steamer to Europe. Psycholgically it is understandable why he exclaimed: "Hurrah!"

Here it is instructive to dwell once again on the good relations which Martens had established with Vitte. In his diary he repeatedly noted the attention and respect on the part of Sergei Iul'evich Vitte. "In general he relates to me very well and even sincerely," he wrote. When saying adieu Vitte deeply moved him: he spoke from the soul and kissed him several times. Martens had wished that the joint work in Portsmouth "had brought me the patronage and disposition of the most intelligent Sergei Iul'evich".[15]

In summing up it should be noted that Martens proved to be very useful to Vitte, especially in processing the text of the peace treaty with Japan, as a highly-qualified and experienced specialist. He exerted no influence on reaching agreement with

[15] AVPR, op. 787, delo 9, ed. khr. 6, l. 70, 73-74.

regard to material questions. Therefore, the assertion that Martens played an important role when concluding the Treaty of Portsmouth does not correspond to the facts.[16] It is remarkable that Martens himself never publicly mentioned his participation in the preparation of the peace treaty. Not only Vitte in his memoirs, but also Nolde, Taube, Wehberg, and other jurists are silent about his services in this matter. If we digress from certain ambitions manifested by Martens, he undoubtedly was right in objecting to his being included in the delegation. He clearly was not suited to determining the conditions of peace, and Taube or another specialist on international law would have been better for legal consultations. Nonetheless, in the situation which unfolded Martens did everything possible for the good of Russia.

[16] See *Encyclopedia Britannica* (Chicago, 1946), XIV, p. 982.

CHAPTER XI
THE SECOND HAGUE PEACE CONFERENCE

The shattering failure of hopes for disarmament or at least a freezing of military expenditures which had been placed on the 1899 Hague Peace Conference should, it seemed, have been sobering. But among the general public of many countries this result not only did not diminish but actually intensified protests against the arms race. The beginning of the twentieth century was marked by an upsurge of the pacifist movement, which furthered the Revolution of 1905 in Russia. The activeness of the societies of the friends of peace grew in Western Europe and the United States. International congresses of pacifists were convoked. Nor did the movement of the friends of peace bypass Russia. The Society of Peace was created at Moscow in 1909, with branches in Odessa, Riga, Revel, and Novocherkassk. Analogous societies emerged at Petersburg and Kiev. In Moscow, as already related, Professor L. A. Kamarovskii conducted the principal work with regard to the Society, and in Petersburg, the noted Russian sociologist, jurist, historian, and ethnographer, as well as the publisher of the journal *Вестник Европы* [Herald of Europe], M. M. Kovalevskii. It was in those years that the great Russian writer L. N. Tolstoi wrote a number of pacifist pamphlets: "Can One Wage War?" (Petersburg, 1901); "Against War" (Berlin, 1903); "Patriotism and the Law of War" (Moscow, 1906), and others.[1] Proposals of various regional associations of States as paths to universal and stable peace were widely disseminated. An example of such views is Kamarovskii's work on the question of a United States of Europe.[2]

On the other hand, the activity of the arbitration court in The Hague, commissions of enquiry, and application of the

[1] L. N. Tolstoi, *Можно ли воевать?* [Can One Wage War?] (Petersburg, 1901); id, *Против войны* [Against War] (Berlin, 1903); id, *Патриотизм и право войны* [Patriotism and the Law of War] (Moscow 1906).

[2] L. A. Kamarovskii, *Вопрос о международной организации Соединенных Штатов Европы* [The Question Concerning an International Organisation of the United States of Europe] (M., 1905).

Convention on the laws and customs of warfare had become visual confirmation of the fruitfulness of the 1899 Hague Conference.

The intention to convoke a new peace conference was maturing in this situation in the ruling circles of some countries. The President of the United States, Theodore Roosevelt, took the first initiative, but the Russo-Japanese War prevented its being effectuated. After the end of the War, the proposal to hold a conference was advanced by the Government of Russia. Therefore, the following formula was later selected to designate the initiators of the Conference: "Second International Peace Conference, proposed first by the President of the United States of America being at the invitation of His Majesty the Emperor of All the Russias and convened by Her Majesty the Queen of The Netherlands ...".[3]

Programme of the Conference In September 1905, immediately after the conclusion of the peace with Japan, the Minister of Foreign Affairs, Lamzdorf, charged the Russian representatives in forty-seven States to seek a view regarding the convocation of a new conference at The Hague. The reaction everywhere proved to be positive. It fell to the Russian Ministry of Foreign Affairs a second time to act as the organiser of the contemplated conference.

The successful work of Martens in preparing for the 1899 Conference recommended him to the organisers of the new conference. When he returned from the United States to Petersburg, at their first meeting Lamzdorf spoke of the Second Hague Peace Conference. The Minister proposed that Martens preside at two interdepartmental commissions: to prepare the programme, and to prepare the draft decisions of the Conference.

Martens turned out to be in a situation analogous to that which had arisen in 1898. On one hand, convocation of the second peace conference was for him something desired and close to his heart. In the programme for the 1899 Conference he had set out the idea for dividing the questions to be raised into two groups so that those most prepared could be discussed at the

---

[3] See *Второй конференции мира 1907 г.* [Second Peace Conference of 1907] (Spb., 1908), p. 303.

first conference and the others carried over to the next. He himself at the 1899 Conference had more than once proposed to defer the discussion of a controversial issue to a future meeting. Moreover, from the standpoint of his theory of the international community and international administration, Martens believed it advisable to hold such conferences periodically. He regarded them as important organs of international administration. His view on the problem he had formulated (in May 1908) as follows: "I look at the Hague Conferences exclusively as governmental attempts *to organise and to put in order* the mutual relations of peoples to the benefit of peace and a better mutual society. But I do not think that any international conference will succeed in introducing eternal peace nor lead to disarmament".[4]

He was offended and then disturbed by the attitude of the Ministry leadership and Imperial court towards him as the organiser of the preparations for the Conference and towards the Peace Conference itself generally. On the basis of the experience of 1898-99, Martens considered himself to be the most appropriate person in the Ministry of Foreign Affairs both to prepare the new conference and to head the Russian delegation. But already he knew that neither one nor the other would be. Lamzdorf awaited from him, as in 1898-99, the drawing up of papers which could be submitted to the Tsar, circulated to foreign States, and discussed at the Conference. He was needed as a work horse who would obediently and quietly pull the heavy load of preparations. There were other people for leadership, representation, and receipt of orders. In addition, the ministers (and the Tsar too) were interested in the Conference as an extensive peaceloving initiative of Russia, important both for foreign (having lost the War with Japan) and internal motives (Revolution in Russia). Lamzdorf did not believe in disarmament, but reacted rather indifferently to the codification of international law and the creation of mechanisms for the peaceful settlement of inter-State conflicts. In 1901, two years after the Hague Conference, Martens declared heatedly that the Petersburg "leaders" did not welcome his efforts at the

[4] AVPR, op. 787, delo 9, ed. khr. 7, l. 118.

Conference, but to a considerable extent condemned them. "The Tsar himself is trying to forget it. My leading role at The Hague I am already being blamed for at the Ministry of Foreign Affairs," he wrote in his diary. When Martens at the end of 1900 proposed to Lamzdorf to put forward the initiative for a solemn opening of the Permanent Court of International Arbitration at The Hague, he did not react at all. In his words, the Tsar supposedly decided that this was a matter for the Government of the Netherlands.[5] Such an attitude did not inspire Martens, and he with dark presentiments accepted to fulfil the commission of the Minister.

As always, he worked rapidly and precisely. In December, without awaiting the convocation of a commission, he submitted to Lamzdorf his own draft of a new circular note. It turned out that the Minister already had one draft drawn up by a bureaucrat in the I Department, and the Minister had approved it. The offended Martens ("evidently they know international law better than I") submitted his own draft and avoided further discussion. And when Lamzdorf invited him on 9 January 1906 for lunch in honour of the Chinese Mission, Martens uttered not a word about preparations for the Conference.

The Martens Memorandum became the basis for the circular note of the Russian Ministry of Foreign Affairs circulated to interested States. The programme proposed in the Note actually circumvented the question of the limitation of armaments and pushed to the side those practical results which were achieved at the preceding Conference. The creation of the Permanent Court of International Arbitration was cited in the circular note as the major achievement of the 1899 Conference, which in fact had proved its vitality, and also the international commissions of enquiry, which had demonstrated a positive role. In development of the results achieved, the Russian Government proposed to discuss the following points:

1. improvement of the provisions of the Convention on the Peaceful Settlement of International Conflicts.

---

[5] AVPR, op. 787, delo 9, ed. khr. 6, l. 119, 139.

2. adding provisions to the Convention on the Laws and Customs of Land Warfare.
3. working out a Convention on the laws and customs of warfare at sea.
4. additions to the 1899 Convention on the application to warfare at sea of the principles of the 1864 Geneva Convention.[6]

The hand of Martens is clearly evident in the programme.

On 8 March 1906 Martens was invited to the interdepartmental meeting on preparation of The Hague Conference. The deputy Minister of Foreign Affairs, Prince Obolenskii, was appointed to be chairman of the meeting. In reply Martens sent a satirical letter to Lamzdorf which said: "I sincerely thank Your Excellency for relieving me from the chairmanship of the interdepartmental meeting" and expressed a readiness to come to it. Lamzdorf immediately sent a letter of reply: "Dear Fedor Fedorovich! I thank You for your letter. I invite You to lunch in honour of the Japanese Ambassador, Motono, to whom I shall present You. At lunch we shall speak about certain of our affairs". Martens immediately replied: "Thank you for the invitation. I accept with pleasure. Mr. Motono I have known for a long time". Martens entered in his diary: "It is necessary to lead Count Lanzdorf by the nose to elicit professions of love". Preparation for the conference was not spoken of at the lunch. Martens steadfastly held to his position of being offended.

At the interdepartmental meeting he conducted himself with studied indifference and answered only when Prince Obolenskii asked him ("the blockhead-chairman"). He was again convinced of the fruitlessness of the meeting. "Our persons on the make thought that having circulated the circular [having in view the circular note of the Ministry of Foreign Affairs – V.P.], they have done everything," Martens wrote. "But now the work begins". Besides Martens, they could not find an appropriate candidate to conduct qualified preparatory work.

[6] See note 3 above, p. 3.

It is difficult to speculate how matters might have proceeded further, but in spring 1906 Lamzdorf was removed from the post of Minister. Vitte was forced to resign, and in his place as Chairman of the Committee of Ministers was appointed Goremykin, who had demanded Lamzdorf be removed as a protege of Vitte. "Finally my most evil enemy, Lamzdorf, has fallen", Martens breathed with ease. On 1 May a farewell to the former Minister and a welcome to the new one, A. P. Izvol'skii, was held. At breakfast Martens was seated next to the Minister. Izvol'skii exchanged several courteous sentences with him. Martens hoped for a certain improvement of his position in the Ministry of Foreign Affairs.

The change of ministers moved preparations in the Ministry of Foreign Affairs for the Hague Conference to the second plane. Martens too did not hurry to an audience with the new Minister on these questions. But, as previously, he already had gathered information, thought out the programme, and possible variant decisions. The following episode was characteristic in this respect. In May-June 1906 he had represented Russia at a conference in Geneva to review the 1864 Geneva Convention on the wounded and sick. Recalling the draft decision prepared in the Ministry of Foreign Affairs for the future conference – to transfer disputes during wartime between States for consideration by the Permanent Court of International Arbitration, Martens proposed to transfer to the Court all disputes relating to interpretation of the Geneva Convention. However, the initiative of the Russian plenipotentiary ("my serene proposal" – wrote Martens) had encountered a categorical "nein" from the German delegate, von Bülow. Martens had not insisted. He merely had wanted to sound out the positions of countries in on the threshold of the Hague Conference being prepared. The results of the soundings were rather pessimistic. Martens had learned that von Bülow was "in the favour of the German Emperor". His position acquired special weight.

With regard to preparing the Hague Conference Izvol'skii turned to Martens only at the very end of 1906. In a conversation with him Izvol'skii sincerely acknowledged that he did not know what had been done before him and why Russia had taken the initiative from the hands of President Roosevelt. He requested Martens to assume the entire preparation for the Conference. Martens answered the Minister that he did not know the reasons and circumstances for the Russian initiative, but now, after such a loud claim, Russia could never lay it down. He agreed to assume the preparation of the Conference, but on condition that he would not bear it alone. The Minister did not object and gave an instruction to transfer all the files to Martens. He also seconded to the disposition of Martens Baron Nolde, whom he knew to be a "distinguished and knowledgable worker".

Martens set about to familiarise himself with the correspondence which the Ministry of Foreign Affairs had conducted for the past eighteen months and gave Izvol'skii a Memorandum in summary. In it he proposed to hold a meeting of the representatives of the five European powers, the United States, Japan, and Holland in Paris for the purpose of preparing the Conference, having appointed as head of the meeting the Ambassador of Russia in Paris, A. I. Nelidov. The idea of an advance meeting of the representatives of the leading States was pleasing to the Minister, but he noted that such meeting would not remain secret and undesirable gossip would ensue. Martens could not fail to concur. Then the Minister suggested that Martens himself be sent to Berlin, Paris, London, Rome, Vienna, and The Hague in order to speak about the preparatory measures on site. Martens agreed and prepared a Memorandum for report to the Tsar. On 19 December 1906 Nicholas II confirmed the proposal, and on 26 December granted an audience to Martens. The Tsar spoke of convoking the Conference as a decided matter. He said that he was aware of the aspiration of the German Emperor to ruin the Conference, but he hoped for a favourable outcome. "I wish You complete success!" – the Tsar said in concluding the conversation. Baron Nolde was appointed to be the secretary accompanying Martens on the trip to the European capitals.[7]

[7] See AVPR, op. 787, delo 9, ed. khr. 6, l. 100-101, 113-114, 117-119, 125-126.

After departure, on 3 January 1907, Martens was once again surprised at Nicholas II. The position of the Tsar on a fundamental issue – disarmament – interested him. Evidently he had recalled the downfall of his proposal to reduce the selection of recruits to the Russian Army. He received no precise explanations, but the Tsar said that one could not speak of "complete disarmament". From this Martens concluded that the Tsar was not against a discussion of the problem of some partial reduction of military arsenals or a limitation thereof.

In conversation with the Tsar the principal idea of Martens' European tour was confirmed: to familiarise himself with the mood of the great European powers relative to the convocation of the Second Hague Peace Conference in spring 1907. The preliminary sounding should assist in agreeing the programme of the Conference, which would ensure its success.

In comparison with the 1899 Conference the working out of the programme for the new conference was simultaneously both simpler and more complex.

The 1899 Conference had in view a general conception for strengthening universal peace – by means of a limitation of armaments and working out means for the peaceful development of inter-State relations. It confirmed the correctness of the programme selected for strengthening universal peace and already had achieved certain material results in the realisation thereof. The new conference should continue the efforts undertaken in 1899. In 1907 the very idea of an international peace conference had not encountered the previous resistance. It was accepted as necessary and useful for all countries. Certain special problems also had disappeared: the period of convocation, place of holding it, and the like. All this facilitated the preparation of the new conference.

On the other hand, there were a number of circumstances which seriously complicated its prospects. Certain questions had been carried over from the first conference to the second (for example, the inviolability of private property in warfare at sea, the extension of certain rules for waging war on land to warfare at sea) which had caused a great diversity of opinion and sometimes material disagreements. The 1899 Conference had put, but had not decided, the problem of the binding nature of decisions of the international court created by it. Thus a heavy burden was placed objectively and irreversibly on the programme for the 1907 Conference which was left over from the 1899 Conference. The earliest appraisal showed that one could not count upon the rapid overcoming of numerous barriers.

Most complex was the situation in the domain of disarmament. In 1899 the governments of all the great powers were sceptical of the direction of the work of the Conference and unanimously were satisfied by a statement of good intentions. In 1907 the situation had changed. The Liberal government which had come to power in England in 1906 had decided to use the international forum to demonstrate its readiness to limit the military burden. The head of the Liberal cabinet, Sir Henry Campbell-Bannerman (1836-1908), personally wrote an article in the *Nation* on the Hague Conference and the limitation of armaments. The article developed the idea that England was ready for such limitation, but the growing armaments of other powers, particularly Germany, compelled it to increase military expenditures. Alarm was growing in English ruling circles about her maritime supremacy, especially in connection with the effectuation in Germany of an extensive programme to enlarge the navy. English ruling circles were full of resolve not to concede. But the strength of the Royal Navy required an increase of the tax burden and could not fail to create strong opposition in the country, which even without this was living through a rise in the strike movement. It was necessary to show the populace and indeed the entire world that Kaiser Germany was at fault for the arms race and thereby the increasing taxes. In accordance with this position England advanced an additional proposal to include in the Conference programme a point about limitation of the military burden.

The Government of the United States proposed to enlarge the programme by including a question on the inadmissability of armed interference of States to recover debt obligations of their subjects (the so-called Calvo and Drago doctrines).[8]

[8] The reference is to L. M. Drago (1859-1921), jurist, diplomat, publicist, and in 1902-3 the Minister of Foreign Affairs of Argentina. The idea of the

Under these complex conditions the achievement of weighty results at the Conference to be convoked seemed more than problematic. Most realistic seemed to be the addition to the Conventions signed at the First Conference, although here too it was complicated to determine those specific domains where it would be possible to anticipate success on the basis of the broad consent of the participants. All this it fell to Martens to elicit at meetings in the European capitals.

European Tour On 6 January 1907 Martens left together with Nolde on a mission for his fatherland. The first stop was Berlin.

By personal experience, the experience of the 1899 Conference, and the materials of the Russian Ministry of Foreign Affairs, Martens knew well the principal obstacles with regard to the question of disarmament and the binding nature of the Hague tribunal, and certain others could be expected from the German side. Berlin was to him the most difficult point on the travel route. He also took into account the close, one could say, special relationship between Nicholas and Wilhelm and their courts. Therefore, he decided to visit Berlin twice, at the beginning and at the end of the tour. He even purchased the railway ticket in advance from Vienna, the final point of the route not directly to Petersburg, but via Berlin. But his intention he for the moment kept to himself.

In Berlin the Russian Ambassador, Count N. D. Osten-Sacken, informed Martens that he already knew from diplomatic papers that: Wilhelm II related to the convening of the Conference "unsympathetically". On 10 January Martens met at the German Ministry of Foreign Affairs with the secretary of State von Bogendorf. The secretary of State informed him that Germany accepted the programme announced by Russia and opposed the inclusion of additional points in it, that is, especially

---

cont'd

inadmissability of armed intervention to recover debts for foreigners was set out in the Note of the United States Department of State in 1902. The delegate of Argentina to the 1907 Hague Conference was C. Calvo, Argentine jurist and diplomat. He set out his conception of the doctrine in the press in 1868.

the English proposal. Martens attempted to explain to his interlocutor that the Russian Government truly had not included the English and American proposals in the proposed programme but did not see a way to prevent their being discussed at the Conference. Bogendorf declared then "everything ends sometime", that is, the conference would collapse at once. To be sure, he then said that he was expressing his own personal opinion, but this reservation did not change the situation. The position of Germany was as before categorically negative with respect to the English initiative. Martens attempted to mitigate it with the following arguments: why at the outset reject the English proposal, it was sufficient to transfer it for consideration to one of the commissions and then "bury" it in the report at the plenary session of the conference. But the arguments of Martens exerted no special effect on Bogendorf nor on other officials of the German Ministry of Foreign Affairs. In a fit of temper Martens wrote in his diary that they "can not see longer than their nose".

In everything else Martens was received in Berlin "excellently". They invited him to a "large" luncheon at the German Chancellery and to an "even larger" luncheon at the Palace. On 18 January Wilhelm II approached Martens at a palace ball in the White Room of the Imperial Palace. He began the conversation with words which Martens considered to be "inappropriate". The Kaiser said that at The Hague Conference they should hang a portrait of Martens travelling about Europe with the "palm leaf of peace". Martens drily objected that he was fulfilling his duty. To the question of the Kaiser, Martens related the route of the trip, the last point of which was Vienna. "And where from Vienna?" asked the Kaiser, and Martens at once used his store of diplomatic cunning. He said that from Vienna he should travel to Petersburg, but was ready to come to Berlin and report on the results of the trip. As Martens supposed, his most August interlocutor reacted positively: "I would be very grateful to you". The Imperial invitation to travel to Berlin upon completing the trip was received.

Despite the splendour of the reception in Berlin, Martens noted: "there is little sincerity". And in summing up the impressions received: they want to take advantage of The Hague Conference in order to inflict minor blows on Russia and England, whom they do not like.

In Paris, where Martens arrived on 19 January and spent ten days, the reception was even more ceremonial and much more sincere. "Dear Paris!" wrote Martens.

The Russian Ambassador Nelidov was dear and kind. The luncheon with ministers, diplomats, and future delegates to the Conference was a warm one. President Falkier[9] gave Martens an audience and discussed for nearly an hour and a half the prospects for the Conference. The President, as expected, did not believe in practical measures relating to disarmament, but saw the importance of this problem. Next the President invited the Russian guest to breakfast in a family setting. In Paris, Martens was fêted as a well-known international arbitrator and awarded a medal. He visited the Senate and the Chamber of Deputies, and the Académie.

The most detailed business conversation for Martens occurred with a long-time acquaintance, Léon Bourgeois,[10] who intended to be a French representative at the forthcoming Conference. He came to Martens at the Hotel Regina, and they discussed for a long time the questions of interest to them. As a result Martens wrote: we are one in that there will be no misfortune if the participants of the Conference are engaged with the consideration of questions of limiting armaments in order to bury the problem in one of the commissions. Moreover, a discussion of the question of limiting armaments would impart to the Conference greater weight in the eyes of the peoples of the entire world. "I am once again persuaded," Martens wrote, "that discussion of the question of disarmament does not represent the slightest danger".

[9] The reference is to Armand Klement Falkier, elected President of the French Republic on 17 January 1906.

[10] The reference is to Léon Bourgeois, French political figure who was Chairman of the Chamber of Deputies (1902-4) and in 1906, Minister of Foreign Affairs of France.

On 28 January Martens arrived in London. The Carlton Hotel, where he stayed, pleasantly surprised him: "The best of all those I have seen in my journeying about the world". The Russian Ambassador, Count Benckendorf, was absent, and therefore the meeting at the Embassy was, although warm, not very substantive.

On 30 January Martens had a first meeting at the Foreign Office with Edward Grey.[11] They conversed for two hours and, since Grey had a poor command of French, then the language of diplomacy, the conversation was in English. Martens drew attention to the fact that to expect disarmament was entirely unrealistic. Grey did not object, but declared that the question of limiting armaments should be discussed at the Conference. Above all it was necessary to stop the increase of expenditures on arms. In the words of the Foreign Secretary, Germany was building more and more naval vessels and forcing England to build more. England intended to adhere to the principle of double supremacy: if the Germans build four ships, then the English would launch eight. Such an arms race was a heavy burden. Moreover, as Grey noted, a discussion of the questions connected with the limitation of armaments would provide valuable material for the future.

Martens made no objections to the Foreign Secretary. He merely requested that the course and completion of plenary debate on this question be agreed with the other great powers. The conversation created for Martens "the most favourable impression", and of Grey himself, "the impression of a very intelligent person".

On the next day Martens was at breakfast with the Prime Minister, Sir Henry Campbell-Bannerman, where he was acquainted with other members of the cabinet, many of whom he found to be "extremely interesting". He attended the ceremony for the opening of Parliament and met with members of the House of Lords. In London, Martens met many good and long acquaintances.

---

[11] The reference is to Edward Grey, Lord Fallodon, English State figure and diplomat, and from 1905-16, Foreign Secretary of England.

On 2 February King Edward VII received the Russian guest. In a conversation of an hour and a half the King said that he was sceptical of the proposal of his government with regard to the limitation of armaments, but as a constitutional monarch may not interfere in such affairs. "An exceedingly intelligent person," wrote Martens and noted the "cherished goal" of the King – to isolate Germany and her Emperor.

An amusing incident happened to Martens in England. On Saturday, when he was ready to depart in the morning at 08:00 hours, he was awakened in the hotel and an invitation from the King to luncheon was transmitted. The departure was moved to Sunday, but on the invitation it said that one should attend luncheon in special dress ("servile short pantaloons and shoes" Martens wrote with irritation), which he did not have. On Saturday all the shops were closed, as the chargé d'affaires informed Martens, and then the Marshal of the Royal Court. They offered Martens their own dress, but he categorically refused. The Marshal reported to the King, who allowed Martens to come to luncheon in ordinary dress.

The best of the English ruling circles assembled in Buckingham Palace for a traditional luncheon on the occasion of the opening of a session of Parliament. The German ambassador was "terribly surprised" to see Martens there in order to learn the course of his soundings. But Martens was an experienced diplomat.

At The Hague, where Martens was from 4-8 February, he was received exceedingly cordially. Meetings were held with the Queen, Prince, Queen Mother, and the like. "They fed me from morning to night," he wrote about the numerous breakfasts, luncheons, and dinners in his honour. An arrangement was reached at The Hague that the future Conference would open on 1 June.

From 10-15 February Martens conducted negotiations in Rome. For about an hour and a half he spoke with the King of Italy, Victor Emmanuel III, who clearly was sympathetic to the idea of disarmament and favoured discussion of the question at the Conference. His conversation with the Italian Prime Minister was successful. "We understood one another," Martens declared.

On 17 February Martens arrived in Vienna. The Russian Ambassador and long a good acquaintance, Prince L. P. Urusov, informed him that Austria-Hungary was following in the German channel. Of this Martens was convinced at an audience with Emperor Franz Josef, who opposed the English proposal. To the arguments of Martens he simply was silent, and Martens wrote in his diary: "He did not make an impression as a very intelligent person". The following conversation with the Minister of Foreign Affairs, Baron A. von Aehrenthal, was more detailed in nature, and as a result of "lengthy disputes" Martens drew the conclusion that the "word" had been put out from Berlin: do not agree to submit the English proposal to the Conference. Martens' counter-arguments were not successful, and he did not detain himself in Vienna.

On 22 March he already was in Berlin. There he was invited at once to breakfast at the palace. Wilhelm II heard Martens' information about the trip, his arguments in favour of discussing the English proposal at the Conference concerning the limitation of armaments, and agreed that the English proposal should be "admitted to the Conference". Martens left for Petersburg "in a wonderful mood".

Izvol'skii had succeeded evidently in hearing the report of Martens, especially about his arrangement with Wilhelm II. But on the next day a Memorandum came to him from the German capital with a complete rejection of what the Emperor had said to the Russian envoy. "Oh, falsifiers!" said Martens in indignation and noted: "Izvol'skii is in despair".[12]

It is advisable to stop a moment to answer a question: was the Martens mission successful? The fact is that with regard to this question there have been debates in doctrinal writings and various opinions expressed. In some works devoted to the 1907 Hague Conference the importance of Martens' tour for the Conference was noted. Others speak of its lack of success, particularly that they remained dissatisfied in Berlin and even

[12] AVPR, op. 787, delo 9, ed. khr. 7, l. 2, 4, 5-6, 7-12, 13-14, 15-16.

in Petersburg with it, where the leadership supposed that he had put forward his own personality too much on the trip.[13]

It should be stressed that the familiarisation and preparatory trip of Martens had a broad resonance and became to a certain extent sensational. For the first time for the purpose of preparing an international conference of such a scale the capitals of the European powers had been deliberately visited by a special envoy of the initiator-country, not a minister, but a university professor, an international lawyer having an advisory post in the Ministry of Foreign Affairs. Martens had acted de facto as a special envoy. At the time this was new and unusual. It is not surprising that those writers who considered the trip of Martens to be unsuccessful describe it as a "noteworthy tour". It is remarkable that in the voluminous literature on the 1907 Hague Conference they always write about the trip of Martens.

The level of Martens' negotiations was highly unusual. The heads of State, heads of governments, and ministers of foreign affairs met with him in Berlin, Paris, London, The Hague, Rome, and Vienna, not to mention other officials and unofficial persons. Everywhere he was accorded enormous respect not only as an envoy of the Russian Emperor, but also as a generally-recognised authority on international law, noted diplomat, and supporter of peace and legality in the inter-State community. Personal authority undoubtedly imparted additional weight to Martens' trip. "I closely saw with what attention and respect all of official Europe greeted him," recalled Nolde, accompanying Martens.[14]

What were the results of Martens' trip? Some writers in essence hold him at fault for not eliminating Anglo-German contradictions. These claims are, naturally, entirely groundless. The very suggestion that Martens, with all of his undoubted authority, could persuade England and Germany to forget, even for a moment, their naval rivalry is naive. As for the collection of information and harmonising of individual positions, this

---

[13] See H. Wehberg, "Friedrich v. Martens und die Haager Friedenskonferenzen," *Zeitschrift für internationales Recht*, XX (1910), p. 356.

[14] B. E. Nolde, «Ф. Ф. Мартенс» [F. F. Martens], *Русская мысль* [Russian Thought], no. 12 (1909), p. 22.

absolutely was a useful contribution to the preparation of the Conference. The trip itself, the international resonance caused by it, increased interest in the Conference, and the heightened attention restrained the parties in dispute.

Martens returned to Petersburg immersed in preparations for the Conference. He even brought with him a specific date for opening: 1 June. However, at home he immediately began to encounter a surprise: it turned out that it was necessary to start from the beginning to convince the Tsar and his "own" Minister of Foreign Affairs about the need to convoke the Conference! Izvol'skii said in his first conversation with Martens that he did not understand why Russia has taken the initiative away from President Roosevelt. The information gathered by Martens during the tour only strengthened his scepticism.

Martens noted in his diary: "Already three weeks I have been in Petersburg, and the matter of the Conference has virtually not moved. Each day I torment myself with editing diplomatic telegrams which Izvol'skii rejects. I strive to convoke the Conference. Will I succeed? Izvol'skii genuflects to Wilhelm and does what he is ordered from Berlin. I prove to him that one can not go back once Russia has sent invitations to 47 States and they have been accepted. However, he tarries. On 13 March he finally reported to the Sovereign the draft circular to convoke the Conference. The Sovereign has signed. I thought that the matter has been resolved. But no, in Berlin they have learned about the note and demand to make changes in it. Izvol'skii has changed the text of the note several times. They still have not sent it".

On 16 March Nicholas II received Martens. Martens tried to explain to the Tsar the "harmlessness of the English proposal" and the senselessness of the position of Berlin and Vienna. He told the Tsar how Wilhelm had promised him consent to inclusion of the English proposal and how then the German side had withdrawn from its word. "Is it possible" How strange!" said the Tsar. He concurred with the reflections of Martens but all the same asked: perhaps the Conference should be deferred? Martens explained that this would be a "great scandal". Nicholas it seems agreed but Martens was not quieted, for he already knew the "weak character of the Sovereign".

On 20 March the Tsar signed the new draft circular note submitted by Izvol'skii. They sent it at once to Russian representations abroad. Martens was able only several days later to familiarise himself with Izvol'skii's amendments. In the new version of the note the complete solidarity of the views of the three Emperors was stressed (Russian, German, and Austrian). The right of Russia, Germany, and Austria-Hungary not to discuss "impractical" proposals also was indicated. Martens read the creation of his minister with great disapproval ("I was horrified").

Reactions to Martens' trip continued to be received in Petersburg. At the end of March Izvol'skii showed him a telegram from Osten-Sacken in Berlin. In conversation with the Ambassador, Wilhelm II had complained about the interview which Martens gave to the French newspaper *Le Temps* on 17 March (30 March, new style). In the interview Martens supposedly had said that in Berlin he had been received coolly and displayed no flexibility. Wilhelm, offended, had said to the Ambassador: "I gave him breakfast, I sat down beside him, and so forth. And he such words!" Martens succeeded in proving that the words offensive to the German Emperor belonged not to him, but to the journalist who did the interview. But Izvol'skii all the same requested that a telegram be sent to Osten-Sacken with explanations and to go to see the German Ambassador in Petersburg.

Although the circular note of the Russian Ministry of Foreign Affairs already had gone and it seemed the bridges were erected, Izvol'skii continued to waver with respect to the new Hague Conference. On 9 April 1907 Martens wrote: "Izvol'skii wishes the downfall of the Hague Conference".[15] The position of the Minister, naturally, did not fill Martens with enthusiasm. But he continued to conscientiously prepare for the Conference.

At the Conference On 15 June (new style) 1907 the Second Peace Conference opened at The Hague. Forty-four States took part in it, including seventeen countries

[15] See AVPR, op. 787, delo 9, ed. khr. 7, l. 20-21, 24, 25, 35.

from Central and South America. A forum with the participation of States of Europe, America, and Asia was unprecedented in scale. A number of States were at such a Conference for the first time. Their delegations, inclusive of ministers, ambassadors, generals, and admirals, were numerous and very representative. Eminent jurists were included. As a whole the Conference assembled the cream of international lawyers. In all 232 delegates were present at the Conference. "Truly an international parliament", Martens entered in his diary.[16] His undoubted success was the adoption by the Conference of both the Russian programme and the reglament which he had worked out. Four commissions were created in all, which might create in turn subcommissions and subcommittees. The materials prepared therein must be considered at the plenary sessions, and then transferred to an editorial committee for final processing and inclusion in the final document.

The Russian delegation was headed by Nelidov, the Ambassador in Paris. The second plenipotentiary was F. F. Martens as a member of the Council of the Ministry of Foreign Affairs. The Russian envoy to The Hague, N. V. Charykov, was a plenipotentiary delegate, and the technical delegates included the envoy to Rio de Janeiro, M. E. Prozor, Colonel at the Admiralty and professor of international law at the Maritime Academy, I. A. Ovchinnikov, and others. Nelidov was elected chairman of the Conference.[17]

Léon Bourgeois, the first plenipotentiary, was elected the chairman of the first commission; of the second commission, the first Belgian plenipotentiary, Auguste M. J. Beernaert; of the third commission, the first Italian plenipotentiary, Count G. Tornielli Brusati di Veragano; and of the fourth commission, the second Russian plenipotentiary, F. F. Martens. All four chairmen were international lawyers. Martens proved to be in the circle of colleagues at the Institute of International Law and partners at earlier international conferences.

---

[16] AVPR, op. 787, delo 9, ed. khr. 7, l. 33.

[17] See note 3 above, pp. 6, 327-329.

In connection with evaluating Martens' role at the Conference it is advisable to briefly consider the intended prospects of this international forum.

Whereas at the 1899 Conference to a great extent new ground was being cultivated and therefore the results obtained were surprising in their novelty and created the impression of great change, a different fate was expected objectively from its repetition in 1907: it was called upon to continue the matters begun and to improve and develop the international legal acts adopted. In 1899 the participants could dwell on insuperable obstacles, deferring them for the future. In 1907 these barriers, for example, the question of the bindingness of the international tribunal, were at the forefront of discussion and could be neither avoided nor postponed. Therefore, objectively the work would be much more profound, more difficult, and less rewarding.

Moreover, in 1907 the influence of the antagonism between two of the more clearly coalescent blocs (on one side, England, France, and Russia; on the other, Germany and Austria-Hungary) was significantly greater than in 1899. This noticeably complicated the achieving of agreement with regard to sometimes even the most petty issues.

The foreign policy conditions materially reduced the objective possibilities for achieving effective results at the Conference. It was rather remarkable that during his trip about the capitals of the European powers Martens had to prove (especially in Berlin) that the discussion (merely the discussion!) of questions of limitation of armaments would not have "catastrophic consequences". Subsequently, in May 1908, there was a talk between Wilhelm II and Martens as follows. Martens, recalling the previous apprehensions of the German Emperor, said that the "question concerning disarmament had not led to a catastrophe". His interlocutor replied: "Yes, that is so, but I hope that this was the last Peace Conference and that at least there will not be a new Conference for a long time".[18] Possibly Wilhelm II rather more openly displayed his feelings, but he was not alone in having such views of the Conference. Certain

[18] AVPR, op. 787, delo 9, ed. khr. 7, l. 118.

influential circles expected no success from it. They looked upon it with apprehension if not doing actual harm.

The insufficiently precise and consistent position of the leadership of the Russian Ministry of Foreign Affairs told negatively on the activity of the Russian delegation at The Hague. Izvol'skii came to the opening of the Conference with great vacillations, and Nicholas II manifested a "weak character". The vacillations persisted during the work of the Conference.

Personally Martens had developed a concern in 1907 which he did not have in 1899, namely, a worsening of his health. In his diary there also appear entries (22 June): "The entire day I lay on the couch because of an acute attack of rheumatism". His illness did not remain unnoticed by participants of the Conference, and Wehberg wrote later that Martens should have left long before the closing of the Conference, but he courageously preferred to remain at his post.[19]

All these circumstances it was necessary to take into account in order to judge the success of Martens' work at the Conference. They should not be overlooked when evaluating the results thereof.

Martens considered his fourth commission, the "maritime" commission, to be the "most difficult". There was every reason for such a view. England for the first time had agreed to a broad discussion of the laws and customs of warfare at sea, and that alone pointed to complexity. Moreover, the Anglo-German rivalry at sea was manifested with particular sharpness in those years. Martens' role as chairman was not easy in this situation of contradictions. He was frequently required not only for his legal knowledge, but for the skills of a diplomat in order to overcome disagreements and not permit deadlock situations. He always endeavoured to restrain the growth of Anglo-German antagonism in the commission. In private conversation he explained to the German representative that England had for the first time agreed to discuss questions of warfare at sea at an international conference and one needed to be greatly flexible so as not to ruin the whole affair.

---

[19] Wehberg, note 13 above, p. 357.

The "conciliation activity" of Martens, however, met with obstructions also on the Russian side. He, for example, as previously actively favoured the strengthening of international justice. And suddenly the maritime minister from Petersburg began to bombard the head of the delegation, Nelidov, with telegrams which said that Russia can not agree to the founding of an international prize court. Poor Nelidov attempted to show that the overwhelming majority of participants of the Conference were persuaded of the need of a "useful and humanitarian reform which would be accepted by all the civilised world with gratitude". However, the arguments had a weak effect on the maritime minister, and the Minister of Foreign Affairs, who, in turn, was more influential with Nicholas II, could not (or did not want to) make him see reason. As a result, the participants of the Conference began to notice the "strange behaviour" of the Russian delegation: the members of the committee elected to work out a Statute on the Prize Court and the representatives of Germany and Austria-Hungary had favoured the election of a Russian specialist (obviously having Martens in view) but, to their astonishment, Nelidov rejected any participation of Russia. They did not know that Nelidov received a regular telegram from Petersburg from the maritime minister with such an instruction.

Colleagues on the delegation also let Martens down. Charykov took it into his head to speak in the fourth commission with his own draft article on the sojourn of vessels in neutral ports, and he turned with a request to prepare such an article to ... the French delegation. The request was satisfied, but then the French delegate approached Martens and asked in bewilderment why he, a noted authority, had not written the draft. Ovchinnikov unexpectedly declared in the name of the Russian delegation objections against the draft submitted by the chairman of the commission, that is, Martens. Martens anticipated a scandal, but it was avoided: some delegates were not listening, others did not understand. "My Russian colleagues don't like me", Martens declared. "That fool Charykov" (the future Deputy Minister of Foreign Affairs), who sat on the fourth commission, interfered especially. The sole consolation for Martens was Nelidov ("a dear, intelligent man"), but he was in touch more with Charykov than with Martens.[20]

Moreover, working out the draft documents in the commission proceeded with difficulty and slowly. On 16 July Martens entered in his diary: "Already seven weeks, and the end is not in sight. Matters are moving forward very poorly. But all intrigues are flourishing".

Feuds enveloped Martens too. On 9 July (21 July new style) the *New York Herald* published correspondence from The Hague in which it was said that "Mister de Martens is now unpopular. One of the delegates describes his organisation of the Peace Conference as hopelessly bad". The article pointed out that the head of the Russian delegation, Nelidov, criticised Martens, that an "incident" had occurred with Martens, and the like. For Martens this was a serious psychological blow, especially when he learned that among the sources of information was a sea captain from his own delegation. "No, the 1899 Conference can not be compared with this one", he wrote.

Although Martens had many troubles in his fourth commission, he worked actively in the commission headed by Bourgeois, especially on the question of international justice so dear to him. When on 19 August the transformation of the Permanent Court of International Arbitration was discussed at The Hague, Martens entered in his diary: "Today is a great day". The American representatives, Horace Porter and James Brown Scott, spoke in favour of the principle of the bindingness of judicial examinations. The addresses pleased Martens, and he spontaneously spoke in the same spirit. His speech made an impression and applause broke out. Bourgeois, presiding, considered it necessary to congratulate his colleague. According to the impressions of participants, Martens and Bourgeois had become the most active supporters of an obligatory international court at the Conference. The German delegation, as in 1899, spoke against.

---

[20] See AVPR, op. 787, delo 9, ed. khr. 7, l. 47-51.

At the end of August, Martens noted in his diary: "Now it is September, and the end of the Conference is not in sight". His mood worsened at the session of the bureau of the Conference at which the heads of all commissions spoke. The American representative at the session, Horace Porter, submitted a proposal concerning the periodicity of the conferences and the need for better preparation. Martens received the proposal as a reproach against Russia and himself personally. Nelidov, to the dissatisfaction of Martens, did not include him nor did he himself join the working group which was charged to study the American proposal.

The early results had emerged from the Conference. As in 1899 the commission under the chairmanship of Martens completed its work first. On 5 September Martens delivered a summary report concerning all drafts relating to the law of warfare at sea. The excellent study of the drafts enabled the discussion thereof to be completed in forty minutes, and they were adopted virtually unanimously. This was an undoubted success of Martens as chairman of the commission and as a jurist, and they deservedly congratulated him at the completion of the work. On 13 September the last session of the fourth commission was organised in an atmosphere of amity. The results of the work of the commission were discussed on 14 September at the plenary session of the Conference and were approved without objections. Nelidov as chairman of the Conference highly esteemed the work of the fourth commission and its chairman. This was a clear success which had important significance: the first step was taken towards the codification of the law of warfare at sea.[21]

On 21 September (8 September in Martens' diary) the fourth plenary session of the Conference assembled. It adopted the Convention concerning the founding of an international prize court at The Hague (37 votes in favour, of 43). This also was an important result, of which Martens justly wrote that he would never have expected this several years ago.

---

[21] AVPR, op. 787, delo 9, ed. khr. 7, l. 45, 46-47, 49, 58, 64-74.

At the plenary session the English representative gave a statement in which he spoke of the aspiration of his Government to reduce military expenditures. He recalled that the previous Hague Conference had adopted a decree relative to limitation of the military burden. Since then expenses on armaments had significantly increased. The English representative called upon the Conference to declare that it was "extremely desirable that the Governments again subjected this question to serious study". As the English also expected, the German delegation spoke against, rather coarsely and sharply. This, with the tacit sympathy of delegates of certain other countries, ruined the discussion of this question. There were not even plenary debates with regard to the address of the English delegate. The entire matter was reduced to the fact that the English proposal, made "outside the framework of the Russian programme," was subsequently entered in the form of a recommendation in the Final Act of the Conference.[22] The English action remained a single act. The work of the Conference concentrated on the codification of international rules.

Work in the other commissions of the Conference moved forward with difficulty. On 21 September the results of the third commission were summed up, but sharp debates were still proceeding in the first commission chaired by Bourgeois. Two clearly distinguishable camps stood out in the commission: on one side, France, Russia, and their allies; on the other side, Germany, Austria-Hungary, and their allies. The debates were carried over to the plenary sessions of the Conference. At the session of 26 September Martens attempted to gloss over the contradictions and submitted a "conciliatory proposal". However, it gathered only 27 votes of 43, and Martens withdrew it.[23]

Results of the Conference

On 18 October (5 October, old style) 1907 the Second Hague Peace Conference adopted a Final Act to which were appended thirteen conventions and one declaration (on prohibiting the throwing of projectiles from balloons). Among the thirteen

---

[22] See note 3 above, pp. 8-9, 12.

[23] See AVPR, op. 787, delo 9, ed. khr. 7, l. 78-79.

conventions, three were revised conventions adopted in 1899 and ten were new. In contemporary doctrine it is accepted to place them as follows: (1) on the pacific settlement of international disputes; (2) on limitation of instances of recourse to force in order to recover contractual debt obligations (the Drago-Porter Convention); (3) the opening of military actions; (4) the laws and customs of war on land; (5) the rights and duties of neutral powers and persons in land warfare; (6) the status of enemy merchant ships when military actions commence; (7) the conversion of merchant ships into military vessels; (8) the placement of automatic contact underwater mines; (9) the bombardment by naval forces during time of war; (10) the adaptation to maritime warfare of the principles of the 1864 Geneva Convention; (11) certain limitations on the use of the right of capture in warfare at sea; (12) the founding of the international prize court (did not enter into force); (13) the rights and duties of neutral powers in warfare at sea.

In addition, the Final Act contained a number of resolutions and *voeux*. One of them already has been mentioned: the recommendation to governments to consider the question of the limitation of armaments. At the initiative of the English and American delegations a recommendation also was adopted to convoke the Third Peace Conference upon the expiry of the period which would approximately coincide with the period between the First and Second Conferences (that is, in 1915).[24]

Today the historical significance of the Second Hague Peace Conference is wholly evident. Usually it is said that it developed the digest of rules which the 1899 Conference had adopted in the domain of the law of war and the peaceful settlement of international disputes. Indeed the conventions adopted in 1899 and 1907 represent a single whole and are so regarded in international law and legal doctrine. The conventions of 1899 can not be imagined without the additions made in 1907.

The Hague conventions also determine the significance of the 1907 Conference as a major event in the history of international relations and the progressive development of

---

[24] See note 3 above, p. 36.

international law. The Hague conventions even now remain a digest of generally-recognised principles and norms of international law relating to warfare. They in significant part are also in our day prevailing international legal documents, compliance with whose provisions is obligatory, and a violation, an international crime. Thus they, in particular, have been classified by the International Military Tribunal which convicted the Hitlerite clique at Nuremburg in 1945-46 as crimes against peace, war crimes, and crimes against humanity. In the indictment in the case of the principal war criminals the violation by them of the 1907 Hague conventions was specially noted.[25]

The principles and norms of the 1899 and 1907 Hague conventions have become the basis for the further establishment of international legal norms in this domain. They served as the point of departure for the Convention on the regime of prisoners of war, signed at Geneva in 1929, for the 1949 Geneva conventions on protection of the victims of war, and the 1977 Additional protocols thereto.

The 1907 Conference developed the provisions concerning the permanent court of international arbitration at The Hague. To be sure, the convention on the international prize court never entered into force.

The institution of international commissions of enquiry received further development. After the Hull Incident, they were used repeatedly. In 1912 they were resorted to in connection with the capture of the French merchant ship *Tavignano* by an Italian cruiser; in 1915, in connection with the sinking of a German submarine by the Dutch vessel *Tubantia*. The United States during 1913-15 concluded about thirty international treaties making provision for the creation of international commissions of enquiry. In 1948 at Bogota, Colombia, a treaty was signed which placed the convocation of commissions of enquiry and conciliation on the Organisation of American States. The institution of international commissions of enquiry has not taken in the United Nations.

---

[25] See *Нюрнбергский процесс: сборник материалов* [The Nuremburg Trial: Collection of Materials] (Moscow, 1952), I, p. 54.

No specific results were achieved in the domain of the limitation of armaments. But the Conference confirmed and reinforced the fact that beginning from 1899 the question of disarmament in one form or another had become a permanent point in the respective international forums. The consideration thereof at The Hague proved to be not an episode, but the commencement of a long and complex journey which is still in progress in the development of international relations.

In this writer's view, when evaluating the results of the 1907 Hague Conference it is never taken into account that the Conference laid the basis for the universal organisation of States which arose after the First World War in the form of the League of Nations, and then rose again after the Second World War as the United Nations. Whereas the 1899 Conference bore the imprint of a one-off occasion, the 1907 Conference already had acknowledged the principle of the periodicity of such international forums. Whereas 27 States had taken part in the 1899 Conference, by 1907 their number had grown to 44 (47 agreed to take part), embracing virtually all independent States of that time. The 1907 Hague forum was of a universal character.

Contemporaries assessed the 1907 Conference somewhat differently. Being closely linked to current events and the emotional perception of eyewitnesses, these assessments often mix proportions, drawing attention to facts which quickly were placed on the back burner or forgotten entirely and ceding place to phenomena of long-term significance. It is not surprising that the assessments were highly diverse and contradictory with respect not only to the entire Conference but also to the role of Martens at it.

Martens himself as a whole assessed the results of the Second Peace Conference as lower than the First. At the same time, he assessed their significance realistically. In a Memorandum to Nolde during the work of the Conference Martens wrote: "All the same much has been done which will remain forever a precious contribution to the treasury of progress of the international community".[26]

---

[26] Cited from Nolde, note 14 above, p. 23.

The personal contribution of Martens was immense. The Conference worked according to the programme which he drew up and the Reglament which he had proposed. In his "very difficult" commission he had achieved certain results. If one takes the conventions as a whole, then three (nos. 1, 2, and 12) were prepared in the first commission; three in the second commission (nos. 3, 4, 5) and one declaration; four in the third commission (8, 9, 10, and 12); and three in the fourth commission (6, 7, and 11).[27]

Ruminating about the results of the Conference, Martens wrote: "I am proud that I helped create the foundations for the common life of nations, as much as my strength permitted. I can contentedly close my eyes. Neither Russia nor the entire rest of the world will forget me after my death, and my activity to the benefit of the development of international law will not be forgotten".[28]

And all the same Martens returned from the Conference without that feeling of elation which should arise, it would seem, from an understanding of the international significance of the legal acts adopted. Amongst other reflections in his diary one can find such expressions as "sorry fiasco". In Petersburg, Martens did not arrange public lectures which gathered a full audience, nor write articles for the journals. He did not conceal his dissatisfaction.

The reasons for Martens' pessimistic mood should, in this writer's view, be sought more in his personal experiences. Taube wrote that the results of the four-month 1907 Hague Conference "inflated in fourteen conventions but rather empty in substance could not fail to disappoint the celebrated proponent of the 1899 Congress".[29] Nolde singled out the fact that at the Conference Martens and his supporters had also failed to achieve general agreement to the creation of a permanent international court and the bindingness of international arbitration. He quoted the

---

27 See note 3 above, pp. 7-8.

28 AVPR, op. 787, delo 9, ed. khr. 7, l. 85.

29 M. A. Taube, *Ф. Ф. Мартенс(1845-1909). Некролог* [F. F. Martens (1945-1909). Obituary] (Spb., 1909), p. 12.

text of Martens' Memorandum to him which showed "how deeply disappointed Martens was about this new failure".[30]

The reason for Martens' disappointment may be the circumstance that the point of the programme proposed by the Russian Government relative to working out a convention on the laws and customs of warfare at sea was not realised in full measure at the Conference. Much was done in this direction. Of the thirteen conventions prepared, eight concerned warfare at sea. But as a whole it did not succeed in adopting that enlarged digest of rules relating to waging warfare at sea which was formalised with respect to land warfare in 1899. The Conference recommended to continue to work out the laws and customs of warfare at sea, and in accordance with its recommendations the regulation of warfare at sea became the subject of a special London Conference in 1909, in which Martens was unable to participate. Since at the Second Hague Conference Martens had headed the commission on maritime law, he evidently considered himself responsible for such an outcome.

A grave upset for Martens was evidently his understanding that his age and illness did not allow him to act as successfully as at the 1899 Conference. Melancholy thoughts gave rise to critical remarks from participants in the Conference. Wehberg pointed out that at the 1907 Conference Martens on the whole acted very energetically, with great passion and enormous erudition, but not as brilliantly as at the 1899 Conference. Referring to participants of the Conference, Wehberg recalled the repeated censures against the address of Martens in that as chairman of the fourth commission Martens "spoke inconsistently" and thereby made the achievement of agreement more difficult.[31]

The fact that Martens simultaneously summed up the results of his life undoubtedly told on the evaluation of the results of the Conference and his own role. The mood was contradictory. On one hand, legitimate pride in the fruits of many years of effort. "I am proud," he wrote in his diary, "that

---

[30] Nolde, note 14 above, p. 28.
[31] See Wehberg, note 13 above, pp. 354, 357.

I helped create the foundations for the common life of peoples as much as my strength permitted". On the other hand, the distress born in the awareness that life was coming to an end balanced the pride in what had been achieved. "The Second Peace Conference has ended, and in all likelihood I will not be at the Third," Martens ruminated.[32]

Previously, although not so strongly as in 1899, he was dispirited that in his Motherland the State leadership related to him worse than was the case abroad. Wilhelm II awarded Count Münster the highest German order of the Black Eagle. "To us Russians, nothing!" Martens noted heatedly.[33] Upon returning to Petersburg, he attempted to inform Izvol'skii about the results of the Conference. But the Minister listened "completely indifferently". On 15 November Martens was received by the Tsar at Tsarskoe Selo. The "Sovereign was gentle", and Martens began to speak to him about how much he had toiled at the Second Hague Conference, that he would not be at a Third, that for 26 years he had been permanently at his post as a member of the Council at the Ministry of Foreign Affairs ... But the reception was crowded, and the intended conversation did not proceed.

And the situation at home did not please him. Having returned to Petersburg, he wrote in his diary: "The internal affairs of Russia continue in their former state of moral decay, intellectual poverty, and State disorder".[34]

Martens' pessimistic evaluation of the 1907 Conference by virtue of his authority left its trace in Russian doctrinal writings. These evaluations seem too one-sided and not entirely substantiated. The personal emotions in them frequently screen off the objective significance of the Second Hague Peace Conference and the prominent role there of Martens himself.

In contemporary doctrinal writings the 1907 Hague Conference is assessed as the "culminating point of a lengthy historical development", and the codification of international

---

[32] AVPR, op. 787, delo 9, ed. khr. 7, l. 161.
[33] AVPR, op. 787, delo 9, ed. khr. 7, l. 161.
[34] AVPR, op. 787, delo 9, ed. khr. 7, l. 88-89.

law undertaken at it, as part of prevailing law. An analysis of subsequent developments enables "certain gaps and certain illusions" to be singled out in the decisions of the Conference, but as a whole these were "innovative provisions which seriously advanced the development of international law". As regards appeals to review the entire law of war as obsolete, it was justly pointed out that "up to now each attempt undertaken in this direction was no more than an addition to or development of the norms contained in the acts signed at The Hague in 1907".[35]

The Hague conventions are a monument to an outstanding Russian jurist, F. F. Martens, a monument the more notable in that they today continue to serve people. Regrettably, the services of Martens in the preparation and conducting of the 1899 and 1907 Hague Peace conferences still have not found sufficient illumination. This also relates to the greatest achievements, for example Martens' "favourite child", the Convention on the Laws and Customs of Land Warfare, and to lesser facts. Almost entirely forgotten, for example, is the fact that the Hague Arbitration Court is obliged to Martens for its magnificent building. The fact is that the American "steel king" Andrew Carnegie, who wanted to make a large donation in support of the idea of peace among peoples, had turned to Martens. And Martens had suggested to him that he build the Peace Palace in The Hague, which was done. In recalling this in 1910, Wehberg expressed just regret that Martens' initiative had not been properly noted when laying the bricks of the Peace Palace in which the arbitration court is situated.[36]

---

[35] S. Nahlik, "Большая гаагская кодификация и ее значение" [The Great Hague Codification and Its Significance], *Panstwo i prawo*, no. 12 (1967), pp. 5-7.
[36] See Wehberg, note 13 above, p. 355.

CHAPTER XII
LAST YEARS

The 1907 Hague Conference was the last international forum in which Martens took part. To be sure, in 1908 the question was raised of his inclusion in the Russian delegation to the London Conference on Maritime Law, and his candidacy was top of the list. And it was he, seeking to avoid the deadlock situation in The Hague, who proposed that a special international conference be convened on the law of naval warfare. He preferred not to travel to London since he did not believe the Anglo-German rivalry had been smoothed over. Consequently he was satisfied when the new Deputy Minister, N. V. Charykov, with whom he had formed close relations after the Hague Conference, settled on the candidacies of Baron von Taube and Boris Nolde.[1] The foreign activity of Martens had come to an end.

He now had more time for his family and for his health, having left the University and the Lyceé in 1903.

Head of the Family

On 18 December 1879 F. F. Martens had married Ekaterina Tur, daughter of the Privy Councillor and Senator, N. A. Tur, a lawyer who specialised in the law of bills of exchange. Martens' wife was an educated lady who had a command of the French, German, English, and Italian languages. The Martens marriage was a harmonious one; while abroad Fedor Fedorovich often would record in his diary how he missed his "friend in life" and his entire family. Often he brought his family with him during his foreign travels. In 1887, for example, they accompanied him to Germany for an extended visit from May until September, returning home after the Red Cross Conference in Karlsruhe.[2] Ekaterina accompanied him to diplomatic receptions, and when he considered the publication of an "underground" pamphlet

[1] See AVPR, op. 787, d. 9, ed. khr. 7, l. 136.
[2] AVPR, op. 787, delo 9, ed. khr. 2, l. 81-82.

against Katkov, she rewrote the German text for the publisher in Berlin so as to conceal the hand of her husband.

How delighted Fedor Fedorovich was to be reunited with his dear wife who awaited him on the pier at Le Havre upon his return from Portsmouth, New Hampshire, and the peace negotiations of 1905. While at The Hague on 27 August 1907 he did not omit to mark the "birthday of my Darling Katiusha". Ekaterina was a Lutheran, and a pastor conducted her funeral services. She died on 30 March 1913 at home in St. Petersburg, her last words "this is the end" were uttered in French. Her son, who was present when she died, wrote in his diary: "Quiet, calm in spirit, of good nature, crystal pure, as she lived so Mama passed away. Beautifully, insofar as life [evidently, death – *V. P.*] can be beautiful".[3]

Many friends visited the Martens family at home. Distinguished foreign scholars and diplomats often came. The home was so closely linked with European culture that Nikolai Martens, the son, supposed himself to be more "European" than "Russian." In any event, he was more accustomed to speaking French than Russian. To be sure, this phenomenon was typical of the families of many Russian diplomats, the nobility in the large cities, and the upper strata of Petersburg society. Fedor Fedorovich often conversed in French with his colleagues at the Ministry of Foreign Affairs.

The Martens family way of life was distinctive in several respects within the milieu of the landed and service aristocracy to which Privy Councillor Martens had access. Most distinctive was his work pace. Having originated in an orphan home, he was not accustomed to lying in bed in the mornings. He worked at home a great deal, at the Ministry, in the University, and in archives. He was accustomed to writing; his hand in the diaries is that of a man for whom writing is an ordinary activity. He also had mastered the fashionable "minute hand" in which every letter of the alphabet is recorded clearly but not more than one millimetre in height. The letters on a line are tiny, like a small "minute hand". Such lines cover his communications to the

---

[3] AVPR, op. 787, delo 9, ed. khr. 8, l. 75.

Minister, Prince A. B. Lobanov-Rostovskii, on 30 November 1895 and 7 June 1896.[4]

Martens lectured at the University, wrote books, journal articles, and newspaper comments, and prepared official memoranda in various languages. To find his way about this sea of publications, rough drafts, notes, and other papers required a trained memory, organisational skills, and a work rhythm. Martens' son recorded in his diary: "Well organised with a vast memory."[5] His son noted that the colossal amount written by his father was achieved by exhausting labour, for example, night vigils, sitting at the desk uninterrupted for hours, constantly poring over papers, and the like. Martens worked assiduously, but the intensity of his labour was facilitated by his organisational skills and talent.

He was capable, at a single sitting, of writing the Reply to a Japanese Note (at Portsmouth, in 1905) and in several days of drawing up and setting out on paper in a voluminous memorandum the programme for an international conference (1898). At the same time, he found time for his family, for guests, and sundry diplomatic receptions. Summer holidays (two-three months) he spent away from sultry, dusty St. Petersburg, in the countryside. There he loved to play tennis.

Martens first purchased an estate in the Vilna Province (village of Pogulianka, near Dvinsk). There he travelled in 1893. But the life at a manor house was not initially satisfactory. His wife became ill with pneumonia at the estate, and then his daughter was taken ill. Martens became so concerned that he ultimately also became ill.[6]

The unfortunate experience in Pogulianka persuaded Martens to seek an estate in another locality, and he acquired one in Livonia. The entire family loved this estate and travelled there every year. Martens constantly spoke of his "Livonian estate", and in 1896 proudly noted on a letter to the Minister: "Waldensee near Wolmar" (Wolmar is presently called Valmiera and is situated in Latvia).

---

[4] See AVPR, op. 731, delo 28, l. 1-2.

[5] AVPR, op. 787, delo 8, l. 4.

[6] AVPR, delo 9, ed. khr. 2, l. 49, 82.

The purchase of the estate gave evidence of the improved material situation of Martens. His wife had brought a dowry upon her marriage, as was the practice then, but the principal source of the family's prosperity was the earnings of the Head of the household. It is difficult to determine precisely how much Martens earned, but certain information reposes in the archives which enables estimates to be made.

In December 1879 Prince Gorchakov assigned to his functionary with special portfolio, 5th class, Councillor of State Martens, 2000 rubles annual salary. If one takes into account the salary at the University, the young man received a not inconsiderable material remuneration. This was then augmented by royalties for numerous publications, payment for arbitral work, and for legal opinions. It is impossible to ascertain the precise amounts, but undoubtedly such remuneration was significant and constantly increased. Teaching at the Lyceé and the School of Jurisprudence brought additional income.

In 1905, to mark his sixtieth birthday, the salary of Privy Councillor Martens as a permanent member of the Council of the Ministry of Foreign Affairs, was increased from 4500 to 6000 rubles per year.[7] After his father's death, Nikolai Martens received as part of his inheritance the estate in Livonia, which he wished to pledge for 150-200,000 rubles, the Petersburg apartment, and a detached house in Petersburg (on Znamenka). Nikolai does not mention the home in Pernov. Although Nikolai was merely the secretary of the Russian mission in Sofia, in 1913 he had money available and intended to invest 60-65,000 rubles in a joint-stock society. In 1912 he was granted leave for three months and three weeks to travel about Europe – Strasbourg, Paris, Berlin, and Stockholm.[8]

In addition to his son Nikolai, Martens had daughters – Edith, Ekaterina, and Maria. Nikolai served in the Ministry of Foreign Affairs. Edith married Count Sollogub. Katia and Mania, according to their brother's diary, did not marry and lived with their mother (Mania in 1912 was about 20 years old). Nikolai,

---

[7] AVPR, op. 773, delo 36, l. 9.

[8] AVPR, op. 787, delo 8, l. 4, 6, 10, 14, 61.

born in 1880, was still a bachelor. He commenced diplomatic service late and lagged behind his colleagues. In the Sofia mission he was the eldest in age of all the secretaries.[9]

Financially speaking, this resident of an orphan home became rather successful. Suffice it to recall that during 1882-91 the average earnings of an agricultural worker in the Courland Province were about 90 rubles per year.[10] A peasant required an entire lifetime to earn as much as Privy Councillor Martens earned in one year.

On the other hand, the financial status of the Martens family hardly compared with the incomes of the capital aristocracy or even the lower strata of the bureaucracy. Count Lamzdorf, for example, when appointed Minister received 75,000 rubles just to furnish his apartment. Such a sum Martens could only dream about. The Minister of Internal Affairs, A. S. Sipiagin, spent 375,000 rubles to refurbish an apartment, and an additional 75,000 rubles for furniture. Sipiagin used treasury money to build a family church, so as not to have to go out on to the street.[11] Embezzlement of public funds and bribery were on the rise. An official with special portfolio attached to the Minister of Finances, I. F. Tsion, for example, received 200,000 French francs from bankers when concluding a loan for Russia in France. This bribe clearly was "not for rank", and Tsion was obliged to leave a cushy job. Then his head, the Minister of Finances I. A. Vyshnegradskii, received, according to Vitte, 500,000 French francs from the Paris banker Rothschild for analogous services and prospered thereafter.[12]

Martens was far removed from the embezzlement of public funds and bribery. "Embodying honour, decency in all relations, and great idealism," his son wrote of him.[13] Private companies paid for the services of their employees rather more than did the Imperial treasury for the labour of university professors.

---

[9] AVPR, op. 787, delo 8, l. 55-56.
[10] *Энциклопедический словарь* [Encyclopedic Dictionary], LI, p. 13.
[11] AVPR, op. 787, delo 9, ed. khr. 3, l. 92-96.
[12] See S. Iu. Vitte, *Воспоминания* [Memoirs] (Moscow, 1960), I, pp. 280-295.
[13] AVPR, op. 787, delo 8, l. 4.

Vitte wrote in his memoirs that at the outset of his career he had no personal income and was obliged to serve on a private railway. They paid him 50,000 rubles per year. Entrepreneurs formed a stratum even more wealthy. The personal income of the noted industrialist Savva Morozov in the years 1895-1904 comprised about 250,000 rubles a year.[14] It should be noted that Morozov was by no means amongst the wealthiest capitalists in Russia.

Thus, materially speaking Martens stood somewhere on the middle rungs of the social ladder. In modern terminology, he was amongst the upper middle class.

Results of His Lifetime Efforts Having reached 60 years of age on 15 August 1905, Martens imagined that his "subscription of life" had ended. This landmark in life abruptly changed his disposition and many of his former views. The time had come to sum up the results, and he began increasingly to mull them over.

Martens had developed a theory of international administration and at numerous international conferences contributed considerably to the organisation of a more structured international community. How many principles and norms of international law had he helped to create! How many initiatives he undertook, how many principles were laid down!

Entire generations of diplomats, public figures, and jurists had studied international law by using his treatise. His fame spread far beyond the frontiers of Russia; he was a widely-acknowledged world authority. His knowledge and experience acquired by his own labours made him a desirable interlocutor of monarchs and presidents, ministers and bankers, eminent jurists and diplomats. By his unceasing labours he raised the prestige of the Russian science of international law and of Russia itself in the world.

An understanding of this principal result of his life inspired him to examine anew many things which in the past had disturbed him. How he had survived the destruction of the plan

---

[14] A. N. Bokhanov, «Савва Морозов» [Savva Morozov], *Вопросы истории* [Questions of History], no. 4 (1989), pp. 73-74.

to become an envoy in The Hague. Now he viewed this differently. Had he moved with his family to The Hague, his daughter Edith would not have come to meet her husband, Sasha. A better pair could not be imagined. Moreover, he himself saw how the humidity in The Hague affected one's health. His fellow diplomat who had worked in the Russian mission at The Hague suffered from rheumatism there. "And what would be my fate – a rheumatic?" wondered Martens. He had deeply regretted that twice he had been passed over for appointment to the State Council. But perhaps this was for the best? He had held his peace when his friend, N. P. Tagantsev, spoke there in favour of abolition of the death penalty and doubtless would have caused general disquiet with his objections ... The malevolence and neglect of the leadership led him to begin to think: should one not cast aside everything and emigrate abroad, where one would enjoy greater esteem? But concerns for his family intervened, and hopes that matters in the Ministry of Foreign Affairs would finally improve. The situation did not improve, but worsened, and another thought was added: "How long will I live? At my age does it make sense to undertake such a step? My daughter-in-law, M. N. Timasheva, was so young, but died from a frivolous operation. And how does one cast aside everything of one's country?"[15]

Melancholy thoughts grew with the death of friends, people with whom he worked and communed. At the Ministry of Foreign Affairs, Martens already was "alone, like a stump". His evil enemy, Lamzdorf, had fallen, to be sure. But there appeared in the post of Deputy Minister a person who was no better – the former envoy to The Hague, Charykov. Vitte had retired, Pobedonostsev has died ... All this led to his being aloof from affairs.

Last Earthly Concerns Despite such moods, Martens continued to lead a rather active life. In November 1907 he had a detailed discussion with Minister Izvol'skii. The Minister expressed an intention to continue to use Martens' knowledge and experience. He said that Martens

[15] AVPR, op. 787, delo 9, ed. khr. 7, l. 116-117.

might hold a diplomatic post in one of the countries of Southern Europe. Regrettably, vacancies there were not foreseen. Martens expressed consent, but did not believe this and remained at peace.

At the beginning of 1908 he decided to write a memorandum on the "Fate of Russia in the Far East". He regarded the memorandum as a "political spiritual testament". Recalling the frictions with the Ministry leadership arising out of a direct appeal to the Emperor, Martens passed the memorandum to Izvol'skii. He knew that the contents of the memorandum would not please the Minister because the policies of Russian in the region were criticised. But Martens all the same sent it to Izvol'skii. "Let him be angry" he decided. Traces of the memorandum can not be located in the Archive of the Ministry of Foreign Affairs. Evidently it found its way into the wastebasket.

In the spring of 1908 Martens travelled to Germany for treatment at a Wiesbaden resort. He was content with the results of the treatment and in an excellent mood accepted an invitation of Wilhelm II to luncheon. In conversation with the Kaiser, Martens did not fail to remind him that "the question of disarmament had not led to any catastrophe". Wilhelm could not object, but all the same expressed the hope that the Second Hague Conference would prove to be the last. He added: the more forces, naval vessels, and cannons, the better is peace secured. Therein is the sole and true guarantee of peace! Martens, naturally, could not concur with the fact that military power secures international peace, but he did not begin to argue with his august interlocutor.

At Wiesbaden, Martens met with his old acquaintance Leopold II, King of Belgium, who also was undergoing treatment at the resort. The meeting was warm, but business was not spoken of.

The months of June-August 1908 Martens spent in "dear Livonia" at "my darling Waldensee". When he returned to St. Petersburg at the beginning of September, he knew that he had "passed from danger". He contemplated a trip to the Conference on maritime law in London, but the malevolence of Charykov led to the confirmation of the candidacies of Taube and Nolde.

In November Martens visited Izvol'skii and chatted with the Minister about the topics of the day: the situation in the Balkans and the question of Bosnia and Herzogovina.

On 5 January 1909 Martens wished to see Emperor Nicholas II. For the first time the Emperor invited him himself, and Martens was quite surprised. The conversation in the working office of the Emperor from the very outset proceeded to the problem of the day: Bosnia and Herzogovina. Martens expressed himself in the spirit that the sham Russophilism of the Minister of Foreign Affairs, Baron Aehrenthal, was an invention, and Austria-Hungary was following the path of Germany. He again spoke of the need for a close alliance between Russia, England, and France.

Martens decided to use the unexpected audience to speak of personal matters. He reminded the Emperor that the right had been given to him to directly hand in political memoranda. "So far there have been none," said Martens, "because I am afraid". The old diplomat counted on the fact that the Emperor was interested in the reason for his timidity. But the Emperor only smiled and did not ask why Martens was afraid. He merely thanked him for an interesting conversation.

Martens then decided to write to the Emperor. He proposed that the Emperor appoint him as a Councillor of State so that he might personally report his views to the Emperor. Evidently the unexpected invitation from the Emperor inspired him to take this step. Martens passed his letter to the Emperor at the beginning of January through the aide-de-camp K. A. Naryshkin, who had studied with him at the School of Jurisprudence. However, the Emperor, "being one of the perfidious Romanovs," and having received the letter, remained silent.

On 16 January Martens visited a reception held by the French ambassador. There he saw Izvol'skii and evidently conversations with the Minister and with diplomats reinforced his intention to undertake yet one more attempt and to send yet another memorandum to the Emperor – this time on the war in the Balkans. Since Naryshkin was on leave, Martens sent the memorandum to Tsarskoe Selo in the name of the head of the military-field chancellery, V. N. Orlov. On 16 February Martens received a reply from Orlov: "His Majesty took the memorandum, expressed gratitude, and said that in the future he will be happy to receive them".[16] There were no consequences from sending the memoranda.

On 1 April 1909 Martens made an entry in his diary which turned out to be his last. He went to his "darling Waldensee", leaving the diary behind. In early June he was required to travel to St. Petersburg. En route there Privy Councillor Fedor Fedorovich Martens died, on 7 June 1909 at the Railway Station in Valga, presently located on the frontier between Estonia and Latvia, aged 64 years.

*****

It is no easy matter to evaluate the character and personal qualities of a man so multifaceted as F. F. Martens.

To many contemporaries he seemed to be an ordinary professor, a commonplace bureaucrat lacking special talents and gifts. Some saw in him a self-serving conceit and quarrelsome disposition. He angered more than a few exalted officials with his scientifically-substantiated objections, which were accepted as an impertinent obstinacy.

On the other hand, he had many outstanding friends and adherents. In 1982 the Swiss international lawyer J. Pictet recalled in a public lecture the "genius" of Martens, and the Russian Academy of Sciences has founded a prize in his name.

It is not the fashion these days to erect monuments to outstanding lawyers, as was done, for example, in ancient Rome. F. F. Martens undoubtedly deserves such a monument: he laboured for Russia, for Great Britain, for Europe, for the entire world.

Martens' aspirations, his credo, were always precise and clear: a human civilisation worthy of this name can only be built on the basis of the rule of law. Illegality is capable only of destroying our planet.

---

[16] AVPR, op. 787, delo 9, ed. khr. 7, l. 92, 116, 118, 157, 160.

MARTENS' ADVERSARIES AS A PUBLICIST: CHARLES MARVIN

W. E. Butler

A proper bibliography of F. F. Martens' publicist publications has never, apparently, been attempted. It doubtless would be lengthy and require researches in the leading newspapers of Europe and North America, so widely were his sallies submitted and so extensively did individual journalists cross pens with him.

One of those who followed his writings closely, and who met with him at least once, in 1882, was Charles Thomas Marvin (1854-1890). A resolute opponent of Russian expansion anywhere, he followed closely the "Great Game" as it was played in Central Asia and the Far East. For some time he served in St. Petersburg as a correspondent for the London *Globe*. He had a good command of the Russian language and was personally acquainted with several Russian generals and other senior military officers. Among his works were: *The Eye-Witnesses' Account of the Disastrous Russian Campaign Against the Akhal Tekke Turcomans* (London, 1880); *Reconnoitring in Central Asia: Pioneering Adventures in the Region Lying between Russia and India* (London, 1884); *The Region of Eternal Fire: An Account of a Journey to the Petroleum Region of the Caspian in 1883* (London, 1884); (ed. & transl.), *Colonel Grodekoff's Ride from Samarcand to Herat, Through Balkh and the Uzbek States of Afghan Turkestan* (London, 1880); *Merv, the Queen of the World; and the Scourge of the Man-Stealing Turcomans* (London, 1881); *The Russian Advance Towards India* (London, 1882); *The Russians at Merv and Herat and Their Power of Invading India* (London, 1883); and *The Russians at the Gates of Herat* (London, [1885]).

On 15 October 1998 a manuscript volume of unpublished articles on Russia and Afghanistan between 1880-88 appeared at auction in London. Among the manuscripts were two dealing specially with Professor Martens. The manuscripts were collected and annotated by Marvin himself, who had them specially bound.[1] All are in his own hand. Never published before, they appear below for the first time as examples of how Martens' views on Central Asia were followed closely and commented upon in the British press of the day.

PROFESSOR MARTENS DISPOSED OF

[Charles Marvin][2]

Professor de Martens, who is a salaried official of the Russian Foreign Office as well as Professor of International Law at St. Petersburg, has forwarded to this country a view of the Afghan question which admits of a very easy answer. The key note of his long and somewhat rambling letter is that the Afghans are a bad lot, the Ameer [not legible] of Russia who is trying to turn England against her, and that it will be a good thing for the two powers concerned when their frontiers match together and Afghanistan is wiped out. To use the Professor's own words: "The contiguity of the possessions of the two powers will prove a positive benefit and not a calamity and will give a practical and solid basis of a thorough understanding between them." This sounds very pretty, but the Professor very carefully omits from his letter where the Cossack and the Sikh are to meet. Herein lies the whole point of the controversy, and one has only to refer to the Professor's past utterances to find how hollow his assurance is. Of course most people will assume that he means that the English shall "man" the Russo-Afghan frontier, as advocated by Mr. Marvin last Friday. But this is the last thing the Professor would dream of. His idea of contiguity is rather that the Russians should have Candahar than that the English

[1] See *Manuscript of Rejected and Wasted Literary Matter. Charles Marvin. 1880-1888.* The volume bears no bookplate or ownership inscription, but the base of the spine bears the word "Marvin", indicating that it was part of his personal library. The volume now reposes in The Butler Collection.
[2] Submitted to the London *Globe*, but not published.

should hold Herat. We print in another column an account of the Professor's real opinions about Afghanistan, which supplied what he so astutely omitted from his letter, and demonstrates how essential it is that England should not be lulled into lethargy while Russia completes the preparations for seizing Herat. It cannot be too clearly understood that Russia attaches quite as much importance to Herat as we do, and that the military parts consider it absolutely essential she should have the place before reopening the Eastern Question in Europe, in accordance with the definite programme Skobeleff drew up shortly before his death. On this account before the Peace Society indulges in any more raptures over the Professor's pacific letter, we would suggest that it should write again to the international decoy duck of Russian diplomacy to ask him to define with precision where he would have the Sikh and Cossack meet.

*****

PROFESSOR MARTENS' REAL VIEWS ON AFGHANISTAN

[Charles Marvin][3]

In a letter to the Peace Society Professor Martens has thrown the whole blame of the present crisis upon the Ameer and suggests that Afghanistan should be abolished and the two empires rendered contiguous. He, however, does not specify where the English and Russians should meet, and as he quotes his pamphlet of 1879, "not a word of which I would change", he says it may be well to point out that he is an advocate for taking the whole of Afghan-Turkestan, with Balkh, Marmene, etc. from Afghanistan, as well as Herat. Quite casually Mr. Charles Marvin repeats in his new work "The Russians at the Gates of Herat" a conversation he had with Professor Martens in 1882, which shows

[3] Submitted to the *Newcastle Chronicle*, but returned unused. Probably c. 1883.

clearly enough what his views really are. "The difficulty," says Mr Marvin (page 162), does not consist in getting troops to Herat, but in making sure Russia will not issue an ultimatum forbidding their advance.

"It may be opportune to repeat what transpired during a discussion which I had with Professor Martens on the subject in 1882. The connection of Professor Martens with the Russian Foreign Office is well known, and some of his utterances appeared to me, at the time, so fraught with warning that I printed them in italics. I give the conversation, and I think it will be found to possess significance of an undoubted character at the present moment.

"The conversation was upon the future of Afghanistan. I mentioned that General Annenkoff had said, 'Take Afghanistan, for the sake of peace.'

"But Professor Martens declared that England would not be able to annex Afghanistan *without Russia's permission*, or as he more delicately put it, 'without informing her first of her intentions;' *while as to Herat, he said that Russia would view an English occupation of the place with displeasure.*

"He would not allow that we enjoyed supremacy in Afghanistan; nor yet that we could regard it as a second Bokhara. He said Afghanistan was an independent state, and a neutral one; and, with reference to Lord Hartington's declaration last year, 'that England would not allow any Power to interfere with the internal and external affairs of Afghanistan,' which I quoted, to show what our Government thought of Russian pretensions he said that the declaration was contrary to the views which Russia and England diplomatically expressed upon the matter, previous to the Marquis's speech. He would not agree that the Afghan war had cancelled those views. 'Herat,' he said, 'is quite as important to Russia as to England. If it is the Key of India it is also the Key of Central Asia. If we were there we could threaten you in India; if you were there you could threaten us in Central Asia.'

"This opinion was expressed also by Baron Jomini, one of the Under-Secretaries of State at the Russian Foreign Office, to

Lord Dufferin in 1879. Writing on July 16th in that year, he states that Baron Jomini said to him: 'Although we don't intend to go to Merv, or to do anything which may be interpreted as a menace to England, you must not deceive yourself, for the result of our present proceedings' (*i.e.*, the operations of General Lazareff for conquering and annexing Akhal) '*will be to furnish us with a base of operations against England hereafter, should the British Government, by the occupation of Herat, threaten our present position in Central Asia.*'

"Professor Martens would not admit that Herat was a much a part of Afghanistan as Cabul or Candahar, and thought that Persia ought to have it. On my pointing out what a rotten State Persia was, and how completely it was under Russian control, he said that if Russia occupied Herat she would make Persia her enemy. My strong dissent from this led him to propose that Herat should be made into a sort of Switzerland, on the buffer state system, although he had previously expressed his disbelief in the possibility of keeping up Afghanistan as a buffer between the two empires. I held that such a project was impossible with Asiatics, but he continued to maintain that England should keep her hands off the place under any contingencies.

"As I gathered from him, he maintains Russia's right to annex all the territory up to the Afghan frontier, if the nomads provoke her to advance; he holds that Russia should also have Afghan Turkestan – *i.e.*, the country between the Oxus and the Hindoo Koosh. He considers that Herat ought not to be treated as an Afghan possession, and, finally, he insists that the rest of Afghanistan should be looked upon as a neutral independent state, in the existence of which Russia has as much interest as England. It is needless to point out that these opinions cannot but be so many red rags to English Russophobists, and that, much as the Professor desires a reconciliation between England and Russia, a cessation of the Central Asian agitation is impossible while they are maintained. I myself would allow Russia to annex up to Afghanistan; but I would give her to understand that that country is English territory, and must not be looked upon as less our property than Mysore or Baroda.

"I used to think that the claims put forward by the *Golos* and *Novoe Vremya*, asserting Russia's right to treat Afghanistan as a neutral state, and Herat as apart from Afghanistan, were merely expressions of Anglophobe feeling. It has surprised me to find them seriously maintained by a person of such weight as Professor Martens."

Since Russia seized the gates of Herat, the St. Petersburg press has repeatedly intimated that she would not allow us to occupy and garrison the Key of India. These opinions have been treated somewhat needlessly by the English press. They have regarded them simply as ravings of irresponsible journalists. But knowing what I do of the aims of Russian statesmen, and with the warnings of Professor Martens ringing in my ears, I cannot but think that the threats of the Russian press possess a very serious significance. In my mind I am persuaded, that if we allow this frontier complication to simmer until Russia masses at Sarakhs and Merv and the gates of Herat a more powerful army than Lumsden and the Afghans control for the defence of the Key of India, she will suddenly throw off the mask and deny our right to send a force thither. Hence, if there is to be any advance for the defence of Herat, it must be done without delay.

INDEX OF PERSONS

www.ingramcontent.com/pod-product-compliance
Lightning Source LLC
LaVergne TN
LVHW020644300926
849161LV00004B/813